DATE DUE

NO 10'98		
MY 2'00		
AG 13'09		

DEMCO 38-296

Ovid's *Fasti*

Ovid's *Fasti*

Roman Holidays

*Translated with Notes and
Introduction by*

Betty Rose Nagle

Indiana University Press
Bloomington • Indianapolis

The paper used in this publication meets the minimum requirements of American
National Standard for Information Sciences—Permanence of Paper for Printed
Library Materials, ANSI Z39.48-1984.
∞™

Manufactured in the United States of America

Library of Congress Cataloging-in-Publication Data
Ovid, 43 B.C.–17 or 18 A.D.
    [Fasti. English]
    Ovid's Fasti : Roman holidays / translated with notes by Betty
Rose Nagle.
        p.   cm.
    Includes bibliographical references and index.
    ISBN 0-253-33967-7 (alk. paper). — ISBN 0-253-20933-1 (pbk. :
alk. paper)
    1. Rome—Religious life and customs—Poetry.   2. Rites and
ceremonies—Rome—Poetry.   3. Festivals—Rome—Poetry.   I. Nagle,
Betty Rose.   II. Title.
PA6522.F2N34   1995
871'.01—dc20   94-21660
            1 2 3 4 5 00 99 98 97 96 95

to the memory of my parents,

Hudson F. and Ruth H. Nagle

CONTENTS

Ovid's *Fasti*

Introduction

OVID'S LIFE AND WORKS

The Roman poet Publius Ovidius Naso, whom we call "Ovid," was born in turbulent times. He came into the world on 20 March 43 BC at Sulmo (today called Sulmone in Italian), a year to the day after the birth of his older brother. A few days before his brother's birth, and 90 miles to the southwest, at Rome, Julius Caesar had been assassinated. Thus began yet another period of civil war culminating in the end of one form of government, the oligarchical Roman Republic, and the beginning of a new one, the imperial Principate. The transition was dominated by one man, Gaius Julius Caesar Octavianus (63 BC–AD 14), the first Roman Emperor otherwise known as Augustus, who gave his name to this period of Roman history and Latin literature.

Ovid and his brother were sent to Rome to receive the education typical for elite males of that time. The focus was on rhetorical training, to equip a young man with the skills at public speaking needed to advance a career in law and politics. Ovid's brother apparently complied with their father's plans for his two sons; Ovid, however, showed an early inclination for a private life of poetry rather than a public career in government, and after holding a few minor political positions, committed himself fully to that preference. Poets at Rome tended to associate themselves with noble patrons. Ovid's first patron was Marcus Valerius Messalla Corvinus (64 BC–AD 8), in contrast to his older contemporaries from the preceding generation of Augustan poets, Horace, Propertius, and Virgil, who belonged to the circle of Gaius Maecenas (?–8 BC), friend and advisor to the Emperor.[1]

Ovid's earliest poetry consisted of highly successful love poems in a verse form called the elegiac couplet. He perfected the form and exhausted the contents of this short-lived genre in five volumes of *Amores* ("The Loves"), of which we have a later three-volume revised edition. Next he playfully adapted the basic situation and conventions of love elegy in a mock-didactic handbook, the famous "Art of Love" (*Ars Amatoria*), two volumes of advice to men (where to find women, how to catch and keep them), and one for women. A single volume, *Remedia Amoris* ("Cures for Love"), offers advice to the lovelorn on how to fall out of love by inverting the advice of the previous work. Also surviving from this period are fragments of another didactic work on cosmetics. In the *Heroides* ("Heroines"), Ovid once again recycles the elegiac conventions in a new form, which he seems largely to have invented. These consist of verse letters from famous women of myth and legend to the famous men who have abandoned, jilted, or otherwise left them in the lurch (e.g., Penelope to Ulysses, Ariadne to Theseus). Of much-debated authenticity is a letter from the poet Sappho, and three pairs of letters in which a man (e.g., Paris) takes the initiative in writing and is in turn answered by his female addressee (e.g., Helen).[2] Since the basic predicament of all the heroines in the single letters is so similar, the form displays Ovid's virtuosity in a characteristic feature of his work, namely, variations on a theme.

Ovid's masterwork is the *Metamorphoses*, a narrative poem based on myths (mostly Greek) of transformation, organized chronologically from the beginning of the world to his own time and composed, unlike the rest of his corpus, in dactylic hexameters, the metrical form associated, since Homer, with epic. Renaissance artists and writers used the work as a sourcebook for Greek mythology; modern handbooks of mythology, from Bulfinch on, owe their chronological organizing principles, as well as much of their contents, to this poem. In it, Ovidian themes, such as love, and characteristic rhetorical strategies, such as variations on a theme or a tradition, which were apparent in Ovid's earliest work, receive extensive elaboration.

While working on the *Metamorphoses*, Ovid was also composing the *Fasti,* a poetic version of the Roman calendar treating religious festivals, historical anniversaries, astronomical lore, and the like. This antiquarian almanac forms an interesting complement to the *Metamorphoses*. Written in elegiac couplets, it treats mostly Roman subject matter; since its organizing principle is the cyclical unit of the year, its months and days, its narrative is episodic. By contrast, the *Metamorphoses* is mostly Greek in content, written in hexameters, organized in terms of linear history; both the linear sequence and the metrical unit produce a continuous narrative (what Ovid refers to as a *carmen per-*

petuum, "a continuous poem"), albeit not a *single* continuous narrative in the same sense as Virgil's *Aeneid.*

In AD 8, as he was putting the finishing touches on the *Metamorphoses* and had half-completed the *Fasti,* Ovid was sent into exile by the Emperor to Tomis (present-day Costanza, Romania) on the shores of the Black Sea. Despite his hopes and efforts, he never was recalled, and he died (according to St. Jerome's chronology) in AD 17 after writing nine volumes of elegiac letters lamenting his situation: five volumes known as the *Tristia* ("The Sorrows") and four as the *Epistulae ex Ponto* ("Letters from the Black Sea"). These urge friends and family to plead with Augustus for recall, or at least relocation to a less remote place of exile. An autobiographical poem appears at the end of the fourth book of the *Tristia;* it is rich in details about his career (it is the basis for virtually all the information in my brief sketch here) and his private life (he was married three times and acquired a stepdaughter with the third marriage), but is no more informative than the other letters, including one, a whole volume long (*Tristia* 2), addressed to the Emperor himself about the reason for his exile. He blames it on "a poem and a mistake" (*carmen et error*). The poem is generally, but not universally, thought to be the *Ars Amatoria* (in view of the Emperor's publicly puritanical attitude, his not very successful endeavors to legislate a reform of Roman sexual morality, and the scandals caused by his daughter's and granddaughter's adulteries). Of the "mistake," Ovid declines to say more than that it was something he saw; this tantalizing vagueness has led to endless speculation by scholars.[3] I wonder, however, if the poem and the mistake were one and the same, since it is possible for a Latin phrase such as *carmen et error* to mean "the mistake of a poem," "the mistake consisting of a poem." And I am inclined to interpret the *carmen* as the *Metamorphoses.* In that case, what he "saw," which is reflected in the poem, was the working of myth in Augustan propaganda and the manipulation of ideology, which disguised the introduction of a new form of monarchy as the restoration of Republican forms of government.

THE UNFINISHED CONDITION OF THE *FASTI*

The first six books of the *Fasti* are apparently all that Ovid wrote, despite his claim to have composed "six books and again as many" (*Tr.* 2.549-50). Although he did not finish the work in exile, there is evidence that he reworked parts of what he had already written at Rome. In Book 4 he refers explicitly to his exile in a reference to the Trojan Solimus, from whom "the walls of Sulmo get their name, / of cool Sulmo . . . where I was born. / Alas, how far that is from Scythian soil! / And I, so far away . . ." (80-83). In Book 1 the prophetess Carmenta consoles her son Evander about his exile from Arcadia by saying, "This was meant to be. Your own fault hasn't banished you, / but a god; you have been exiled by an outraged god" (1.481-82). In his poetic letters from exile, Ovid frequently refers to himself as the victim of an outraged god; consequently, scholars have conjectured that he wrote these lines in exile, too. Further on in this episode, when Carmenta and Evander step ashore at the future site of Rome, Ovid exclaims, "Lucky man, whose exile brought him to that spot!" (1.540); this line too has been interpreted as written in exile.

Because we know that Ovid was exiled in AD 8, we can tell that the address to Tiberius (42 BC–AD 37) as "general we revere," victor in Germany, and founder of a Temple to Concord in AD 10 (1.645-48), must have been composed in exile. There are two references in Book 1 (533, 615) to the accession of Tiberius in AD 14 after the death of Augustus. In Books 2-6, Augustus is generally the addressee, but the work opens with a proem, or introduction, dedicating the work to Germanicus (15 BC–AD 19). When Augustus adopted his stepson Tiberius in AD 4, he required that Tiberius in turn adopt his own nephew Germanicus, the son of his brother Drusus (38–9 BC). In doing this, Augustus was trying to assure that he would be succeeded by male members of his family for several generations. Germanicus was a popular prince and had literary interests of his own (to which Ovid alludes in the proem); his translation of Aratus' astronomical poem *Phainomena* made him an appropriate dedicatee of the *Fasti*. Ovid wanted his support, not only for the poem, but also for his recall from or relocation in exile. To Germanicus is addressed the sad reference in Book 4 to his hometown of Sulmo "so far away." These inconsistencies of address, some to Germanicus, some to Tiberius, and some to Augustus, result from the different periods of composition and indicate that the *Fasti* did not receive a final revision. In the Latin text, these inconsistencies are not so conspicuous, because Ovid could address both Augustus and Tiberius as *Caesar* (when Tiberius was adopted, his change in status was reflected by the change of his name from Tiberius Claudius Nero to Tiberius Julius Caesar), but I have eliminated that ambiguity in the interests of clarity for my reader. As evidence for the poem's original introduction, scholars have long pointed to the beginning of Book 2 (3-18), but more recently that passage has been defended as suitable in its own context.[4]

Paullus Fabius Maximus (46 BC–AD 14), whose wife Marcia was a friend of Ovid's third wife, was one of the prominent persons at Rome to whom Ovid addressed requests for assistance in his poetic letters from exile. The last Book of the *Fasti* ends with praise of the "rank and beauty and character" of "virtuous Marcia" (6.802-806). The occasion is a reference to a monument built by her father Philippus (801), and the passage, put in the mouth of the Muse Clio, concludes, "'The Emperor's aunt was once married to Philippus' father. / What a glorious woman, worthy of this hallowed household!'" (809-10). The second husband of Atia, Augustus' mother, was Lucius Marcius Philippus. His son by a previous marriage, whose name was the same as his (this is the Philippus Ovid refers to in 801), married his stepmother's younger sister; their daughter was Marcia. Praise of his wife Marcia would have gratified Fabius, as praise of his aunt Atia and cousin Marcia would have gratified Augustus; hence this is another passage Ovid is thought to have composed in exile.

Evidence of a strategy to win Fabius' favor also appears in Book 2. One long section deals with the battle of Cremera, at which a Roman army consisting entirely of members of the Fabian clan was massacred. Ovid dates "that famous day" (2.195) to 13 February, but the traditional date is 18 July. The alternative date may come from a family tradition of the Fabii;[5] if so, the choice of date would presumably be part of the effort to win Fabius' support. The episode of Cremera leads into praise for Fabius' famous ancestor, Quintus Fabius Maximus Verrucosus Cunctator (consul in 233, 228, 215, 214, and 209 BC; died 203 BC), whose strategy of non-engagement led to Hannibal's defeat in the Second Punic War (218–210 BC). Moving the Cremera episode from July allows Ovid to combine that Fabian material with his allusion to the two branches of the priesthood of the Luperci, the Luperci Fabiani or Fabii, and the Luperci Quinctiales, or Quinctilii. This is how Ovid concludes his narrative of a legend explaining the origin of the priesthood: "He [i.e., Romulus] laughed, but still he was stung that Remus and the Fabians / could win, but not his own Quintilians. / The appearance of the exploit survives. The Luperci run undressed / and what ended well is thus memorialized" (2.377-80).

Finally, a last piece of evidence reflects the poem's unfinished condition. There are several "doublets," or repeated passages, suggesting the poet had not made his final decision about their location. The most striking is the appearance in both Books 1 and 6 of a story explaining why the ass is sacrificed to Priapus. In both, the ass interrupted an attempted rape by the god, in Book 1 of Lotis, in Book 6 of Vesta.

THE CONTENT AND STRUCTURE OF THE *FASTI*

The Fasti contains diverse material. As the framework of the calendar, there are sections on the traditional festivals and entries noting astronomical phenomena. These are elaborated with narratives from Roman legend and history, as well as Greek myths. One category of the latter are so-called "katasterisms," stories telling the origin of stars and constellations. Anniversaries are mentioned: of famous battles won and lost, of temple dedications, and of titles conferred on Augustus.

As for the organization of this content, one might assume that Ovid's work was done once he had chosen the calendar format and decided to allocate one book per month. Indeed, Ovid is careful in his first two books to establish the correspondence of book to month so that the year and the poem progress in parallel. His entry for 1 January begins, "Look, Germanicus, Janus heralds a happy year for you, / and here he is to inaugurate my poem" (1.63-64). Ovid ends the first book with a couplet that states, "And now the first installment of my work is done / and this book ends with the month it treats" (1.723-24). Book 2 begins "January has ended. The year and its poem continue to grow. / With the second month comes a second installment" (2.1-2), and ends "I have come into port at the end of the month and the book. / Let my skiff soon sail through other waters" (2.863-64). Having made his point, Ovid does not belabor it; at the end of Book 3 he remarks only that the month has ended (3.883-84). The rhythm of time progressing is enhanced by the transitions from one date to the next. Notable in the *Metamorphoses* are the clever, even ingeniously unpredictable transitions from one myth to the next. In the *Fasti*, on the other hand, Ovid develops a repertoire of varied ways of saying "on the next day," or "so many days later," or "when such-and-such has happened." A sort of "punctuation" occurs when Ovid mentions, briefly, the date for various astronomical phenomena: the sun entering a new sign of the zodiac, the rising and setting of certain stars, the midpoint of winter, the beginning of spring, the vernal equinox.

A characteristic feature of books of poetry written in the Augustan period are organizational schemes involving elaborate patterns of thematic and verbal correspondence within and between books. This is true of both long narrative poems, such as Virgil's *Aeneid* and Ovid's own *Metamorphoses,* and collections of short poems, such as Virgil's *Eclogues*, Horace's *Odes*, and Ovid's *Amores*. It has generally been assumed that the formal requirements of the calendar prevented Ovid from developing such patterns in the *Fasti*, but scholars have begun to recognize patterns which imply a greater exercise of choice on Ovid's part.[6] For one thing, the books form pairs on the basis of how they begin: the first two open with an address to an imperial patron, and the second two with remarks on the month's name. In the last two, three goddesses offer competing explanations for the month's name. Peace is a prominent theme in Book 1, both in the section on Janus and again at the end. To develop this theme at the end, Ovid postponed discussion of "Sowing Day" (a moveable feast) to 23 January and chose to treat the Altar of Peace on its dedication date (30 January 9 BC) rather than the date it was consecrated (4 July 13 BC). Likewise, Ovid's choice of an untraditional date for the massacre of Cremera (in February rather than July) allowed him to develop a "Fabian" theme in Book 2. For festivals lasting several days, Ovid usually discusses them on the first day, but the Parentalia, which started on 13 February, he treats on its last day, 21 February. The Floralia began on 28 April, but Ovid explicitly postpones his discussion of that holiday to Book 5.

In the case of katasterisms, Ovid had some leeway: he could decide whether to narrate one at all, on which of the four possible dates (morning rising, morning setting, evening rising, evening setting) to include that narrative, and which variant account of its origin to choose. Ovid hints that he has been involved in choosing among different options by alluding to one version of a katasterism before telling another one. His katasterism of the Hyades begins, "Some think they wet-nursed Bacchus, others believe they were / the granddaughters of Tethys and old man Ocean" (5.167-68). It is the second of these alternatives which he develops in what follows (5.169-82). Ovid records that the Dolphin became a constellation as a reward for rescuing the mythical singer Arion, after beginning his narrative like this: "He [sc. the Dolphin] once was a lucky go-between for a secret love affair / or else he rescued the maestro of the Lesbian lyre" (2.81-82) Later in the same book Ovid tells how the Fish (Pisces) were rewarded for rescuing Venus and Cupid (2.457-74). Ovid's choice of the Dolphin variant makes these two narratives thematically parallel.

The narrative material concerning the twins Romulus and Remus and the founding of Rome appears in six major passages. The exposure of the twins and their rescue is told in Ovid's discussion of the Lupercalia (2.383-422). The death of Romulus appears during a passage on the Quirinalia (2.481-510). Book 3 begins with an account of their conception, birth and exposure (as well as a brief sketch of their adolescence and the foundation of Rome) as part of the explanation that March is named after Mars, the twins' father (3.9-70). The reconciliation of the Sabines and Romans after the Rape of the Sabine Women is included in Ovid's discussion of the Matronalia (3.187-228). Ovid's account of the Parilia features the foundation of Rome and death of Remus (4.807-56), and his treatment of the Lemuria includes a story about Remus' ghost (5.451-80). In addition, Ovid anticipates two passages from the unfinished second half: at 3.55-58, when introducing Mars and his month, Ovid proceeds to describe the twins' reception by their foster parents, Faustulus and Acca Larentia, which he promises to elaborate upon in his entry for the Larentalia (23 December); at 3.199-200, when treating the Kalends of March, Ovid alludes to a passage on the Rape of the Sabines, to be treated in his section on the Consualia

(21 August). It might seem a disadvantage to split up the narrative in this way, but the recurrence of episodes about the city's founders does have an effect similar to the cyclical recurrence of the dates and festivals as the pattern of the year repeats itself over time. To a lesser extent, a similar effect is created by recurring episodes involving Evander and Hercules. When the Tiber says to Ovid, "You've often heard mention of Arcadian Evander's name" (5.643), this could well be a subtle allusion to Evander's appearances in the *Fasti* itself.

To vary his presentation, Ovid alternates long and short episodes, specifically long narrative passages with short astronomical "notices." Each book has two or three episodes developed at length. As for organization and structure within episodes, especially the long passages about the major festivals, Ovid follows several procedures. Frequently he discusses a series of different aspects of the festival. Other times, he presents a sequence of alternative explanations for a single custom or feature. Within those schemes, he may arrange the material in approximately chronological order, beginning in Greek myth and ending in Roman legend or history. Within the entry for the Lupercalia, Ovid offers four roughly chronological reasons why the priests run naked. The Greek god Pan himself runs naked (2.285-88). The primitive Arcadians who originally worshipped Pan didn't wear clothes (2.289-302). The Roman god Faunus dislikes clothes because of a sexual contretemps caused when Hercules and Omphale exchanged clothes (2.303-58). Once, at a feast for Faunus, Romulus and Remus and their followers were exercising in the nude when they had to rush off, still undressed, in pursuit of cattle rustlers (2.361-80). This principle also appears within the entry for the Megalensia, a festival in honor of Cybele. Overall this entry is presented as a series of observations on various aspects of the rites. The three longer sections in this series are arranged chronologically: the noise made to drown out the crying of the infant Jupiter and to prevent his father from finding him (4.197-214); the self-castration of Cybele's priest-lover Attis (4.223-44); and the events surrounding the importation of the goddess to Rome (4.249-347). The whole segment on the Megalensia is organized as an interview, with Ovid asking questions and the Muse Erato supplying the answers. Ovid also uses the scheme of interrogating a divine informant with Janus on New Year's Day in Book 1 and with the goddess Flora for her festival, Floralia, in Book 5. Since the interview with Janus forms the entry for the first date on the calendar, in a sense it establishes a paradigm or model for the contents of a typical entry. It too is organized roughly chronologically: first the god claims that originally he was Chaos (1.103-14); later he says he was a king in Rome in the era before all the gods had left the earth (1.235-54); finally he tells how he helped the Romans fight off an attack by the Sabines under King Tatius (1.259-76).[7]

8

One feature of the way that Ovid presents and organizes his material is his emphasis on the relationship between narrator and reader, and his representation of the narrator as occupying various roles relative to the reader. The narrator of the *Fasti* refers to himself, and is several times addressed by divinities, as *vates*. Sometimes I render this word "poet," sometimes "inspired poet." The later translation conveys more of the nuances of the Latin word. For the Augustan poets, it had an intentionally archaic flavor, and it conveys ideas of a prophet and a community spokesman. Ovid portrays himself also as a researcher of antiquities, who has dug up his material in archaic calendars. The *Fasti* is the record of these research efforts; the narrator lets us in on the process as well as the results. Just before Janus appears to answer the poet's questions about him in Book 1, Ovid reports, "With notebook in hand I was pondering these topics" (1.93). Toward the end of Book 1, the poet persists in "leafing through calendars which marked the seasons" (1.657) in a vain search for a moveable feast, "Sowing Day." Book 6 opens with the poet in a grove, "researching the origin of the month just begun" (6.11). Some of his information comes from interviews, usually impromptu: with the veteran he finds himself seated next to at the games, with an old host in Paelignian territory, an old woman in the Tuscan Quarter, a priest of the god Quirinus. A distinct category of informants consists of gods (singly or in groups) with whom he has extended conversations (Janus; Mars; Flora; the Muses; Juno, Hebe, and Concordia). More generally, Ovid constantly refers to tradition with various locutions meaning essentially "people say" or "the story goes" (the verbs *ferunt, dicitur, memorant,* and the like).

Reporting on his sources of information is one way for Ovid to create the illusion of the poem as a work of scholarship. Another is a feature characteristic of didactic works, the presentation of alternative explanations, as found, for instance, in Lucretius' philosophical *De Rerum Natura* ("On the Nature of the Universe"). Such alternative explanations appear frequently in the *Fasti*, as when Ovid offers a series of possible reasons for the purificatory use of fire in the Parilia ritual (4.783-806). A special category is formed by alternative etymologies; in Book 1, for example, Ovid begins his account of the Agonalia by offering six possible derivations for the name of that festival (1.319-32).

The narrator imagines himself addressing a reader who shares his antiquarian interests. The *Fasti* is punctuated with rhetorical questions such as "Do you want to know?" and "Are you asking?" (e.g., *rogas*, 2.284; *quaeras*, 2.381; *requires*, 2.583). Often the verbs *rogas, quaeres, requires* are used as a kind of formula for introducing a new topic; they are also a way of sustaining the reader's attention. On several occasions, Ovid says something that suggests a reader with as deep an interest in antiquarian research as his own. Ovid tells his reader to look something up if he has the time (3.87); he assures him that if he is fond of archaic rites, he'll be hearing about them (1.631-32); and after asserting that in the original calendar, 1 March was New Year's Day, Ovid suggests a way "to convince yourself" (3.135-36). Elsewhere he recommends "checking out" an inscription (6.211-12).

Ovid's reader is also imagined to share an active fascination with astronomy. Interspersed throughout the poem, between longer sections of religious and other antiquarian lore, are brief astronomical "notices" about such events as the rising or setting of constellations. Quite often, rather than reporting these in third-person narrative, Ovid records them in terms of his reader's perception. Of the Dolphin's setting, he says, "The Dolphin you saw 'til now . . . / will escape from view on the following night" (2.79-80). Similarly, "You'll see the neck of Pegasus" (3.450), "You'll see all the Pleiades" (5.599), "You'll find Jupiter's eagle is rising today" (6.196). Sometimes this role is played not by the reader, but by some hypothetical observer, for example the sailor who makes a remark about the Dolphin (6.471-72) or the drunk on his way home from late-night carousing who comments on the imminent appearance of Orion (6.785-88). Another variation involves telling the reader what he will *not* see. Examples of this are "in vain will you look for the ram" (4.903), and "If you look for Boeotian Orion in the meantime, you'll be mistaken" (5.493).

Occasionally Ovid adopts the role not of a somewhat detached scholarly investigator, but of an active participant in worship. He is still an "expert," but rather than an antiquarian describing the rites, he is a director telling the worshippers what to do and say. This is the case with "Sowing Day" in Book 1, near the beginning of which he says, "Circle the district, farmers, / and offer the district's altars their yearly cakes" (1.669-70); he concludes a prayer to Ceres and Earth by saying, "I wish these things for you, farmers. Wish them for yourselves" (1.695). The Parilia rituals are presented in a series of imperatives: "People, go and ask for fumigant" (4.731), "Shepherd, sprinkle water and sweep the ground" (4.735), "Hang up leaves" (4.737), "Make smoke rise" (4.739), "Bring her food . . . / then pray . . . to Pales" (4.745-46). After the prayer are more commands to conclude the ceremony (4.777-82). Other festivals presented this way are the Matronalia (3.253-58) and the Veneralia (4.133-58).[8]

THE *FASTI* IN THE CONTEXT OF OVID'S OTHER WORKS

"They say a lover denied admission sang the first song / while keeping watch at the barred door" (4.109-10): This couplet employs the conventions and describes an archetypal situation of Latin elegiac love poetry, the form in which

Ovid first won success (*Tr.* 4.10.57-60). Here Ovid attributes the first elegy to the plight of the *exclusus amator* ("the locked-out lover"), associating this type of poetry with the *paraclausithyron* (a serenade, literally, a poem "in front of a closed door"), whose goal is to persuade the woman to let the singer in. In this genre, the poet devotes his work to the service of his mistress, and he declines to write poetry in genres, such as epic, traditionally considered more important. At the beginning of his own *Amores,* Ovid claims he set aside an epic in progress when Cupid interrupted him (*Am.* 1.1.1-4; the rest of the elegy develops this notion).

The subject matter of the *Fasti,* then, is unexpected content for the elegiac form. Knowing that his readers will be surprised ("The poet's the same, but the theme is religion and dates on the calendar. / Who would believe the road from there led here?" 2.7-8), Ovid calls attention to this change of topics a number of times, especially at the beginning of a book, traditionally a point for poets to discuss their aims. Introducing his subject to Germanicus, he asserts that "Augustus' arms [are] a theme for others, mine is Augustus' altars / and the days he added to the ritual year" (1.13-14). Here, the antithesis in elegy between love and war (as celebrated in epic poetry) has become the distinction between religion and war. In the proem to Book 2, often regarded as the original introduction to the whole poem before the rededication to Germanicus, Ovid characterizes his earlier elegies in the standard, self-deprecatory fashion as light, erotic, non-serious, and youthful (2.4-6), by contrast with this, their "first voyage under full sail" (2.3). The present work he represents as his "active duty" (2.9) in service to Augustus as "an eager enlisted man" (2.15). This is a switch on the situation in *Amores* 1.9, which claimed that "every lover is a soldier," that the life of a poet in the service of love is actually more demanding than a military career. At the beginning of Book 3, Ovid imagines Mars himself wondering "what's a poet's business with Mars" (3.3). When he starts Book 4 by invoking the aid of Venus, she reacts by asking "'What do you want with me? Surely you were singing a grander song'" (4.3). As in the proem to Book 2, he characterizes the earlier work in her service as youthful and non-serious (4.7-9). There he expressed the grander scope of the current project in a nautical metaphor (the "first voyage under full sail"); here the conveyance is a chariot: "now my horses are running on a bigger track" (4.10).

Finally, Juno captures the incongruity of form and content when she addresses Ovid as the "'bold reporter / of matters great in light-weight measures'" (6.21-22). Ovid pretends to be dismayed by his choice of form as he begins to treat "the greatest honor heaped on the calendar" (2.122), i.e., Augustus' title of "Father of his Country," conferred on 5 February. He calls it "a crazy idea" to load "such weight / on elegy[.] This is the stuff of epic poetry" (2.125-26).

Indeed, he opens the entry by wishing for the "inspiration and power" which Homer manifests in the *Iliad* (2.119-20).

At the time he was composing the *Fasti,* Ovid was absorbed in the question of both elegiac and epic form and content, since he was simultaneously at work on the *Metamorphoses* in dactylic hexameters. There is overlap in the contents of both works, Greek myths and Roman legends. Further, Ovid makes a point, it seems, of calling attention to passages in the *Fasti* which treat topics also dealt with in the *Metamorphoses,* thus nudging the reader to interpret the *Fasti* in the context of the *Metamorphoses.* In introducing the topic for 17 March (the Liberalia), he dismisses a series of possible Bacchic topics, the god's fiery conception and unusual birth, his early triumphs, his punishment of those who, like Pentheus and Lycurgus, resisted his worship (3.715-22). He finally gets to his subject this way: "Look, I'd like to tell about the Tyrrhenian sailors, suddenly / dolphins, but that's not the function of this passage. / The function of this passage is to set down the reasons why / the vine planter summons people to his libation cakes" (3.723-26). The repeated phrase *carminis huius opus,* which more literally means "the function of this poem," points up the contrast between the present work and the *Metamorphoses*, which features the transformation of Tyrrhenian sailors into dolphins when Ovid relates a story about Bacchus in its third book.

In his treatment of the Cerealia, Ceres' festival, Ovid asserts that "This section of my work demands an account of the Rape of Proserpina: / much will be familiar, but you'll learn a few things" (4.417-18). This is especially true for the reader of the *Metamorphoses*, which contains an extensive version of this story, told by the Muse Calliope, in its fifth book. An early twentieth-century monograph by Richard Heinze used a comparison of these two versions to distinguish between genres of "epic narrative" and "elegiac narrative." Recently Stephen Hinds has re-evaluated Heinze's study and concluded not that the two works represent different narrative genres, but that viewed in terms of each other, the Proserpina narratives in the *Fasti* and the *Metamorphoses* examine and stretch the possibilities of elegy and epic.[9]

Besides these two instances in which Ovid broadly reminds the reader about his other version of the same tale, the story of Callisto appears in the second book of both works. The gist of the story is this: Callisto, one of Diana's band of chaste nymphs, is raped and impregnated by Jupiter. When Diana discovers her pregnancy, she expels her from the company. After she has given birth to a son, she is transformed by Jupiter's wrathful wife Juno into a bear. Fifteen years later, the bear Callisto encounters her son, a hunter, who would have killed her if they had not been transported to the sky as the constellations of the the Great Bear and the Bear Guardian. Still irate, Juno asks as a favor of the ocean that it refuse to bathe those stars, which accounts for why they never set. In the *Fasti* this story appears as a katasterism in the context of a reference to those constellations (2.153-92). Two long sections which comprise the beginning and the end of the episode in the *Metamorphoses* (2.401-530) appear in very condensed form in the *Fasti*. In the *Metamorphoses*, Jupiter, disguised as Diana, accosts Callisto—the nymph is resting from the noonday heat—and then rapes her; when she next encounters Diana, she is afraid it may be Jupiter again (2.417-44). In the *Fasti* all this is abbreviated as "She avoided men, but Jupiter got her in trouble" (2.162). The version in the *Metamorphoses* concludes with Juno going to the sea gods Tethys and Ocean and making her request (2.508-30). This is condensed into the final couplet of the *Fasti* version: "Juno is still furious, and asks the foaming Sea / not to bathe—or even touch—the Arcadian Bear" (2.191-92). Ovid avoids repeating himself, but in such a way as to remind the reader familiar with both works of what has not been repeated. Such a reader would be attuned to similarities and differences, reading each version in light of the other. In the *Fasti* one reads: "Wounded pride drove Juno crazy and she transformed the girl. / Whatever for? Jupiter had her against her will" (2.177-78). "Whatever for?" is addressed to Juno, and more literally means "What are you doing?" Within his report of Callisto's futile struggle with Jupiter in the *Metamorphoses*, Ovid addresses a parenthetical remark to Juno: "I wish you had seen that, Juno, you would have been more merciful!" (2.435). After the transformation in the *Fasti*, Juno "told her husband, 'Go to bed with *that*'" (180). In the *Metamorphoses*, the transformation is preceded by Juno's taunts to Callisto herself (2.471-75). One last difference in the *Fasti* can be seen as an interpretation of a detail in the *Metamorphoses*. When she escapes the noon heat in the *Metamorphoses*, Callisto unstrings her bow and takes off her quiver to use it as a pillow (2.419-21); it is at that moment that Jupiter sees her and rapes her. When she finally escapes, she almost forgets to take her bow and quiver (2.439-40). Thus, the emblems of her association with Diana represent her virginity. This is made explicit by the scene which opens the *Fasti* version but does not appear in the *Metamorphoses*: "With her hand on the goddess' bow, she took a solemn oath: / 'I swear by this bow to remain a virgin'" (2.157-58).

THE *FASTI* IN THE CONTEXT OF GREEK AND ROMAN LITERATURE

Two works of Hellenistic Greek literature of the third century BC were especially influential on the *Fasti*, the *Phainomena* of Aratus (ca. 315–240/239 BC) and the *Aitia* of Callimachus (ca. 305–ca. 240 BC). The former is a poem in hexameters on astronomy and weather signs. At Rome, the statesman Cicero translated it into Latin, as did the prince Germanicus, to whom Ovid rededicated the *Fasti*. Fragments of an abridged adaptation of Aratus by Ovid himself are extant. The *Aitia* was profoundly influential, not only on the *Fasti*, but on Roman poets in the Augustan period as well as several of their predecessors in the generation known as the Neoterics, or innovators. Callimachus was a scholar as well as a poet who tutored the children of one of the Ptolemies of Egypt and catalogued the famous library at Alexandria. His *Aitia* is an elegiac four-book collection on the origins (*aitia*) of various obscure customs. Part of Callimachus' *persona* is that of a scholar collecting the lore which he presents. In the first two books, a framework for the diverse *aitia* is provided by a dialogue between the poet and the Muses. Thus Ovid's debt is clear: the aetiological conception in general, the notion of conversations with divinities, and the poet's role as a scholarly antiquarian. Ovid introduces his subject as "The dates—and their origins" (1.1: *tempora cum causis*; *causa* is the Latin equivalent of the Greek *aition*).

Ovid shared his interest in origins with the other Augustan writers. Virgil, in his national epic the *Aeneid*, wrote about the original founding hero, Aeneas, a Trojan who came to Italy as a refugee from Troy after its defeat by the Greeks. In his fourth book of elegies, Propertius turned from love elegies to *aitia* about various monuments and cults in the city of Rome. Livy wrote a multi-volume history of Rome from its beginnings to his time; because of his interest in the cause of Rome's greatness, he stressed the origins of her various institutions.

Frequent themes in the *Fasti*, as one might expect in an antiquarian work, are the good old days, the contrast between then and now, between past simplicity in the appearance of the city and the behavior of its inhabitants, and present sophistication. This is one of the points in the dialogue with the god Janus on New Year's Day, a passage which in many ways is paradigmatic for the whole poem; the theme of past simplicity appears in the god's answer about why he is given small coins (1.191-226). The gods Mars and Tiber make similar observations in Books 3 and 5 respectively, when Mars briefly explains why the earliest Romans had to abduct their wives (3.178-92), and when Tiber is asserting that he can remember far enough back in time to answer Ovid's question about the Argei (5.639-42). This theme of antique simplicity comes up again when Ovid talks about the Liberalia and the *toga liberalis* and recalls an earlier time when senators and consuls worked their own land (3.779-84), and when he discusses the origins of animal sacrifice and contrasts that with the forms of sacrifice in simpler times (1.337-46). To explain the custom of eating fat bacon, beans and barley on 1 June, he notes that the date is the festival of an old-time goddess from the period before Romans developed luxurious tastes (6.169-80).

Ovid shares this theme with other Augustans, as well as the theme of a Golden Age and the role in that period of the Arcadians, who "lived on earth before Jupiter was born," and are of a "race [that] even predates the moon" (2.289-90). These literary motifs also correspond to themes in the Augustan political program and its propaganda, since the Emperor presented his reforms as returns to earlier ways, in government, religion, sexual morality, and so on. The first poem in Propertius' aetiological fourth book provides a stranger to Rome with a tour of its current monuments and includes comments contrasting the opulent present with the simpler past. In Book 8 of the *Aeneid*, the hero Aeneas is taken on a tour of the future site of Rome by the Arcadian king Evander at his settlement Pallanteum (the future Palatine Hill). In that same book, Evander tells how Hercules came to the area and got rid of the monster Cacus, who had been terrorizing the inhabitants. This episode provides an *aition* for the Ara Maxima, the monument which is the subject of Propertius' aetiological elegy 4.9. Ovid includes a narrative of Hercules and Cacus in Book 1.543-82, concluding with the foundation of that altar.

Two other sections of the *Fasti* also reflect the influence of the *Aeneid*. When discussing the Carmentalia, Ovid tells of Evander's flight from Arcadia as an exile, accompanied by his mother Carmenta, who guides him to the site on the Tiber, and, upon arrival, prophesies the Roman future (1.469-540). These details correspond to the plot outline of the first half of the *Aeneid*. There, Aeneas flees from Troy as a refugee, accompanied by his father Anchises, though Anchises dies before they arrive in Italy. Aeneas visits him in the Underworld and hears an extensive prophecy about Rome's future just before reaching his destination. Likewise, in Book 3 Ovid gives one explanation of the goddess Anna Perenna as Anna, the sister of Dido, queen of Carthage. According to Ovid, after Aeneas abandons Dido and she commits suicide, Anna escapes with some other Carthaginians and wanders in search of refuge until she is shipwrecked at Aeneas' settlement in Italy. This narrative forms both a sequel and a parallel to the first four books of the *Aeneid*; Ovid presents Anna as a counterpart to Virgil's Aeneas, who escapes from Troy and wanders the Mediterranean until he is shipwrecked at Dido's Carthage.[10]

Propertius' elegy 4.2 treats the statue of the god Vertumnus in the Tuscan Quarter. In this poem the statue talks, mostly about the etymology of its name. Ovid reiterates some details from Propertius' poem in the explanation he has an old woman give for the custom of going barefoot in that part of the city (6.395-416). She claims it dates from the time when the Tiber flooded the neighborhood, when "Yonder god Vertumnus hadn't yet taken a name from averting / the stream, that also fits his versatile shapes" (6.409-10). Those explanations correspond to two of the three derivations discussed by Propertius' talking statue; the first is one of two the statue rejects as incorrect, the second is the one he claims is right.

Material in the *Fasti* about the Roman monarchical period, from the time of the founder and first king, Romulus, to that of the last king, Tarquin the Proud, also appears in the first book of Livy's history, including the plot against King Servius by his daughter Tullia and son-in-law Tarquin (1.46-48), the refusal of the god Terminus to budge from the site of the Temple of Jupiter at the Capitoline Hill (1.55), and the sequence of events from the war with Gabii to the rape of Lucretia and the resulting end of the monarchy with the expulsion of the Tarquins (1.53-60). In this first Book, Livy's antiquarian interests frequently coincide with those of Ovid in the *Fasti*. He credits King Evander with introducing the ritual of the Lupercalia (1.52) and the worship of Hercules at the Ara Maxima (1.7). He discusses the foundations of the earliest temples: of Jupiter Feretrius, the very first, by Romulus (1.10.5-7); of Janus by Numa (1.19); and of Jupiter on the Capitoline by Tarquin the Proud (1.55). He recounts the innovations of the several kings, including Numa's calendar reforms (1.19) and priesthoods (1.20). He dates the first bridge over the Tiber to the reign of Ancus Martius (1.33), and later discusses Tarquin's construction of the Circus Maximus and the Cloaca Maxima (1.56). He outlines the formal procedure for the declaration of war (1.32) and explains the custom of shouting "Thalassius" at weddings in terms of an occurrence during the Rape of the Sabine Women (1.9.12).

In the *Fasti* we find echoes from earlier Roman literature as well. The story of Ariadne and Theseus told in connection with Ovid's description of a constellation, Ariadne's Crown, not only recalls Ovid's own version of the same story in his letter from Ariadne in the *Heroides*, but also one by the Republican love poet Catullus. Catullus 64 is a long poem on the marriage of Peleus and Thetis, the parents of Achilles. Within that poem, narrated as the description of a scene embroidered on the coverlet for the marriage bed, is the story of Theseus' desertion of Ariadne. The story of Attis and Cybele, related during Ovid's discussion of the Megalensia, recalls Catullus 63, but with a significant difference, as usually is the case when Ovid adapts another author's version. The story of Attis' self-castration is a myth explaining Cybele's eunuch priests. Catullus' poem recounts the arrival of the young man Attis in Phrygia, his self-castration in a frenzied moment of religious ecstasy, and his remorse afterward when he realizes what he has done. In Ovid's version Attis is Cybele's lover, and he castrates himself when the goddess drives him mad for an act of infidelity. Lucretius' *De Rerum Natura*, also from the late Republic, begins (1.1–43) with a hymn to Venus, *Aeneadum genetrix* ("mother of the descendants of Aeneas"), and includes a tirade against animal sacrifice as one of the horrors for which religious superstition is responsible. Ovid recalls these passages in his praise of Venus near the beginning of Book 4 (87-114), and in his discussion of the origins of animal sacrifice in Book 1.

THE *FASTI* AND THE IMAGE OF THE EMPEROR AUGUSTUS

In the proem rededicating the *Fasti* to Germanicus, Ovid tells the prince that in this poem ". . . you'll find your family's special observances / and often read the names of your father and grandfather" (1.9-10), and refers to the "red-letter days which both of them earned" (11). On four dates, Ovid's entries commemorate a title won by Augustus: on 13 January, "Augustus" itself; on 5 February, *pater patriae* ("Father of His Country"); on 6 March, *pontifex maximus* ("chief high-priest"); and on 16 April, *imperator* ("Commander"). Throughout the poem other aspects of Augustus' public image are treated, both specifically and generally. For a better appreciation of this important theme, it will be useful to consider it in light of Augustus' own official version of the events from 44 BC to AD 14, the *Res Gestae* ("Accomplishments").

The "Restoration of the Republic" was a central element in the program and propaganda of Augustus. On 13 January 27 BC, he felt securely enough established in power that he announced this "Restoration." Ovid says, "On that date . . . all power was restored to the people / and your grandfather got the title 'Augustus'" (1.589-90). Augustus' version of this event climaxes the *Res Gestae*, forming its penultimate section (*RG* 34): "In my sixth and seventh consulship, after I had extinguished civil wars, and at a time when with universal consent I was in complete control of affairs, I transferred the republic from my power to the dominion of the senate and people of Rome. For this service of mine I was named Augustus by decree of the senate, and the doorposts of my house were publicly wreathed with bay leaves and a civic crown was fixed over my door and a golden shield was set in the Curia Julia. . . ."[11] The "civic crown" (*corona civica*) originally was a military decoration awarded to a soldier who had saved a fellow-citizen's life in battle. The Senate's rationale was to honor Augustus for saving all the citizens from the ravages of civil war. This "civic crown" appears in Ovid's prayer at the end of the entry for 13 January: "May his [i.e., Jupiter's] oak-leaf wreath safeguard your palace doors" (1.614). Ovid alludes to this decoration again at the end of Book 4 in referring to the "house with the oak-leaf cluster" (4.953; literally, "the house bordered [*praetextata*] with oak").

Ovid's entry for 13 January discusses the *cognomen* "Augustus," asserting that it is the most glorious of all the various Roman honorifics, and climaxing with it a list of other famous *cognomina* (1.593-608). As with the Ides of January, so the Nones of February commemorates a title honoring the Emperor, "Father of His Country" (2.127-44). This is the title Augustus mentions last in the *Res Gestae*: "In my thirteenth consulship the senate, the equestrian order and the whole people of Rome gave me the title of Father of my Country . . ." (35). Ovid's development of the topic involves an extended invidious comparison between the first king and founder Romulus (who is told to "take second place," 2.133) and Augustus. "Romulus" may even have been considered as a possible title for Octavian (as a sort of second "founder") before "Augustus" was decided upon; Dio Cassius claims, in his early third-century AD history of Rome, that Octavian himself was eager to receive that title until he realized its suggestion of royal ambitions (53.16.7). Line 139 of Ovid's comparison of Romulus and Augustus—"You took wives by force, his laws kept them chaste"—contrasts the Rape of the Sabine Women with Augustus' marriage legislation. This legislation, forbidding marriage between members of Rome's highest and lowest classes and criminalizing adultery, represented the Emperor's endeavor to restore old-time sexual morality and raise the elite birthrate. The assertion that Romulus "harbored criminals" (2.140) refers to the Asylum he reputedly established on the Capitoline Hill; elsewhere (3.431-34) Ovid presents that in a favorable light. In line 142 Ovid contrasts their titles: *dominus* ("king"; literally, "lord" or "master") for Romulus, the first king, and *princeps* ("a leading citizen"). The word *princeps* (the source of the English word "prince") developed into a title for the emperor during Augustus' lifetime. He himself claimed to be *primus inter pares* ("first among equals"), being careful to avoid the suspicion of monarchical ambitions which had led to Caesar's assassination. In the next point of comparison between the first king and the *princeps,* the former's murder of his twin brother Remus is put in the balance against Romulus. In his actual narratives of the murder and its aftermath, however, Ovid presents Romulus in as favorable a light as possible (4.835-56; 5.467-72). In the latter passage, the ghost of Remus blames Romulus' assistant Celer and exonerates his brother. To this fratricide, Ovid contrasts Augustus' famous *clementia* toward enemies (2.143). Along with the title "Augustus," the Emperor had been awarded a gold shield inscribed with his virtues—"courage, clemency, justice, and piety" (RG 34.2). The policy of "clemency," which Augustus shared with Caesar, is stressed near the beginning of the *Res Gestae*: "I undertook many civil and foreign wars, and as victor I spared the lives of all citizens who asked for mercy. When foreign peoples could safely be pardoned I preferred to preserve rather than to exterminate them" (RG 3.1-2).

Augustus' reign inaugurated a period called the "Augustan Peace," which was characterized by military successes and increased security abroad and the end of a century of intermittent civil war at home. The arched gate of Janus Quirinus at the north side of the Roman Forum was kept closed in peacetime and open in time of war. The importance of this practice in Augustan propaganda can be seen in *Res Gestae* 13, in which Augustus boasts that the gate, although closed only twice in the entire period of Roman history prior to his reign, was closed three times during his principate. It is Janus Quirinus to which Ovid alludes in his interview with the god Janus when he asks, "'With so many doors, why are you worshipped in just this one, / where the Roman Forum and the Julian meet'" (more literally, "here where you have a temple joined in two fora"; 1.257-58). Later, Ovid asks, "'Why do you hide in peace and open when war breaks out?'" (1.277). Janus replies (in part), "'In peace I shut my doors to keep the peace from escaping. / Under the Caesars I'll be shut a long time'" (1.281-82). Earlier, in discussing his role as cosmic opener and closer, Janus alludes to his connection with war and peace, while reversing the logic: "'When I have felt like dispatching Peace from her calm abode, / then she freely walks the long highways. / The whole world will be a welter of deadly bloodshed / unless strong bars keep wars locked away'" (1.121-24).

The theme of peace and the responsibility of the imperial house for that peace is strong at the end of Book 1. At the end of his entry for "Sowing Day," a moveable agricultural festival, Ovid concludes his prayer, "I wish these things for you, farmers. Wish them for yourselves, /. . . . / Wars have long kept men from the fields. . . . / . . . / . . . / Thanks be to the gods and your imperial house; under your foot / Wars have long lain bound in chains" (1.695-702). The final entry of this book concerns the dedication of the magnificent Altar of Augustan Peace, originally in the Campus Martius, now on display near the Mausoleum of Augustus. In the *Res Gestae*, Augustus mentions the senate's consecration of this monument in his own honor in a section immediately preceding that on Janus Quirinus (12.2). Ovid begins, "Peace, wreathed in honor of the end of civil war, / be with us, as a gentle presence throughout the globe" (1.711-12) and concludes, "Pray that the house which brings us peace may last forever / with that peace . . ." (1.721-22).

To divert attention from the fact that he was one party in a civil war, Augustus represented his actions against the assassins of Julius Caesar as the vengeance of a dutiful son. As he puts it near the beginning of the *Res Gestae*, "I drove into exile the murderers of my father, avenging their crime through tribunals established by law; and afterwards, when they made war on the republic, I twice defeated them in battle" (*RG* 2). Two dates on the calendar provide opportunities for Ovid to develop this theme. The first, of course, is the Ides of March. Of the assassins Ovid says, "But whoever dared such wickedness, forbidden by the power of the gods, / and violated the person of the chief high-priest, / lies dead as he deserves. Bear witness, Philippi, / and the battlefield white with their scattered bones. / This was the task, this the duty, this the foundation / of Augustus avenging his father in a righteous war" (3.705-10). Philippi is the battle in which Brutus and Cassius were defeated by Antony, then Octavian's ally, in 42 BC. The second occasion is 12 May, the dedication day of the Temple of Mars Ultor ("the Avenger"), the main temple of the Forum of Augustus (5.545-98). Mars is imagined to have come to earth for the commemorative festivities and to be looking over the temple and the two colonnades flanking it. Two couplets in the description allude to the statues in niches of the colonnades: "From here he sees Aeneas loaded with a priceless burden / and so many ancestors of the noble Julian line. / From here he sees Romulus shouldering spoils from a general, / and exploits inscribed beneath a row of statues" (5.563-66). Ovid recreates a scene in which Augustus vows the temple at the outset of war, "'If my father, Vesta's priest, is my inspiration for going to war, / and if I intend to avenge the divinity of them both, / be with me, Mars, glut my sword with the criminals' blood, / and back the better cause with your support. / If I am victorious, you'll get a temple and be called the Avenger'" (5.573-77). The remainder of that date's entry (579-94) concerns another event important in Augustan propaganda, the recovery from the Parthians in 20 BC of the standards they had captured from Crassus at the battle of Carrhae (9 June 53 BC; cf. *Fasti* 6.465-68 and *RG* 29.2).

The Augustan Peace was won by the military successes of the Emperor's generals, which he claimed as his own. In listing his triumphs and other honors for military victories, Augustus notes that he "was twenty-one times saluted as *imperator*" (*RG* 4.1). On 16 April, Ovid commemorates one such occasion, probably the first, which seems to have honored Octavian for breaking Mark Antony's siege of Modena in 43 BC (4.673-76; cf. 627-28 on Modena). There he uses the circumlocution *titulum imperii* (676; literally, "the title of command") for *Imperator* ("Commander"). This title, which became included as part of Augustus' and later emperors' names, is the origin of the word "Emperor." Originally, a victorious Roman general had to be acclaimed *Imperator* by his troops in order to petition the Senate to celebrate a triumph.

Augustus' activities in the religious sphere were another part of his public image. On 6 March 12 BC, he became *pontifex maximus*, a position his adoptive father Caesar had also held, as Augustus himself points out in his account of this honor in the *Res Gestae* (10.2). The core of Ovid's entry reads, "To Augustus' countless honors (which did he prefer to earn?) / has been added the office of chief high-priest" (3.419-20). Several times Ovid acknowledges the special relationship between the goddess Vesta and the *pontifex maximus*. In treating the Ides of March, Ovid has Vesta herself claim that Caesar's person was actually unhurt by the assassins since she had taken him to heaven and substituted a phantom (3.701-702). Ovid concludes Book 4 by saying, "Vesta has been welcomed in the palace / of her kinsman Augustus. . . . / Apollo has a share; a second share has gone to Vesta; / the third that remains he occupies himself" (4.949-52). This conceit, of Augustus, Apollo, and Vesta sharing a residence ("a single house for three immortals," 4.954), refers to the location on the Palatine hill of Augustus' house, a temple of Apollo, and a shrine for Vesta. The Temple of Palatine Apollo was dedicated on 9 October 28 BC and is one indication of a special relationship the Emperor claimed with that god, to whom he gave credit for his defeat of Antony and Cleopatra at Actium in 31 BC. The shrine for Vesta he built immediately adjacent to his own house on the Palatine, to avoid moving into the Regia, the official residence of the *pontifex maximus*.

One of Augustus' prominent and conspicuous religious activities was the restoration of temples which had fallen into disrepair. This was, in a way, a visible corollary to his claim of restoring the moral standards credited to earlier times. He mentions some of this activity in the *Res Gestae*: "In my sixth consulship I restored eighty-two temples of the gods in the city on the authority of the senate, neglecting none that required restoration at that time" (20.4). Ovid alludes to his efforts at restoring religious monuments from time to time when he names a temple's original founder and its imperial refounder. He mentions it most explicitly on a very slight pretext in Book 2. On 1 February, he tells us, a temple was founded for Juno Sospita, but it disappeared as a result of the ravages of time (2.55-58). From that lead-in, Ovid continues to praise the "Founder of temples, the temples' holy restorer" (2.63), "Our hallowed leader's far-sighted concern has taken measures / to keep the rest from toppling with a similar crash. / Under his regime temples don't show their age. / Just like us, the gods are indebted to him" (2.59-62).

Throughout the *Fasti*, Ovid refers to the divine status of Augustus and members of his family. This cult of the emperor was introduced very gradually during his reign, to avoid offending Roman sensibilities. This happened sooner in parts of the Roman world where the concept of deified rulers was familiar, i.e., the Hellenistic East, which had been ruled by deified successors to Alexander the Great. In Rome itself the divine associations of the Emperor began when his "Genius" (the spirit of his procreative powers) was joined in worship with the Lares Compitales (the "Lares of the Crossroads"). Ovid alludes to this practice when he claims that "The City has a thousand shrines to the Lares and the spirit of the leader / who restored them. Every parish worships those three" (5.145-46). In that passage, however, Ovid conflates the

Lares Compitales with the Lares Praestites (the "Standby Lares," actual subject of that entry). After his assassination, Julius Caesar was deified; his divinity was declared on 1 January 42 BC. Hence his adopted son Octavian began to refer to himself as "son of a god." After Augustus' own death and ensuing deification, his adopted son Tiberius could logically be called "son and grandson of gods" (1.533). In AD 6, Tiberius rededicated the Temple of Castor and Pollux, in his own name and that of his late brother Drusus. Ovid alludes to this artfully: "For those divine brothers, brothers from a deified clan / founded it close to Juturna's pool" (1.707-708). Ovid has Carmenta conclude her prophecy of Roman history in this way: "'As I will someday be worshipped on everlasting altars, / so will Julia Augusta become a new god'" (1.535-36). Augustus' wife Livia was adopted as Julia Augusta in his will, but Ovid's prediction was premature. When Livia died, her son, the Emperor Tiberius, vetoed the Senate's deification of her. Only later did the Emperor Claudius, her grandson, deify her.

ROMAN RELIGION

Roman religion, like the rest of Roman culture, is an amalgam of native and imported elements. Primitive, animistic forms relating to farms and family combine with the great anthropomorphic deities of the Roman state, products of contact with Greeks and Etruscans. Later, there were imports from the Near East, such as Cybele, the Great Mother. Finally, under Augustus, there was both religious restoration and the beginning of emperor worship in the imperial cult.[12]

The chief deity of the Roman state was Jupiter. An early temple on the Capitoline Hill housed him with Juno and Minerva; this triad is Etruscan, however, rather than Roman. Mars was an Italian god of both war and agriculture. Under Greek influence, the god Quirinus was identified as the deified first king Romulus, but an ancient tradition maintains that he was Sabine in origin. Diana was the chief deity of the Latin League. Vesta seems to have originated as the spirit of the king's hearth. Venus and Fortuna were both Italian imports; Apollo, Mercury, and the hero Hercules were Greek. Liber was an Italian wine-god who became associated with the Greek Dionysus, as Ceres was an Italian grain-goddess associated with the Greek Demeter. Well before Ovid's time, the gods of the Roman pantheon had assimilated the myths about the Olympians from Greek literature: Jupiter was equated with Zeus, Juno with Hera, Venus with Aphrodite, and so on.

The gods were worshipped under various cult-titles.[13] In the *Fasti,* for instance, there appear Jupiter Elicius and Jupiter Pistor, Juno Lucina, Juno Sospita and Juno Moneta, and both Venus Erycina and Venus Verticordia. The god Janus refers to two of his titles when he says, "You're going to laugh / at the names the priest invokes when he sets out a cake / and salted meal. One and the same, I'm called now Opener [Patulcius], / now Closer [Clusius] by the celebrant's lips" (1.127-30). This passage also reflects the importance in Roman worship of addressing the divinity by exactly the right title. In some ways the cult-titles are vestiges of the multiplicity of spirits (*numina*) which, at an earlier stage of Roman religion, were believed to preside over specialized subdivisions of human life and activity. F. E. Adcock has joked about these "functional spirits" in a telling way, saying that if the Romans had had bicycles, they would have had a divinity named "Punctura."[14]

Religion at Rome was not a matter of individual conscience but of corporate ritual for the welfare of the state. The goal of religious practices was the maintenance of good relations between the Roman people and their gods (the *pax deorum*, "peace of the gods"). Conduct of the cult was in the hands of various priesthoods. Being a priest did not require any special vocation or training, nor was it, generally, a full-time occupation. The Roman nobility supplied members for the priesthoods, just as it did the candidates for elected office; participation in the priesthoods was one aspect of a political career, just as was election to what we would call "secular" public office. If any of the priests could be viewed as the head of the state religion, it was the *pontifex maximus* ("greatest pontiff"), head of the college, or board, of sixteen *pontifices* (singular, *pontifex*); in the translation I render *pontifices* as "high priests" and *pontifex maximus* as "chief high-priest" or "chief priest." Under the supervision of the *pontifex maximus* were the six Vestal Virgins, dedicated to the service of Vesta and her eternal flame. The association of the *pontifex maximus* with the Vestals can be seen in Book 6, where Ovid describes the *pontifex* Metellus as first exhorting the Vestals to rescue Vesta from her burning temple, then in desperation doing so himself (6.437-54). The official residence of the *pontifex* was the Regia (literally, "the palace"), one indication that the earlier religious functions of the Roman kings had devolved onto him. A similar indication is the association with the pontifical college of the priest called the *rex sacrorum* (literally, "king of sacrifices"; I render this as "king-priest"). The gods Jupiter, Mars, and Quirinus each had a priest called a *flamen* (I have retained the Latin term). These and twelve minor *flamines* were also associated with the pontifical college. Jupiter's *flamen*, the *flamen Dialis*, had a life circumscribed by numerous taboos so onerous that in the late Republic the position went unfilled for 75 years until Augustus' restoration of lapsed offices and collapsed temples. His wife (the *flaminica*) also had to satisfy certain requirements and perform certain rituals (cf. 2.27-28; 3.397-98); at 6.229-32, the *flaminica* discusses some of these with Ovid. Other priesthoods which appear in the *Fasti* include the Luperci (2.301) and the Salii (I render this as "the Leaping Priests"; see 3.259).

Prayer and sacrifice were the two basic elements of worship. A prayer invoked the divinity's presence (hence the importance of precise address) and petitioned to win favor, avert harm, or expiate offense. The prayer was not a magic spell which bound the god to grant the request, and so it also included an endeavor to persuade him or her, by reminding the deity of past favors, or by insisting that the favor was within the deity's sphere of influence. In the *Fasti*, a prayer to Terminus, the god of boundary markers, first cites past occasions when the divinity maintained boundaries, and then asks him to continue to do so (2.659-78). When the *flamen* of Quirinus prays to Robigo, spirit of mildew and rust, he reminds the deity that "Your power is not slight" (4.915) and pleads "Don't harm the crops; the power to harm is enough" (4.922). Sacrifice took place either before the prayer, to predispose the god, or afterward, to seal it. After the *flamen*'s prayer to Robigo, he offers sacrifice (4.911-36), whereas sacrifice precedes the prayer to Terminus (2.643-78). In addition to animal sacrifice (which Ovid discusses at length, 1.335-456), there were offered special cakes (3.733-36), libations of wine (e.g., to the Lares, 2.633-38) or milk (e.g., to Pales, 4.745-46), and *mola salsa* (a mixture of salt and grain meal; cf. 1.337-38); different sorts of sacrifice were appropriate to different gods. The sacrifice had to be something living, i.e., organic, since it not merely won the god's good will, but in origin was thought to sustain his power to enable him to comply. The formula *do ut des* ("I give so that you give") concisely expresses the contractual, even legalistic, aspect of Roman sacrifice. The gist of this appears in a couplet in which Ovid mentions offerings made by merchants to Mercury: "Everyone whose line is selling merchandise offers incense / to you and asks you for profits in return" (5.671-72). Gods received sacrifice on the occasion of festivals in their honor and on the anniversary of a temple dedication. Jupiter and Juno received monthly sacrifice, she on the Kalends, he on the Ides.

Gods were also honored by the dedication of temples. Temples housed the cult statue of the divinity in whose honor it had been built and a storeroom for valuable offerings dedicated to that divinity; at a stone altar outside the temple, animal sacrifice took place. To the fire on the altar were offered chopped up portions of the internal organs (the Latin word for these is *prosecta*, which at 6.163 I have simply translated as "innards"); the meat might be consumed by the priests or worshippers. These permanent altars had been, at an earlier stage, temporary structures, like the one erected for the offerings to Terminus (2.645-53). Temples were often dedicated in thanksgiving, sometimes in satisfaction of a vow made during a time of crisis, sometimes as an act of appeasement. One such vow in the *Fasti* is the temple to Concord promised by Camillus: "Camillus . . . had vowed / the original temple and fulfilled his vow. / The occasion was a popular revolt against the ruling class / when Rome lived in fear of her own manpower" (1.641-44). Another is the temple vowed by the Senate to *Mens Bona* ("Good Sense"): "Good Sense has divine power too. We see that a shrine was promised / to Good Sense from dread of war with shifty Carthage" (6.241-42).

As another way of honoring the gods, at festivals the Roman officials held *ludi* (I render this word as "shows," but they are usually referred to as "games"). Entertainments at these "shows" included theatrical performances, chariot races, gladiator fights, and animal hunts. The gladiatorial combats were derived from the Etruscan and Campanian practice of giving such combats as funeral games. The chariot races, in the Circus Maximus and other later racetracks, date from at least the monarchy and also reflect Etruscan origins. The theatrical performances, the more recent form of *ludi*, were a Greek import. Ovid mentions gladiator fights in honor of Minerva on the Quinquatrus (3.813-14). As part of Flora's festival, the Floralia, he mentions "races and cheers from the theater" (5.189) and inquires about the animal hunts: "Why are there netted at your shows, not African lions, / but harmless roe deer and twitching hares?" (5.371-72). These shows in Flora's honor were not originally annual, but became so as the result of a vow made to appease the goddess (5.295-330).

Rites of purification were also important in Roman religion. Ovid derives the name of "February" (2.19-34) from *februa* ("the means of absolution," 2.19), and discusses the concept of purification (2.35-46). In April at the Parilia, livestock and their keepers were purified. In June, Vesta's temple was swept and the refuse disposed of in the Tiber (6.227-28). An act of purification might precede prayer and sacrifice, as in the procedure Ovid describes in Book 6, when a merchant prefaces prayer and sacrifice to Mercury by sprinkling himself and his goods with water drawn from the god's spring (5.675-79). As that episode illustrates, not only did priests conduct rituals on behalf of the Roman state, but individuals offered prayers and sacrifice, and made and satisfied vows, on their own behalf. Ovid gives the case of the merchant a satirical twist, since the latter asks both forgiveness for his intentionally deceptive practices in the past and profit for such practices in the future (5.681-90).

Roman religion was pragmatic and functional, aimed at maintaining the good will of the gods. The exact performance of the ritual actions and words was essential. Consequently, the religious experts (the priests) performed these while the attending crowd observed but did not participate, as Ovid indicates in his report on the Robigalia: "a crowd in white stood blocking the road. / A flamen was entering the grove of ancient Rust, / to offer dog guts and sheep guts to the flame" (4.906-908). Because the crowd did not participate, there was no danger of their doing or saying anything incorrect or ill-omened. At the beginning of a rite, in fact, the priest enjoined silence; hence the "reverent silence" of the crowd at the Terminalia (2.654).

Since the aim of religious practices was maintenance of divine favor, it was necessary to have a means of ascertaining the will of the gods. Divination, as it was called, did not attempt to predict the future, but to determine divine approval or displeasure. Elected officials, rather than priests, were responsible for "taking the auspices," to determine in advance of any significant public event (e.g., elections, meetings of the Senate, the commencement of military campaigns) whether the gods approved. The officials were assisted in this by a college of priests known as "augurs," in charge of augury (*augurium*), which involved observation of the flights or songs of birds, and of thunder and lightning from a special watchpost on the Capitoline hill; at 6.674 I have translated *augurium* as "bird report." Another form of divination, also imported from the Etruscans, was based on observing the organs, especially the liver, of sacrificial animals. The gods did not always wait to be consulted in these forms of divination; the Romans believed that extraordinary phenomena were expressions of divine will. Portents or prodigies (such as two-headed calves, bleeding statues, and so on) were reported to the pontiffs, who endeavored to interpret them and kept permanent records of them. The last resort for interpretation was to consult the collection of oracles called the Sibylline Books (named for their reputed source, the Sibyl of Cumae, an oracle of Apollo). In times of special trouble or crisis, a board of fifteen priests consulted the books, stored in the temple of Jupiter on the Capitoline until Augustus moved them to the Temple of Apollo on the Palatine. At various points in the *Fasti*, Ovid refers to such consultation. He accounts for the temple of Venus Verticordia in this way: "Sexual morality at Rome once slipped from ancestral standards; / the ancients consulted the Sibylline Books, / which demanded a temple for Venus . . ." (4.157-59). The importation of Cybele, the Great Mother, from Asia Minor, was the result of such consultation (4.255-60), undertaken in the panic brought on by Hannibal's successes in Italy during the Second Punic War with Carthage.

Many of the practices of Ovid's time, when Rome had become an urban and cosmopolitan world capital, betray their origins in an earlier era, when Rome was a small, agricultural community and the rituals concerned the welfare of small farmers and citizen-soldiers. The Terminalia involves a sacrifice by landholders at their joint boundary-marker (2.639-78). The Parilia, in honor of the pastoral goddess Pales, involved purification of livestock, their stalls, and their keepers (4.721-82). Both of these festivals developed aspects appropriate to Rome's growth; at the Terminalia there was a sacrifice at the sixth milestone on the Via Laurentina (2.679-84), and the Parilia was celebrated also as the anniversary of the founding of Rome (4.806-58). In both those cases, Ovid treats the rustic aspect of the celebrations first, and in the case of the Terminalia, the sacrifice on the Via Laurentina forms only a very brief coda. In Ovid's day, service in the Roman army was a professional career. Some of the ceremonies Ovid records date from a much earlier phase, when citizen-soldiers were drafted to meet a military emergency and demobilized at the end of the crisis. In March, Ovid discusses the hymn and shields (*ancilia*) of Mars' priests, the Salians (3.259-392). Put in simplest terms, the Salians' activity is a war-dance. In March (3.849-50) and in May (5.725-26) he briefly records ceremonial "Trumpet Purification" (Tubilustrium). At the temple of Bellona, the ritual declaration of war was made (6.199-208).

Although Ovid's focus is on state cult, he does have occasion to describe some rites concerning the family. In February he treats two festivals, the Feralia (2.533-70) and Caristia (2.616-38), at which Romans honored their dead ancestors. In March he considers the rite of passage when Roman boys received the *toga liberalis* ("free toga," also called the *toga virilis*, "toga of manhood," 3.771-88). In several months—February (2.557-62), March (3.393-96), May (5.487-90), and June (6.219-34)—he cites beliefs that certain periods were not auspicious for marriages.

Some of the practices Ovid reports show their origin in magic. The Lupercalia in February, during which naked priests run through the streets striking women with strips of goat hide, is a fertility ritual. In May, at the Lemuria, householders perform a ceremony to exorcise ancestral ghosts (5.419-92). In February, Ovid describes a rite performed for Muta, which has voodoo-like aspects (2.573-82).

THE ROMAN CALENDAR

In the *Fasti* there are two passages, near the beginnings of Books 1 (27-62) and 3 (75-166), in which Ovid treats the general arrangement and history of the Roman calendar. My discussion of those passages here can also serve as a general introduction to the calendar.[15] Originally, the Romans had a ten-month calendar, beginning with March and ending in December, which they attributed to the first king, Romulus. According to Ovid, he named the months as follows: "The first month went to his father Mars, / the second to

Venus, who started his line. / The third was named for the elders, the fourth for the young. / Numbers designated the following bunch" (1.39-42). Ovid explains the names of the months in greater detail at the beginning of the respective books. The numbered months of September (the seventh) through December (the tenth) are familiar to us; Quintilis (the fifth) was renamed July after Julius Caesar and Sextilis (the sixth) was renamed August after the first Emperor Augustus.

To the second Roman king, Numa, was traditionally attributed the introduction of the two months of January and February. When Ovid first alludes to this attribution (1.43-44), he simply says that "Before the original months he added two" (44). A brief passage near the beginning of Book 2 (47-54), however, offers a more complicated account of the arrangement, asserting that January was first and February *last*, until "the ten commissioners" (as I have translated Ovid's reference to the Decemvirs, *bis quini . . . viri*, 54) "joined together" those periods.

Until two years before Ovid's own birth, the Roman year consisted of 355 days, with the result that the calendar was increasingly out of sync with the solar year. This problem was solved by the occasional insertion, called "intercalation," of a 22- or 23-day period by the priestly board of pontiffs. Perhaps because of the role of the pontiffs and because of their more general responsibility for drawing up the official calendar, Julius Caesar, then the *pontifex maximus*, undertook the reforms which produced what we know as the "Julian calendar" (3.155-66), which went into effect on 1 January 45 BC. Because Caesar had been *pontifex maximus* since 63 BC, however, this symbolically significant reorganization of time was more immediately connected with his increasing political supremacy (in 46 BC he was named dictator for ten years). After the Julian calendar reforms, Fasti (calendars) were set up publicly; some of them have survived (see below). The one in Praeneste contained material by the antiquarian Verrius Flaccus, whom Augustus later chose as a tutor for his grandsons. In 8 BC Augustus made some further adjustments to the calendar. A more striking indication of the first Emperor's interest in time and the calendar is the *Horologium Augusti* ("the Sundial of Augustus").[16] The sundial face occupied a large area in the Campus Martius (about half the size of St. Peter's Square); the pointer was an obelisk brought from Egypt to commemorate the Roman conquest of Egypt. It has been calculated that on the Emperor's birthday and conception day, the shadow pointed to other Augustan monuments in that part of the Campus Martius—the Altar of Augustan Peace and the Mausoleum of Augustus. All of this may have contributed to Ovid's decision to write a poem based on the calendar.

The ancient Roman month was not subdivided into weeks as we know them. Dates were reckoned by counting *backward* from three fixed points. The first of the month was the Kalends; dates in the second half of a month were said to be a certain number of days *before* the Kalends of the next month. The Ides was in the middle of the month, and the Nones was, as the Latin word implies, nine days before the Ides. In the months of March, May, July, and October, the Nones was the 7th and the Ides, the 15th; in the other months, the Nones was the 5th, the Ides, the 13th. From this method of calculation, one can see that the Roman counted inclusively; we would say that the Nones was *eight* days before the Ides. In my translation I have retained the inclusive method of counting; incidentally, this accounts for Ovid's references to a 10-month period of pregnancy (1.33; 3.124; cf.5.534). The peculiarity of counting days *backward* becomes comprehensible when one realizes that the three "dividing days" are vestiges of an original lunar calendar. The Kalends was the day after the night when the crescent moon first appeared (this only approximates the new moon). The Nones was the first quarter, the Ides, the full moon. Originally, one of the pontiffs kept watch for the appearance of the crescent moon. Then the pontiffs announced the number of days until the Nones, the day on which the people gathered from the countryside and heard an announcement of the date of the first festival of that month.[17]

Our knowledge about the Roman calendar relies upon the *Fasti* itself, some other written sources, and various archeological remains found in Rome and nearby Italian towns, of calendars inscribed in stone (and in one case, painted on plaster). One is pre-Julian, the others, Julian; the Julian calendars date from the reigns of Augustus and his successor Tiberius. From these materials, we know that the Kalends, Nones, and Ides were indicated on such calendars; in addition, each day was marked with a letter between A and H and might be marked with abbreviations in the form of additional letters, including F, N, EN, and C.

It is to all these subdivisions of the month which Ovid alludes in the discussion he prefaces by saying: "So you won't misunderstand the rules for the different days, / not every dawn serves the same function" (1.45-46). What I have translated as "legal holiday" (47) is *nefastus*, abbreviated N. What I call "a work day" (48) is *fastus*, abbreviated F. A day which is *nefastus* in the morning and *fastus* in the afternoon (50) was marked with EN, standing for *endotercissus*, "cut between." The "days for holding elections" (53, actually, more generally for holding "assemblies"; these bodies voted on legislation as well as on candidates for office, and originally had a judicial function as well) were *dies comitiales* ("assembly days"), abbreviated C. The "weekly marketdays" (1.54; my translation glosses Ovid's more allusive reference to the day that recurs in a cycle of nine, i.e., eight) were the *nundinae*; these were tracked on the calendar by the recurring cycle of the letters A-H, beginning on 1 January and running continuously through the year. Finally, Ovid says that the days after the Kalends, Nones, and Ides were "black" (57-58). Black days (*dies atri*) and taboo days (*dies religiosi*) were considered unlucky, and so no new activity could be undertaken and religious activity was avoided. Ovid alludes to the traditional origin of the *dies atri* when he says, "The curse comes from historical events; for on those days / Roman armies suffered terrible reverses" (59-60). In 390 BC a Roman army was totally defeated at Allia by Gauls on 18 July, and subsequently the city was occupied by the enemy. When the Senate investigated the disaster, they discovered that the defeat at Allia occurred two days after the auspices had been taken on the day after the Ides, and that similar disasters had occurred when the auspices had been taken on days after the Kalends, Nones, and Ides. To avoid this in the future, the pontiffs instituted the custom of the *dies atri*.

As mentioned above, some of the surviving stone calendars were found in Italian towns outside of Rome, including the largest, from Praeneste (present-day Palestrina). In an earlier period of time, however, the Italian towns had not yet come under Rome's sway and had independent cultural institutions, including their calendars. Twice Ovid refers to these calendars and their differences from the Roman one. In his account of the name of March, he advises his readers: "If you have the time, take a look at neighboring Italian calendars. / In these there's also a month named for Mars" (3.87-88), and gives a list of local calendars in which March is the third, fourth, fifth, sixth, or tenth month (89-96). In defending her claim that June is named for her, Juno maintains that "The neighboring towns pay me the same tribute" (6.58), and urges the poet to "Take a look at the calendars" of five towns that also have a month of June (6.59-63). In both places, the speaker (Ovid to his readers, Juno to Ovid) commands "take a look at calendars" (*inspice fastos;* 3.87, 6.59). Repeated diction and phraseology in similar contexts is a feature typical of Ovidian style.

BRIEF REMARKS ON OVID'S ASTRONOMICAL INFORMATION

The reader may notice that Ovid refers to stars rising or setting on more than one occasion. The reason for this is rather complicated. First, ancient astronomers distinguished between "apparent" risings and settings and "true" ones. The "apparent" ones are determined by empirical observation, the "true," by mathematical calculation. The early Greek astronomers compiled almanacs (called *parapegmata*), listing day-by-day the positions of the sun and the fixed stars, along with remarks on changes in the weather (which the ancients believed were caused by the astronomical changes). These observations depended, of course, on the horizon of the observer, i.e., the latitude of the place where the observations were made, so observations made at Athens would not agree with those made at Alexandria, and neither would agree with those made at Rome. Confusions also arise between references to "true" and "apparent" risings and settings, because ordinary language did not distinguish between these scientific terms. Further, there are risings and settings in both the morning and the evening. As the Roman author Pliny the Elder (Gaius Plinius Secundus, AD 23/24–79) puts it, "the day on which the risings and settings of the stars begin or cease to be visible at the rising or the setting of the sun, these being designated the morning or evening rising and setting according as each of them occurs at dawn or dusk" (*Natural History* 18.219; trans. H. Rackham, Loeb Classical Library).

Caesar's calendar, remember, went into effect 1 January 45 BC. Our evidence for the astronomical details of that calendar includes fragments in Pliny the Elder (according to *NH* 18.57, he is explicitly following Caesar's calendar). Another first-century AD Roman writer includes astronomical information, Columella (Lucius Junius Columella), whose work on agriculture (*De Re Rustica*) was written AD 60–65. Columella uses Caesar less exclusively than did Pliny; the information in the *Fasti* agrees more closely with that in Columella than with that in Pliny, and closely enough to suggest that they relied on the same source.

Put simply, with all its confusions and discrepancies, the astronomical data in the *Fasti* would not have been accurate and reliable even for its original audience. In fairness to Ovid, however, one needs to recognize that readers would not have turned to his poem primarily (if at all) for scientific information. The modern reader interested in pursuing Ovid's astronomy in detail will find information in the commentaries of Frazer and Bömer (see below, note 22), both of whom rely upon the early nineteenth-century German treatise on the astronomy of the *Fasti* by H. Ideler, as I do myself.[18]

REMARKS ON THE TRANSLATION

My inspiration for undertaking this project was David Slavitt's translation of Ovid's poetic letters from exile.[19] I was impressed by his success in making an ancient, allusive text modern and immediately accessible. One means of achieving this success was the inclusion of explanatory material, not in cumbersome and annoyingly frequent footnotes, but in what I call "internal glosses." This is a feature I have adopted. It does entail, of course, some degree of tampering with the text.

Ovid's original readers expected and enjoyed indirect references to, for instance, characters from mythology and geographical places. A sample is 3.81-84: where I have "Athenians," Ovid actually wrote "the descendants of Cecrops" (*Cecropidae*), an allusion to their first king; my "Lemnos" glosses Ovid's "Hypsipylaean land," alluding to the queen Hypsipyle, who entertained Jason and the Argonauts; and "Arcadia" replaces the "Maenalian region," referring to the Arcadian mountain, Maenalus. These allusions are very straightforward. Ovid's more cryptically opaque allusions can be illustrated by the following two examples. Ovid refers to straw dummies being tossed off a bridge into the Tiber *Leucadio . . . modo* (5.630; literally, "in the Leucadian manner"). To understand this, one must recall first the Greek promontory of Leucas (off the coast of which in 31 BC Antony and Cleopatra were defeated at the Battle of Actium), and then the legend that the poet Sappho committed suicide by jumping from there, supposedly because of unrequited love. Hence my translation of "lover's leap." Elsewhere, the goddess Flora refers to the flower she made *Therapnaeo . . . sanguine* (5.223; literally, "from Therapnaean blood"). This refers to Hyacinthus, whose cult was associated with the Spartan town Amyclae; Therapne is another Spartan town, and from the description of the flower in line 224, one can identify the flower as a hyacinth, recall the myth of its origin, and thus, working backward, come to understand "Therapnaean" as "Spartan." This kind of indirection may seem like more trouble than it is worth. To appreciate the delight of the author in showing off a recondite bit of knowledge, and the reader in recognizing it, it may help to think of the appeal of the games "Jeopardy" and "Trivial Pursuit." In a somewhat different category of internal gloss are my translations of references to Roman cultural institutions and historical events and characters which would have been obvious to Ovid's original readers.

A specific category of internal gloss involves the many examples of etymological wordplay throughout the work. It was a common belief in antiquity that words were not accidental or merely conventional but had an inherent connection with the things they designated.[20] Among the explanations in the *Fasti* are many explanations of the origins of words, most often names. Since the explanation hinges on a sort of pun, it is essential to convey this with a pun in English as well. Sometimes it is possible to do this without deviating from the literal meaning of the Latin text. When it has not been possible, I have tampered with the literal meaning to produce an English pun, as close as possible to the general sense, and have supplied footnotes.

In addition to the internal glosses of allusions, I have also tampered with two other features of Ovidian style. The first involves Ovid's frequent use of apostrophe, i.e., he regularly addresses characters and even things. Believing that this would strike my readers as an oddly artificial intrusion, I have generally rewritten those second-person apostrophes as third-person narrative. I have made exceptions when Ovid heightens the emotional pitch of his narrative by addressing one of the major characters at a critical point in the plot (e.g., Arion 2.97, Lucretia 2.794, Tarquin 2.811-12). The second stylistic feature I have altered concerns narrative tenses. It is common for Latin poets to use the present tense within a narrative of past events; this increases immediacy and vividness. Ovid does this in the *Fasti* and also shifts back and forth between present and past tenses within the same narrative. Believing that this might appear arbitrary and confusing, I have, for the most part, used past tenses. Occasionally, however, usually at emotional high points in the story, I have used a present tense to increase the vividness.

Of course there have been lost in translation many of the effects which depend upon Latin word order and the versification of the elegiac couplet. Here is a sample of what is missing. The disposition of proper names to accommodate the requirements of metrical form was a trick Latin poets liked to perform. In 4.288 Ovid arranges the names of the three Cyclopes in one pentameter line: *Brontes et Steropes Acmonidesque solent*. While the meaning is prosaic, "Brontes, Steropes, and Acmonides are accustomed to," the arrangement makes it interesting; the technical term for such a series of increasingly longer items is "ascending tricolon." The poet tops this in 2.43, completely filling an hexameter with proper names: *Amphiareides Naupactoo Acheloo*. Supplying the verb from the next line, this means, "The son of Amphiaraus [i.e., Alcmaeon] said to Achelous [a river] near Naupauctus." A line like this combines the effects of allusion and arrangement. The catalogues, or lists, of the places to which Ceres wandered in search of Proserpina (4.467–502, 563-74) and of the places on the Great Mother's route to Rome (4.277-90) are full of such combined effects. Catalogues like these are alien to modern taste but were a regular feature of ancient poetry, starting with the catalogue of ships in the second book of the *Iliad*.

The following line (2.499) is prosaic in meaning; the arrangement of words makes it interesting: *sed Proculus Longa veniebat Iulius Alba* ("but Julius Proculus was coming from Alba Longa"). Split up as they are, and divided by a verb (*veniebat*), they produce a so-called "golden line," in which a pair of adjectives (here, *Proculus Longa*) is separated from the pair of nouns they modify (*Julius Alba*) by a verb (*veniebat*). Another example of a golden line is yet again mundane in meaning (4.824): "and the hearth enjoyed its newly kindled flame." Here is the line in Latin with the English meaning beside each word: *et* (and) *novus* (new) *accenso* (kindled) *fungitur* (it enjoys) *igne* (fire) *focus* (hearth). This line is also arranged chiastically; the adjective-noun pairs occur in concentric circles, so to speak, around the verb, with *accenso* and *igne* immediately on either side and *novus focus* on the outside.

Because these effects are so difficult to capture in English, I have sometimes compensated by supplying an effect in a line where Ovid does not use it. My version of 1.707, "For those divine brothers, brothers from a deified clan" has a chiastic arrangement which allows for the emphatic juxtaposition of "brothers" (juxtaposition often naturally results from chiastic arrangement). The actual arrangement of Ovid's Latin line is closer to "for brother gods, brothers from a clan of gods."

Roman poets and their audiences were apparently quite attuned to recurring words, phrases, and lines. To be sure, not every repeated word is significant, but for the most part I have endeavored to preserve this feature, especially when the repetition seems more likely to be significant, because the repetition itself it is conspicuously frequent or the repeated words are close together. The careful reader will perhaps notice these, and so approximate the ancient reader's sensitivity. In the story of the constellation of the Raven, Snake and Bowl (2.243-66), for example, forms of the word *mora* ("delay") occur in four of the episode's 24 lines, and so become a leit-motif. I have rendered these with forms of the phrase "to keep waiting": "my little story won't keep you waiting long" (248), "'. . . nothing should keep the service waiting,'" (249), "[the bird] kept on waiting . . ." (256), and "'Here's what kept me waiting'" (259). Generally such repetition is not nearly so obvious, as in the recurrence of *perit* (literally, "it perishes") in 2.227 and 233: "Courage is brought down by deceit" and "but soon [the boar] is brought down. . . ."

The *Fasti* is written in elegiac couplets, the verse form of all of Ovid's works except the *Metamorphoses*. This consists of dactylic hexameter alternating with pentameter. The hexameter line consists of four feet which are either dactyls (-⌣⌣) or spondees (--), a fifth foot which is almost always a dactyl rather than a spondee, and a sixth foot spondee. The pentameter line consists of two halves divided by a strong break (caesura); simplifying a bit, each half consists of two dactyls plus one extra long syllable. The basis of Latin meter is not the alternation of stressed and unstressed syllables (as it is in English poetry), but the alternation of syllables which take a longer or a shorter time to pronounce (this feature is called "quantity"). Having decided to render the

Fasti into a metrical form of English, I chose a pattern based on stress accent, i.e., one natural to English. It is considerably looser than Ovid's own strict form, of which he is a master, but it does maintain a poetic form. In it, I alternate between lines with five to six stresses and lines with four to five.

For my text I have used the Teubner edition.[21] Generally, my line numbering corresponds to the numbering of the Latin text in that edition. My couplets always correspond to Ovid's; that is, something from the hexameter line may be in the pentameter, or vice versa, but couplet for couplet the translation and text correspond. I have also consulted the texts, translations, and commentaries of Franz Bömer and Sir James George Frazer.[22] Indeed, every page of my translation is indebted to Bömer's commentary. The dates were not in Ovid's original but are supplied for the reader's convenience.

Book
1

January

The dates—and their origins—arranged through the Latin year,
    stars setting and rising—of that I'll sing.
Germanicus Caesar, accept this work with a peaceful glance
    and guide the course of my anxious ship.
Don't turn your back on modest tribute, but be at my side   5
    to support this service pledged to your godhead.
You're going to learn about rituals dug up in archaic calendars
    and how each day won its special mark.
There too you'll find your family's special observances
    and often read the names of your father and grandfather.   10
The red-letter days which both of them earned, you and your
    brother Drusus are going to earn too.
Let Augustus' arms be a theme for others, mine is Augustus' altars
    and the days he added to the ritual year.
Smile on my efforts to hymn your family's praises   15
    and banish fear from my pounding heart.
Give me your indulgence, and you'll give my poem strength.
    My talent waxes and wanes at your glance.
Under the scrutiny of a learned prince, my page reacts
    as if the critic were Apollo himself.   20
For I have felt the effects of your well-trained eloquence

battling in court for your anxious clients.
I also know how the mighty torrents of your talent rush
    when inspired to my own field of poetry.
If it is right and proper, guide my reins as a fellow poet.   25
    Under your auspices may the year go well.

When our city's founder was arranging the dates in his year,
    he decided on a calendar ten months long.
Naturally, Romulus, you studied war more than astronomy,
    and conquering your neighbors was more on your mind.   30
And yet, Germanicus, his plan had a certain logic
    and he has grounds to defend his mistake.
The time that suffices to carry a child to term,
    he decreed should suffice for a year.
For the same length of time from the death of her husband   35
    a widowed wife remains in mourning.
So this was what Romulus had on his mind when he gave
    the year's rules to his primitive people.
The first month went to his father Mars,
    the second to Venus, who started his line.   40
The third was named for the elders, the fourth for the young.
    Numbers designated the following bunch.
King Numa didn't neglect Janus nor the ghosts of our ancestors.
    Before the original months he added two.

So you won't misunderstand the rules for the different days,   45
    not every dawn serves the same function.
On a legal holiday, no verdict is pronounced;
    on a work day, you may go to court.
Don't think the rules always last the whole day through.
    Some work days are legal holidays until noon: 50
as soon as the god gets his sacrifice, court is in session again
    and the honorable judge is free to speak.
And besides, there are days for holding elections.
    And besides, there are weekly marketdays.
Attention to Juno has a claim on the Italian Kalends.   55
    A bigger white lamb falls to Jove on the Ides.
The Nones has no patron deity. The days after these three
    (make no mistake) will be black.
The curse comes from historical events; for on those days

Roman armies suffered terrible reverses.   60
What I've said here once applies to the rest of the year.
    Now I won't have to break my thread.

1 January

Look, Germanicus, Janus heralds a happy year for you,
    and here he is to inaugurate my poem.
Two-headed Janus, silent source of the year that slips by,   65
    alone of the gods you see behind your back.
Stand by our generals whose efforts bring carefree peace
    to the fertile land, peace to the sea as well.
Stand by your senators and the people of Romulus.
    Unlock shining temples with a nod of your head.   70

The happy day is dawning. With heart and voice attend.
    Lucky words are required on this lucky day.
Let lawsuits fall on deaf ears, and frenzied disputes be gone;
    adjourn your work, you jaundiced horde.
Do you see how the atmosphere shines with scented flames   75
    and saffron crackles on the lighted hearth?
The gleaming firelight strikes the temples' gilt and reflects
    a flickering radiance to the buildings' tops.
The procession to the Capitol's peak is clad in spotless white
    so the people match the holiday spirit.   80
Consuls-elect, newly and duly attired and escorted,
    sit on their new chairs of office.
Unbroken bulls offer their throats to be slit, bulls
    which grew fat on grassy Falerian fields.
When Jupiter surveys the whole world from his stronghold's vantage,   85
    there's nothing to watch over that isn't Roman.
Welcome, happy day, and many happy returns, fit object
    for worship by the people who rule the world.

"And yet, what sort of god should I call you, two-faced Janus?
    For Greece has no deity the likes of you.   90
Tell the reason why alone of the gods you see both
    what is behind you and what lies ahead."
With notebook in hand I was pondering these topics,
    when my house seemed brighter than a moment before.

Then holy Janus, an amazing sight with those two heads,   95
    suddenly met me faces to face.
Frightened out of my wits, I felt my hair stand on end
    and suddenly an icy chill gripped my heart.
With a staff in his right hand, and a key in his left, the god
    uttered these words from his foreward mouth: 100
"Don't be afraid, industrious poet of the calendar; learn
    what you want, and take my words to heart.
The ancients called me Chaos, because I'm a primitive matter.
    See how I sing about events of long ago.
Here the clear air and the other three elements—   105
    fire, water, earth—were a single heap.
Once a dispute among its components broke up this lump
    and the parts went off on their separate ways.
Fire rose to the top, air took its place nearby,
    earth and water settled in the middle.   110
Then I, who had been a featureless spherical hulk, assumed
    a face and figure suitably divine.
Even now, as a trace of my once homogenous shape,
    I look the same both coming and going.
Here's another reason for the shape you've asked about,   115
    so you'll know it and my job as well.
Whatever you see all around, sky and sea, clouds and dry land,
    my hand opens and closes it all.
In my control alone is the safekeeping of the huge cosmos,
    and the right to open it hinges on me.   120
When I have felt like dispatching Peace from her calm abode,
    then she freely walks the long highways.
The whole world will be a welter of deadly bloodshed
    unless strong bars keep wars locked away.
Along with the Seasons I am in charge of heaven's doors;   125
    it's my job to let Jove himself come and go.
Accordingly, I'm called Janus the Doorman.[1] You're going to laugh
    at the names the priest invokes when he sets out a cake
and salted meal. One and the same, I'm called now Opener,
    now Closer by the celebrant's lips.   130
Of course by those successive names rough antiquity
    intended to convey my revolving roles.
My power I've told you. Now learn the reason for my shape,
    but you've almost got that yourself by now.

Every door has a pair of surfaces, inside and out;   135
    one faces the public, the other is private.
The way your own doorman is posted near the entrance
    and watches the comings and goings,
that's how I, doorman of the heavenly hall, survey
    Eastern and Western directions at once.   140
You see how Diana of the Crossroads faces three directions
    to guard the intersection where three roads fork.
I too can stay put and see two things at once
    without wasting time by turning my neck."
He had finished speaking, but the look on his face let me know   145
    that a follow-up question would not be amiss.
I took heart, fearlessly offered my thanks to the god, and
    spoke some more as I stared at the ground:
"Tell me, now, why the new year begins in cold weather.
    It would have been better to begin in the spring.   150
Everything then is in bloom, then the cycle of seasons is new,
    new buds are bursting from swollen branches,
the trees are covered with leaves newly opened,
    and sprouting seeds break through the soil,
birds delight the warm air with their choruses,   155
    and herds frisk and frolic in the meadows.
Then sunny days are inviting, and the swallow returns to build
    its nest of mud high under a rafter.
Then the fields undergo cultivation and renewal by the plough.
    We would rightly call this the year's renewal."   160
I had inquired at length. In brief he replied without pausing
    and conveyed his response in these two lines:
"The winter solstice is the first new sun and the last old one.
    The sun and the year have the same beginning."
Next I wondered why court was briefly in session on the first   165
    of the year. "Learn the reason," says Janus.
"I began the new year with business to attend to,
    to set an example for a whole busy year.
Likewise everyone dabbles at tending his shop, to give
    just enough proof of his usual work."   170
Me again: "Janus, why do you always get offerings first,
    no matter which god I intend to appease?"
"Through me, who guards the entrance, you gain access
    to whichever god you desire," says he.

"So why are happy words spoken on the first of your month,   175
    and why the exchange of greetings then?"
Leaning on the staff he carried in his right hand, the god
    then said, "Beginnings set the tone for things.
You prick up your anxious ears at the first sound,
    the augur interprets the first bird he sees.   180
Gods' ears are open like their temples, so nary a tongue frames
    a prayer in vain; words carry weight."
Janus had stopped. I didn't pause long and my next words
    were hard on the heels of his last.
"What is the purpose of giving dates and wrinkled figs   185
    and shining honey in a snow-white pot?"
"For luck," he explained, "so this flavor will stick to things,
    and the year continue as sweetly as it began."
"I see why sweets are given. Add the reason for the cash donation.
    I don't want to miss a single detail."   190
He laughed and said, "You sure don't get these times of yours,
    if you think that honey is sweeter than cash.
Even in the reign of Saturn I hardly saw a soul
    whose mouth didn't water at a full cash-box.
With time the love of possessions, now at its height, increased.   195
    It hardly has room to go any further.
Wealth is valued now more than during the archaic age
    while folks were poor, while Rome was new,
while a tiny hut sheltered Romulus, the son of Mars,
    and river grass served as his meager bed.   200
Jupiter's statue was cramped in his temple's tight quarters
    and the statue's thunderbolt was plain terra-cotta.
Garlands then decked the Capitol instead of the gems of the present,
    and senators grazed their sheep themselves.
Sleeping peacefully on straw was nothing to be ashamed of,   205
    nor was resting one's head in the hay.
The judge delivered his verdict fresh from his plough.
    Even thin silver plate raised eyebrows.
But after the luck of this place raised its head
    and Rome looked the gods in the eye,   210
wealth increased, as did the mad passion for wealth,
    and those with a lot just long for lots more.
They strive to get so they can spend, and get again
    what they've spent, fueling, not quenching the fire.

On a binge there's never a single drink, but always   215
    "one more round" and "one more for the road."[2]
Your worth is worth your while. Net worth wins you friends,
    net worth gets you votes. The poor are trampled on.
But I digress. You wanted to know if cash augurs well
    and why our palms itch for old copper coins.   220
People used to give pennies; now gold augurs better.
    New money has driven out the old.
And gilded temples tickle us, however much we approve
    the ancient ones. Grandeur suits a god.
We praise the good old days, but enjoy the present age.   225
    Both ways are worthy of equal respect."
He had finished his lecture. Once again as before
    I calmly addressed the god with the key,
"I've surely learned a lot. But why is the penny minted
    with a ship on one side, two heads on the other?"   230
"So you could spot me in that double image, if time
    had not erased the ancient handiwork.
And the ship? A ship brought the god with the sickle to the Tiber
    after he'd wandered all over the world.
I well remember when this land welcomed Saturn   235
    after Jove banished him from the heavenly kingdom.
For a long time the name "Saturnian" stuck to the people,
    and Latium was named for the lately evicted god.[3]
Following generations duly minted pennies with a ship
    to commemorate the divine stranger's arrival.   240
The sandy waters of the peaceful Tiber scour the left bank
    of the land where I myself resided.
Where Rome now stands, a virgin forest grew; a mighty nation
    was pasture for a paltry few head of cattle.
My stronghold occupied the hill which the present age   245
    commonly calls by my name, the Janiculum.
I was king in the days when gods still walked the earth
    and divinities travelled in human circles.
The wickedness of men had not yet driven Justice away;
    she was the last god to quit the earth.   250
Not fear, nor force, but conscience guided folks.
    Honorable men made "his honor's" job easy.
No wars for me; peace and portals were my watch, and this
    was my side arm," he said, holding up his key.

The god had closed his mouth. I opened mine again,   255
    conjuring a god's words with my own.
"With so many doors, why are you worshipped in just this one,
    where the Roman Forum and the Julian meet?"
Stroking the beard that reached to his chest, he right away
    related Sabine Tatius' siege of Rome and how   260
the fickle guard Tarpeia was bribed with bracelets to show
    the stealthy Sabines the route to the stronghold's top.
"Then, as now, a steep slope led you down from there
    through the fora to the valleys beyond.
The enemy had already reached the gate, unbolted   265
    by Saturn's spiteful daughter Juno.
Wary of a frontal assault against so great a power,
    I shrewdly made use of my expertise.
I opened (my strong suit) an underground spring
    and suddenly jets of water shot out.   270
But first I threw sulphur into the dripping channels
    to make a geyser block Tatius' route.
After the spring had served its purpose and drove the Sabines off,
    I restored the place to its former appearance.
An altar was erected for me beside a tiny shrine,   275
    where fires burn spelt and piles of cakes."
"Why do you hide in peace and open when war breaks out?"
    Right away I got the answer to my question.
"When our boys are in the field my unlocked door stays open,
    to be open when they come marching back.   280
In peace I shut my doors to keep the peace from escaping.
    Under the Caesars I'll be shut a long time."
He spoke, and looking up (with all four eyes) surveyed
    whatever exists in all the world.
There was peace, the reason for your victory parade, Germanicus,   285
    the Rhine's surrender of its tributaries to you.
Janus, keep the peace forever, and with it the servants of peace,
    and keep the peacemaker forever at his task.

On this date, as I could find out right from the calendar,
    the senate consecrated two temples.   290
The island which parts the Tiber as it passes Rome received
    Aesculapius, son of Apollo and the nymph Coronis.
Jupiter got his share; a single spot received them both,

and the grandson's temple adjoins his mighty grandfather.

3 January

What's to stop me from writing about the stars as well?   295
    Their rising and setting is a part of this project.
Lucky souls, astronomy's founding fathers, who troubled
    to learn these things and ascend to higher realms.
I can well believe they also transcended human folly
    when they rose above human heights.   300
Too high-minded to be distracted by wine and women,
    civic duty or military service,
they weren't bothered by trivial ambitions, the purple
    of status or hunger for great wealth.
In their imagination they approached the distant stars   305
    and subjected heaven to their intellectual might.
That's how to aim for the stars, not like the Giants did it,
    piling Mount Ossa on top of Pelion.
I too will survey the heavens with them to guide me,
    and assign the right dates to the constellations.   310

And so, three nights before the coming Nones,
    when the ground is sprinkled with the dew from heaven,
you'll search in vain for the claws of the eight-legged Crab,
    since it will plunge beneath the western waves.

5 January

Signs that the Nones are here will be dark clouds,   315
    pouring rains, and the rising Lyre.

9 January

Count from the Nones four days in a row, and Janus
    must be appeased on Agonal day.
The origin of the name[4] could be the vested priest
    who strikes the victim dead for the gods.   320
Before he bloodies the knife in his hand, he always asks
    "should I go on," awaiting the command to "go on."
Because the beasts must be goaded to come, some people believe
    day is called "Agonal" from a goading.

45

Others think this festival was called Agnalia by the ancients,   325
    but one stray letter has now been added.
Or, because the victim fears the knife's reflection,
    does the day bear the mark of the creature's agony?
It also could be that the day took a Greek name
    from the antagonistic contests of an earlier time.   330
Besides, archaic Latin called a beast "agonia."
    In my opinion, this final reason is correct.
That point is moot, but the king-priest must appease
    the gods with the mate of a woolly ewe.
What falls to a victorious hand, is called the "victim";   335
    the "hostage" gets its name from vanquished hosts.[5]
It used to be that spelt and a crystal grain of salt
    were enough to win the gods' good will.
That was before strange ships had sailed the watery seas
    transporting tears that the myrrh tree wept,   340
before Syria sent us frankincense, and India, balsam,
    before anyone knew what saffron looked like.
Altars were content to give off smoke from Sabine juniper,
    and laurel crackled loudly as it burned.
Whoever had violets to weave in a garland of meadow   345
    wildflowers, that was a wealthy man.
The knife that now lays bare the slaughtered ox's guts
    had no function in religious rites.
Ceres was first to take pleasure in the blood of a greedy sow,
    avenging her damaged crops as the pest deserved.   350
She found out that the bristly-snouted sow had rooted up
    the succulent shoots of early spring.
The sow paid with her life, which should have been a lesson
    to you, billy goat, to leave grapevines alone.
The person who saw him sinking his teeth into the vine   355
    loudly gave vent to his dismay:
"Keep right on chewing, but when you're at the altar, that vine
    will furnish something for sprinkling your horns."
The prediction came true. Held personally liable for damages,
    your enemy, Bacchus, has his horns drenched with wine.   360
The sow's mischief did damage, the goat's did damage too.
    For what can cows and docile sheep be liable?
Aristaeus was weeping at the sight of hives abandoned
    by his bees, every last one of them dead.

His sea-goddess mother could hardly comfort his distress 365
    and concluded by speaking these final words:
"Stop crying, my boy. Proteus will relieve the damage
    and give you a way to recover your losses.
Don't let him fool you and escape by changing shape.
    Make sure strong chains confine both hands." 370
The young man came upon the wizard sound asleep.
    Old Man of the Sea was quickly caught and bound.
Craftily he tampered with his looks and took on other shapes,
    but quickly chained he resumed his own appearance.
Lifting his face with its sea-wet beard, he said, 375
    "You want a technique to recover your bees?
Sacrifice a young bull and cover its body with earth.
    What you want from me, the covered body will give."
The shepherd followed instructions. From the rotting cow swarms
    boiled out. One life gave life to thousands. 380
The sheep was doomed. It wickedly browsed on twigs a devout
    old woman had been bringing the country gods.
What else can be exempt, when woolly sheep, and cows
    bucolic, lay down their lives at the altars?
The Persians appease the Sun and his rays with a horse, 385
    a swift sacrifice for a god so fleet.
His sister Diana once took a deer in place of young Iphigenia
    and now the deer falls without that excuse.
I have seen the Sapaeans offer dogs' entrails to Hecate.
    Other Thracians do the same thing. 390

An ass is killed for Priapus, erect guardian of the fields.
    The reason is indecent, but it fits that god.
Greece was thronging the rites of Bacchus with his ivy crown,
    for his biennial mid-winter festival.
The gods had also congregated to worship Bacchus 395
    with anyone else in the mood for good times.
There were Pans and a young pack of sex-crazed Satyrs
    and the nymphs of rivers and of lonely fields.
Old Silenus had come as well, riding a sway-backed ass,
    and also the ithyphallic terror of the birds. 400
They found a grove just right for a pleasant party
    and settled down on couches of grass.
The Wine-God poured the drinks, everyone made himself

47

a garland; water for mixing came from a brook.
    Some of the nymphs came with hair let down and uncombed,   405
        others with skillfully arranged coiffures.
One bustled to serve with her skirt hitched above her calves,
        another's blouse was unbuttoned revealingly.
This one is bare-shouldered, that one's skirt trails in the grass.
        No sandal-straps confine their delicate feet.   410
Some of these lovelies kindle the Satyrs' desires,
        others arouse pine-garlanded Pan.
They burn you too, Silenus, you with your unquenchable lust.
        At your age, you ought to be ashamed.
But ruddy Priapus, glory and guardian of gardens,   415
        was taken with Lotis, out of all of these.
He needs her, he wants her, he pants for her alone,
        he pesters her with winks and gestures.
Pretty girls are stuck-up and naturally proud of their looks.
        Lotis looked down her nose and laughed.   420
Night came on and wine brought sleep. Bodies overcome
        by drowsiness lay all around.
Furthest away, under a maple tree, Lotis rested
        on a grassy spot, exhausted from the party.
Her admirer gets up, and holding his breath,   425
        silently sneaks toward her on tip-toe.
When he reached the snow-white nymph's secluded bower,
        he was careful not even to breathe too loud.
And now his body was poised on the grass beside her,
        but she was completely sound asleep.   430
Overjoyed, he lifted her skirt from her feet, and began
        to travel the happy route to his desires.
Listen! Silenus' mount, the hoarsely braying ass,
        broke the silence with an untimely blast.
The frightened nymph got up, shook off Priapus,   435
        and woke the whole grove as she made her escape.
But the god, his shameless member all too ready,
        was everyone's moonlit laughingstock.
The cause of the uproar paid with his life, and at Lampsacus
        this victim still pleases the god.   440

As yet unscathed were the birds, which cheer up the countryside,
        denizens of the forest, a harmless race.

You make your nests, and hatch your clutch of eggs,
    and effortlessly utter sweet measures.
No help in that, since your sin lies in your voice;   445
    the gods think you reveal their will
(and they aren't wrong, since you, being closest to them,
    make true revelations in flight and in song).
Safe for so long, the race of birds at last was slaughtered,
    and the gods took pleasure in their informers' guts.   450
And so, abducted from her mate, a white dove
    is often burned on altars to Venus.
The Capitol's rescue from sneak attack doesn't help
    keep the goose's liver from Isis' plate.[6]
At night the rooster is slain for the goddess Night, because   455
    his watchful voice calls forth the warming day.

Meanwhile the Dolphin constellation rises above the sea,
    and pokes his snout from the waters of his origin.

10 January

The next day marks the turning point of winter.
    What remains will equal what has passed.   460

11 January

When Dawn next leaves Tithonus' bed, she will survey
    the high-priests' rites for Arcadian Carmenta.
This day also welcomed you, Juturna, into a temple,
    where the Maiden Aqueduct enters Mars' Field.
Where may I find the origins of these rites and their practice?   465
    Who will steer the sails of a poet at sea?
Teach me yourself, you whose name derives from the charms of song.[7]
    Support my project so your homage is correct.
Created before the moon (if you believe its own traditions),
    Arcadia is named after mighty Arcas.   470
From there Evander came, well-connected on both sides
    but nobler on his holy mother's side.
As soon as a heavenly spark had ignited her mind,
    she gave voice to predictions divinely inspired.
She spoke of disturbances besetting her son and herself   475
    and much besides which time proved true.

For indeed the young man did leave his Arcadian hearth and homeland,
    banished with his all-too-accurate mother.
As he wept his mother said to him, "Please dry your tears.
    You have to endure misfortune like a man.   480
This was meant to be. Your own fault hasn't banished you,
    but a god; you have been exiled by an outraged god.
You are not suffering your just deserts, but a deity's wrath.
    Innocence is worth something in times of trouble.
A man's conscience determines if, in his heart of hearts,   485
    what he's done makes him hopeful or anxious.
Don't grieve as if you're the first to suffer this way.
    Great heroes have been sunk by storms like this.
Cadmus suffered this fate when, driven from Phoenician shores,
    he landed, an exile, on Theban soil.   490
Diomedes suffered this fate, as did the Argonaut Jason
    and many others too numerous to mention.
The brave man feels at home wherever on earth he is,
    like fish in the ocean, and birds in the sky.
Rough weather doesn't rage the whole year long.   495
    Believe me, your spring will also come."
His resolve was strengthened by the words his mother had spoken,
    and Evander sailed his ship westward to Italy.
Following Carmenta's sage advice, he had steered that ship
    into the Tiber and was sailing upstream.   500
She scanned the bank next to the future docks of Rome
    and the houses scattered through lonely spots.
She stood on the prow with her hair blowing wild
    and frantically checked the hand on the tiller,
and reaching her arms to the far-off starboard bank,   505
    stamped madly three times on the pinewood deck.
Evander just barely restrained her by force from jumping
    overboard in her haste to stand on dry land.
"Hail," she said, "to the gods of the place we have sought,
    and the land that will give new gods to heaven,   510
to rivers and springs which this welcoming land enjoys,
    to woodland groves and bands of nymphs.
Be a sight of good omen for my son and for me
    and may it be lucky to set foot on that bank.
Unless I'm mistaken, these hills will become great walls.   515
    Other lands will turn here for law and order.

To these hills the whole world is promised one day.
    Who could believe the place has such a destiny?
And ships from Troy will soon reach these shores.
    Here too a woman will again cause war.   520
Dear grandson Pallas, why put on the fatal armor?
    Put it on. Your death will be nobly avenged.
Conquered Troy, you will yet conquer, toppled, you will rise again.
    Your downfall crushes the homes of your foe.
Conquering flames, burn down the Troy that Neptune built.   525
    Won't it rise from the ashes above the whole world?
Devoted Aeneas will soon bring his venerable gods and his
    venerable father. Vesta, welcome Trojan gods.
The time will come when the same man will be your guardian
    and the world's; a god himself will conduct your rites,   530
and the state will remain a ward of Augustus.[8] It is right
    for this family to be at the reins of command.
Then Tiberius, son and grandson of gods, despite his demurral,
    will bear his inherited burden with a god-like mind.
As I will someday be worshipped on everlasting altars,   535
    so will Julia Augusta become a new god."
When she got down to the present day, speaking this way,
    her prophetic tongue abruptly stopped.
Disembarking, her exiled son stood on Latin turf.
    Lucky man, whose exile brought him to that spot!   540
It wasn't long before new buildings were standing
    and Evander was supreme on the hills of Rome.
Here comes the hero with the club driving Geryon's cattle,
    measuring out his journey across the wide world.
While Evander's house provided him hospitality,   545
    his cattle, unguarded, ranged the wide fields.
Morning had come. Awakened from sleep, the drover from Tiryns
    noticed two bulls were missing from the count.
He searched in vain for traces of the theft. Savage Cacus
    had dragged them backwards into his lair,   550
Cacus, the terror of the Aventine and a blot on its woods,
    a serious nuisance to neighbors and strangers.
The man's face was dreadful, his manliness fit his size, and his size
    was huge (Vulcan was the creature's father).
His home was a cavern with extensive tunnels, so hidden away   555
    that wild animals could scarcely find it.

Heads and arms hung nailed up over the doorway,
    and the filthy ground was white with human bones.
Jupiter's son was leaving with the poorly guarded remnant
    of his herd. The stolen goods bellowed hoarsely.   560
"I heed your call," he said. Following the sound, he came
    through the woods to the wicked lair, bent on revenge.
Cacus had blocked the entrance with a mountain top. Ten teams
    of oxen could hardly have moved that bulwark.
Hercules put his shoulders to it (they'd supported the heavens once)   565
    and made the mighty burden shake and quake.
Once it was dislodged, the crash alarmed the very heavens
    and the earth sank under the weight.
At first Cacus battled hand to hand, and savagely
    conducted the engagement with logs and rocks.   570
When those had no effect, the coward resorted to his father's
    element, and spat out fire from his roaring mouth.
Each time he breathed out, you'd have thought the giant
    under Mount Etna was spewing flashes of lightning.
Hercules grabbed him and wielded his knotty club, sinking it   575
    again and again in the man's upturned face.
Cacus fell and spat out bloody smoke, and dying,
    struck the ground with his broad chest.
The victor offered one of the bulls to you, Jupiter,
    summoning Evander and the countryfolk,   580
and set up an altar for himself, called the Greatest,
    here in the city's Cattle Market district.
Evander's mother didn't hide that the time was near
    when the earth would be done with Hercules' services.
As the happy prophetess lived very much in the gods' favor,   585
    so, a goddess, she has this day in Janus' month.

13 January

On the Ides in great Jupiter's temple, his pure priest
    offers a gelded ram's guts to the flames.
On that date too all power was restored to the people
    and your grandfather got the title "Augustus."   590
Study the family portraits displayed in noble halls.⁹
    No other man received so great a title:
Victory in Africa won "Africanus" that title.

"Creticus" commemorates mastery of Cretan might.
Deeds in Numidia make "Numidicus" proud. The fall 595
    of Numantia gave "Numanticus" his mark.
Drusus, called "Germanicus," met death and distinction in Germany.
    What a pity courage like that was so short-lived!
If Augustus went looking for titles among the conquered nations,
    he'd have as many as this great world contains. 600
Some famous generals won their honorifics in single combat,
    like "Torquatus," who stripped off the loser's torque.
Pompey the Great, your title is the measure of your deeds, but Caesar,
    your victorious opponent, won a greater name.
The surname of the Fabii is a superlative one. For its services, 605
    that family is called "the Greatest."
But still, all these are famous with merely mortal honors,
    while Augustus shares an epithet with Jupiter most high.
Our elders term hallowed things "august," and "august" is the term
    for temples duly dedicated by priestly hands. 610
The word "augury" is another related derivation,
    and whatever Jupiter "augments" with his might.
May he augment our leader's power, and augment his span of years.
    May his oak-leaf wreath safeguard your palace doors.
May the successor to that title assume the weight of the world 615
    with the same divine auspices as his father did.

15 January

When the Sun rises two days after the Ides, services
    will be repeated for the Arcadian goddess.
Roman matrons used to ride in wagons called "carpenta"
    (derived, I think, from Evander's mother Carmenta). 620
Soon this privilege was taken away, and every matron resolved
    not to continue her ungrateful husband's line.
To avoid giving birth, she recklessly groped and gouged,
    aborting the burden growing in her womb.
They say the senate censured the wives' atrocities, 625
    but restored the right they'd been deprived of,
and ordered the same rites now be repeated for the Arcadian
    mother, in thanks for sons and daughters.
Animal skins must not be brought inside that shrine,
    to keep the pure altars free of death's taint. 630

If any of you is fond of archaic rites, during the prayers
　　you will hear epithets you didn't know before.
"Porrima" is appeased, as is "Postverta," maybe Carmenta's
　　sisters, or maybe her fellow refugees.
The one is thought to have reported imminent matters,　　635
　　the other posted advertisements of coming events.[10]

16 January

The next day, fair Concord, installed you in a snow-white temple
　　where the steps of Moneta's temple[11] steeply rise.
Now, as you rightly keep an eye on the Roman multitude,
　　hallowed hands have established you.　　640
Camillus, who conquered the Etruscan town of Veii, had vowed
　　the original temple and fulfilled his vow.
The occasion was a popular revolt against the ruling class
　　when Rome lived in fear of her own manpower.
The latest occasion is better. Tiberius, general we revere,　　645
　　Germany, in mourning, surrenders to your command.
You offered up the conquered nation's spoils
　　and built a temple to the goddess you adore.
This your mother Livia seconded by her actions and an altar,
　　the only spouse worthy of our Jove-like Augustus.　　650

17 January

When that day has passed, the Sun-God will leave Capricorn
　　and drive his chariot through Aquarius' sign.

23 January

When the seventh rising sun has set beneath the waves
　　the Lyre will shine nowhere in the sky.

24 January

On the following night the fire that flashes　　655
　　in Leo's chest will have sunk from sight.

I kept on leafing through calendars which marked the seasons,
　　but "Sowing Day" was nowhere to be found.
Aware of my confusion, the Muse said, "This is the appointed day.

Why search the calendars for a moveable feast? 660
The date of the observance isn't fixed, although the season is,
   when the fields are fruitful with scattered seed."
Young bulls, stand garlanded by your full mangers.
   Your work will resume with the spring thaw.
Let the country fellow hang up his veteran plough on a peg. 665
   Frozen ground flinches from every blade.
Overseer, give the earth a rest after the sowing's done.
   Give the men who farm the earth a rest.
Let the district keep the feast. Circle the district, farmers,
   and offer the district's altars their yearly cakes. 670
Let the harvest-mothers, Ceres and Earth, be appeased with spelt
   they produced and the flesh of a pregnant sow.
Ceres and the Earth safeguard a joint responsibility.
   One gives the crops their origin, the other, their place.
Partners in the task, who improved old-fashioned ways, 675
   and replaced acorns with more nutritious food,
glut the ravenous farmers with boundless harvests
   so farming gets the rewards it deserves.
Grant constant increase to the delicate newly sown crop
   and don't let the shoots be nipped by snow. 680
When we clear and sow, clear the sky with freshening winds.
   When the seed lies hidden, sprinkle it with rain.
Keep the birds, a danger to farming, from decimating
   the fields of grain in destructive flocks.
You ants should also spare the kernels underground. 685
   After the harvest there'll be more to plunder.
'Til then, let the grain grow free of scruffy mildew
   and don't let bad weather turn it yellow.
Don't let it wither and fail, but don't let it grow too fast
   and choke on its own rank excess. 690
Keep the fields free of darnel that hurts the eyes
   and keep wild oats out of cultivated ground.
Let the field pay a big dividend in wheat and barley,
   and spelt one must parch before baking it.
I wish these things for you, farmers. Wish them for yourselves, 695
   and may Ceres and Earth make our prayers come true.
Wars have long kept men from the fields. The sword was handier
   than the plough; the ox gave way to the war horse.
Hoes were lying idle, mattocks were turned into javelins

55

and helmets were made out of metal rakes.   700
Thanks be to the gods and your imperial house; under your foot
    Wars have long lain bound in chains.
Let the ox get into harness and the seed into ploughed land.
    Peace nurtures Ceres, foster child of Peace.

27 January

The sixth day before the next month's Kalends is the one   705
    on which a temple was dedicated to Castor and Pollux.
For those divine brothers, brothers from a deified clan
    founded it close to Juturna's pool.

30 January

This poem itself has brought me to the Altar of Peace,
    dedicated on the day before the end of the month.   710
Peace, wreathed in honor of the end of civil war,
    be with us, as a gentle presence throughout the globe.
So long as enemies are missing, too, triumphs won't be missed.
    You'll bring our generals greater fame than war.
Let our troops bear arms only to keep arms at bay,   715
    and let the wild trumpet herald nothing but parades.
May the ends of the earth tremble at the race of Aeneas.
    If any land didn't fear Rome, let it love her now.
Priests, burn incense on the altar of Peace and strike down
    the white victim with its wine-drenched brow.   720
Pray that the house which brings us peace may last forever
    with that peace; the gods heed patriotic prayers.

And now the first installment of my work is done
    and this book ends with the month it treats.

Book
2

February

January has ended. The year and its poem continue to grow.
    With the second month comes a second installment.
Elegies, now is your first voyage under full sail.
    Recently, I recall, you were only light verses.
I had your able assistance in matters of the heart   5
    when I dallied with your verse-form in my early youth.
The poet's the same, but the theme is religion and dates on the calendar.
    Who would believe the road from there led here?
This is my active duty. I shoulder what arms I can.
    My right hand doesn't dodge every form of service.   10
Maybe I don't hurl javelins with a powerful throwing arm,
    or ride on the back of a cavalry mount,
or strap on a helmet or buckle on a well-honed sword
    (anybody can master the manual of arms).
Just the same, Augustus, I'm an eager enlisted man,   15
    falling in behind your glorious banner.
So be with me and give my services a slightly indulgent look
    if ever you're on furlough from pacifying the foe.

Our Roman forefathers called the means of absolution "februa."
    Even today much evidence attests to this meaning.   20

The high-priests ask the king-priest and the flamen for bits of wool.
    The word for these in archaic Latin is "februa."
The means of atonement which the honor guard[1] collects,
    toasted spelt and salt, is termed the same thing.
The same name applies to the bough cut from a pure tree   25
    to cover the priests' chaste brows with its leaves.
I myself have seen the flamen's wife requesting "februa."
    Requesting "februa," she was given a pine bough.
In sum, anything used to purify our bodies was named
    "februa" by our full-bearded grandfathers.   30
The month is named after this, because the Luperci purify
    everywhere with leather straps as an act of atonement,
or because the period is pure after the tombs are appeased
    when the festival of the dead is over.
Our ancestors used to believe that absolution   35
    could remove all sin, all source of evil.
The Greeks started the practice. That culture thinks wrongdoers
    remitted wicked acts by ritual purification.
Patroclus and Peleus each spilled innocent blood. Absolved
    by Acastus, the latter washed the former's stains away.   40
When the witch Medea fled the scene of her murdered sons,
    gullible Aegeus gave her unwarranted sanctuary.
His father's avenger by matricide, Alcmaeon asked a river-god
    "Wash away my sin," and he washed the sin away.
Oh, you are much too lax if you think that river water   45
    can remove the awful crime of spilling blood!

So you won't remain in ignorance of the original order,
    the first month was Janus', then as now.
The one that follows Janus was the last of the ancient year.
    Terminus' festival closed the ritual cycle.   50
The first month is Janus', just as the door is also first.
    The one sacred to the Afterlife, used to come after the rest.
Later, we believe, the ten commissioners joined together
    periods that originally were far apart.

1 February

On the first of the month Juno the Deliverer reportedly was enhanced   55
    with a new temple adjoining the Great Mother's.

Where is it now, the temple hallowed to the goddess
    on this day? It collapsed from the effects of time.
Our hallowed leader's far-sighted concern has taken measures
    to keep the rest from toppling with a similar crash.   60
Under his regime temples don't show their age.
    Just like us, the gods are indebted to him.
Founder of temples, the temples' holy restorer, I hope
    the gods have comparable concern for you.
May the gods prolong your life, as you prolong their temples,   65
    and may they stay on guard for your family.
Also today the grove of nearby Alernus is crowded,
    where the Tiber wanders in search of the sea.
At the temples of Vesta and the Capitoline Thunderer,
    and on Jupiter's high stronghold they sacrifice a sheep.   70
Often the sky, covered with clouds, lets loose
    heavy rains, or the ground lies covered with snow.

2 February

When next the sun is about to sink in the western waves
    and unhitches his rosy steeds from their jewelled harness,
that night someone will lift his face to the stars and say,   75
    "Where is the Lyre which shone here yesterday?"
Looking for the Lyre he'll also note that Leo's back
    has suddenly sunk into the clear waves.

3 February

The Dolphin you saw 'til now in relief against the sky
    will escape from view on the following night.   80
He once was a lucky go-between for a secret love affair,
    or else he rescued the maestro of the Lesbian lyre.
What sea doesn't know Arion, what land hasn't heard of him?
    He used to hold back strong currents with his song.
His voice often stopped a wolf in its tracks and the lamb   85
    would stop fleeing from that ravening wolf.
Hounds and hares often lay in the same patch of shade,
    and a doe would stand on a rock right by a lioness.
The chattering crow perched at peace with Athena's owl,
    and the dove and the hawk were reconciled.   90
Melodious Arion, they say your cadences have often amazed

Diana as much as her brother Apollo's.
Arion had made his name throughout the cities of Sicily,
 and the music of his lyre took Italy by storm.
Returning home from there Arion boarded a ship,   95
 bringing along the receipts of his tour.
Unlucky man, did winds and waves cause you alarm?
 The deep proved a safer haven than your ship.
For the pilot drew his sword and took a stand;
 the conspiring crew were armed and ready.   100
Sailor, what's with the sword? Keep your ship on a steady course.
 You mustn't lay a finger on any other tackle.
Shaking with fear, Arion said, "I do not beg for my life,
 just let me take up my lyre and play a bit."
They granted this stay with sardonic smiles. He took a garland   105
 fit to grace the god of song himself,
and donned his costume dyed with a deep royal purple.
 The strings he strummed produced their notes,
in those mournful strains which a white swan sings,
 when an arrow has fatally wounded it.   110
In full regalia he dove at once into the water
 and splashed the stern when he broke the surface.
Then—would you believe it?—a dolphin with arching back
 surfaced beneath this unusual load.
Sitting and holding his lyre, Arion pays his passage   115
 with a song and calms the waters of the deep.
The gods know devotion when they see it, so Jupiter took the dolphin
 into the sky and awarded nine stars to him.

5 February

Homer, I wish I had the inspiration and power
 with which you celebrated Achilles' deeds,   120
now as my couplets treat the hallowed Nones,
 the greatest honor heaped on the calendar.
My talent fails me, the matter at hand is beyond my strength.
 This day demands exceptional verse.
What gave me the crazy idea of loading such weight   125
 on elegy? This is the stuff of epic poetry.
Holy "Father of His Country," this title was conferred by the people,
 by the senate, and by my class, the knights.

But history conferred it sooner. Belatedly you received your proper
    title; you've long been father of the world.   130
You have the same title here on earth as Jupiter has in heaven.
    You are father of men as he is father of gods.
Romulus, take second place. Augustus exalts your walls
    by his protection. You let Remus jump over them.
Sabine Tatius and his tiny towns experienced your might.   135
    With this leader the sun never sets on Roman soil.
You occupied a scant whatnot of conquered ground.
    Everything under high heaven Augustus occupies.
You took wives by force, his laws keep them chaste.
    You harbored criminals, he has banished them.   140
Force was to your taste. Augustus fosters the rule of law.
    Your title was "King," he's a "leading citizen."
A murdered brother reproaches you, he showed mercy to the foe.
    Your father Mars made you a god, he made his father Caesar one.

And now Aquarius is already half-visible on the horizon.   145
    The cup-bearer Ganymede still serves the nectar.
Here now, you who were shivering in the cold North Wind,
    cheer up: a milder breeze is blowing from the west.

10 February

The Morning Star has raised his shining light from the sea
    five more times. Today is the beginning of Spring.   150
But don't be fooled: frosty days are still in store;
    winter left its traces on the way out.

12 February

Let three nights pass, and at once you will behold
    the Bear Keeper[2] stride across the sky.
Among the wood-nymphs and Diana with her hunting spear,   155
    Callisto was a member of that hallowed troop.
With her hand on the goddess' bow, she took a solemn oath:
    "I swear by this bow to remain a virgin."
Diana commended her and said, "Keep the promise you've made
    and you will be my favorite companion."   160
She would have kept her promise, if she hadn't been so pretty.
    She avoided men, but Jupiter got her in trouble.

Diana was returning from hunting scores of woodland beasts,
    when the sun had reached—or maybe passed—its zenith.
Setting foot in her grove (a deep dark grove of oak   165
    with a spring of icy water at the center),
she says, "Arcadian virgin, let's bathe here in the woods."
    That form of address made Callisto blush.
Diana had spoken to the nymphs as well. The nymphs undressed;
    Callisto was ashamed and dawdled suspiciously.   170
Her tunic was off. Her swollen belly gave her away
    with obvious evidence of her condition.
The goddess told her, "Callisto, you liar, leave this assembly
    of virgins and do not stain our chaste waters."
Ten times the moon had gone from new to full.   175
    The supposed virgin was now a mother.
Wounded pride drove Juno crazy and she transformed the girl.
    Whatever for? Jupiter had her against her will.
When Juno saw her rival's ugly bestial face,
    she told her husband, "Go to bed with *that*."   180
Through mountain wilderness she wandered as a shaggy bear,
    the erstwhile object of great Jupiter's affections.
After their bastard boy had reached the age of fifteen,
    his mother encountered her son again.
Out of her wits, she stood as if she knew him,   185
    and growled. The growl was a mother's voice.
The boy would have stabbed her unwittingly with his hunting spear,
    if they both weren't whisked to a home in the sky.
They shine as neighboring constellations. The Bear goes first.
    The Bear Keeper seems to trail behind.   190
Juno is still furious, and asks the foaming Sea
    not to bathe—or even touch—the Arcadian Bear.

13 February

On the Ides the altar of pastoral Faunus smokes
    where Tiber Island splits the parted stream.
This was that famous day on which there fell six and   195
    three hundred Fabians to the arms of Veii.
A single family undertook the burden of the city's defense.
    The family's hands took up the arms it had volunteered.
From the same camp blue-blooded troops marched out,

any one of them fit to be their leader.   200
  The direct route went through the right arch of the Carmental Gate.
    Don't go through it, anyone. It has a curse.
Legend reports that the Fabians sallied forth from there.
    The gate isn't to blame, but it still has a curse.
Marching at the double they reached the raging Cremera   205
    (the river flowed in muddy winter flood),
and pitched camp on the spot. With swords drawn they launched
    a powerful assault on the Etruscan line,
not a bit differently than when the lions of Africa
    attack a herd scattered across wide fields.   210
In retreat the foe receives disgraceful wounds in the back.
    The ground is red with Etruscan blood.
Again and again they were routed like that. When they couldn't win
    a pitched battle, they prepared an ambush.
There was a plain, and the ends of it were blocked by hills   215
    and a forest fit for hiding mountain beasts.
In the middle they left the bait—men and some straggling cattle.
    The rest of the horde lay hidden in the underbrush.
Look! Just as a torrent swollen with showers of rain
    or with snow melted by a warm West Wind   220
is carried over fields and over roads, and doesn't keep
    its waters confined in their usual banks,
so the Fabians pour into the valley in a wide sweep
    and fell everything in sight with no fear of reprisal.
Where are you rushing, family of blue-bloods? You trust your foe too much. 225
    Guileless nobility, beware of treacherous arms.
Courage is brought down by deceit. Into the open fields
    from every side pounces the foe and surrounds them.
What can a few good men do against so many thousands?
    What help is left in this desperate situation?   230
Just as a boar driven deep in the woods by barking,
    scatters the hounds with his lightning tusks,
but soon is brought down, so the Fabians died
    fighting, and gave as good as they got.
A single day sent all the Fabians off to war.   235
    The men sent off to war a single day brought down.
But I can believe that the gods themselves made plans
    to insure that Hercules' line would survive,
since an underage boy not ready yet for bearing arms

was the sole survivor of the Fabian clan, 240
plainly in order, Maximus, that one day you could be born
    to rescue the state by your Fabian tactics.[3]

14 February

Three constellations lie in a row, the Raven and the Snake
    with the Bowl in the middle between them both.
On the Ides they lie in hiding; they rise on the following night. 245
    I'll tell you the reason for their close association.
Apollo once was fixing Jupiter's usual celebration
    (my little story won't keep you waiting long).
"Bird of mine," he said, "nothing should keep the service waiting.
    Go fetch clear water from a running spring." 250
With his hooked feet the raven lifted a gilded bowl
    and flew up high in his path through the air.
There stood a fig tree covered with fruit that was still hard.
    Pecking proved it wasn't ready to pick.
Disregarding directions, they say, the bird settled under the tree 255
    and kept on waiting 'til the fruit got soft.
Finally stuffed, he grabbed a water snake in his black claws,
    and returned to his master with this fabrication:
"Here's what kept me waiting. This one blockaded the running water,
    this one kept me from my errand at the spring." 260
Apollo said, "Your lying only makes it worse. How dare you
    try to fool the god of prophecy?
You won't quench your thirst from any cooling spring
    so long as figs hang unripe on the tree."
He spoke, and as a permanent reminder of that deed of long ago, 265
    snake, bird, and bowl twinkle together.

15 February

The third morning after the Ides beholds the naked Luperci,
    and two-horned Faunus' ritual gets under way.
Tell me, Muses, the source of these rites, where they were found
    before they came to our Latin homes. 270
They say the ancient Arcadians worshipped Pan, the god
    of herds, who haunted Arcadian mountains.
Mount Pholoe will vouch for this, as will Lake Stymphalus,
    and the Ladon river running swiftly to the sea.

So do the pine-clad ridges of the Nonacrine grove,   275
    lofty Tricrene and snowy Parrhasian peaks.
There Pan was a god of cattle and horses, who received
    thanks for sheep kept safe and sound.
Evander brought this forest spirit with him when he came
    to the vacant spot where our city is now.   280
And so we observe the rites of a god imported from the Greeks.
    Jupiter's flamen keeps the archaic custom.
So why do they run, you may ask, and why do they run that way,
    taking off their clothes and going naked?
The god himself loves to run fast in the high mountains.   285
    Panicky flight is inspired by him.
The god himself is naked, and naked his acolytes must be.
    Clothing isn't loose enough for running.
They say Arcadians lived on earth before Jupiter was born,
    and that race even predates the moon.   290
They lived like wild animals and had no use for work,
    still uncivilized, a primitive crowd.
For shelter they used leafy boughs, for food, wild plants.
    Their nectar was water drunk from cupped hands.
No bull strained under the curved plough's weight,   295
    no land was under a cultivator's control.
No use for horses yet; everyone went on his own two feet.
    And sheep got to wear their own woolen coats.
They toughened their bodies out in the open, going naked,
    masters at enduring heavy rains and hot winds.   300
Unclothed to this day, the Luperci bear a reminder of ancient
    practice and vouch for old-fashioned resourcefulness.

A funny old story has been handed down to explain
    why Faunus has a special aversion to clothes.
Young Hercules from Tiryns happened to be escorting his lady;   305
    Faunus spied the couple from a lofty ridge.
What he spied got him hot. "Mountain nymphs," he said,
    "you're not for me. This one's my flame."
As Omphale went by, her perfumed hair spilled over her shoulders,
    something to see with her golden neckline.   310
Warding off the warm sun's rays was a golden parasol
    held by none other than Herculean hands.
When she finally reached the grove of Bacchus and the vineyards of Tmolus,

dewy Evening's dusky steeds were approaching.
She entered a cave tiled with natural tufa and pumice.   315
    A brook was babbling right at the entrance.
While her servants prepare a banquet and wine to drink,
    she arrays the hero in her finery.
She hands over a dainty royal purple chemise,
    hands over the belt she had just undone,   320
a belt smaller than his belly. He unhooks the chemise
    so he can shove his big hands through.
First he'd burst bracelets not designed for those arms and
    then his big feet split petite sandal straps.
In exchange she took his heavy club, the lion's pelt,   325
    and the arrows stowed in their quiver.
Dressed like this they dined and retired to sleep like this,
    lying on separate adjoining cots.
The reason for this was their chaste preparation for attending
    the next day's rites for the vine's discoverer.   330
At midnight—filthy lust will try anything, won't it?—
    Faunus approached the grotto in the dark.
When he saw the servants sprawled out drunk and asleep,
    he hoped the same might be true of their masters.
The would-be rapist went boldly in, bumbling this way and that,   335
    groping his way with careful hands.
He'd reached his objective, the chamber where the cots were made up,
    and would have got lucky on his first try.
When he felt the tawny lion's shaggy hide,
    he was thoroughly shocked and withdrew his hand.   340
Stunned with alarm he recoiled, the way a startled traveller
    steps back in panic at the sight of a snake.
Next he felt the delicate clothes on the nearby cot
    and was duped by this misleading clue.
He clambers aboard the nearer cot, and lies down,   345
    his tumescent crotch harder than his horns.
Meantime he lifts up the chemise by the hem of its skirt.
    Rough calves were bristling with coarse hair.
The hero from Tiryns abruptly foiled further advances.
    Faunus came tumbling down out of the cot.   350
At the crash, the lady shouts to her servants and calls
    for a light. Torches made everything clear.
Violently thrown from the cot to the ground, Faunus

groaned and gingerly picked himself up.
Hercules laughed with the others who saw him lying flat,   355
    and the Lydian girl laughed at her suitor.
Made a fool of by clothing, the god is not fond of concealing attire,
    and invites his worshippers naked to his rites.

Add Latin reasons, Muse of mine, to foreign ones.
    Let my poem's chariot run on its native track.   360
A she-goat had been duly sacrificed to horny-hooved Faunus
    and the crowd came as invited to the meager feast.
While the priests were fixing the innards skewered on spits
    of willow, as the sun was in mid-course,
Romulus and his brother and their youthful band of shepherds were giving 365
    their naked bodies exercise in the sun.
They were putting their arms to tests of strength with fencing
    foils, and javelins, and throwing stones.
From a rise a shepherd called, "Romulus and Remus, rustlers
    are driving our bulls through the pathless fields!"   370
No time to get dressed. The twins went off in different directions.
    It was Remus who found and recovered the spoils.
When he returned, he pulled the sizzling innards from the spits
    and said, "None but the winner gets to eat these."
He and his Fabians⁴ were as good as his word. Thwarted, Romulus   375
    returned to bare tables and bare bones.
He laughed, but still he was stung that Remus and the Fabians
    could win, but not his own Quintilians.
The appearance of the exploit survives. The Luperci run undressed
    and what ended well is thus memorialized.   380

Maybe you also want to know why that place is the "Lupercal,"
    and the reason for a day with a name like that.
Impregnated by a god, the Vestal Silvia had given birth
    while her uncle the usurper held the throne.
He ordered the little ones carried off to be killed in the river.   385
    What? One of those boys is going to be Romulus.
His servants reluctantly carried out the king's deplorable command,
    in tears as they brought the twins to a lonely spot.
The Albula, renamed the Tiber after King Tiberinus
    was drowned, happened to be in winter spate.   390
Here where the fora are now, and the low-lying Circus Maximus,

you'd have seen skiffs plying their course.
When they had come here (for they couldn't proceed any further),
    the servants exchanged the following remarks:
"How alike they are! How handsome each of them is!   395
    But that one is the livelier of the pair.
If breeding shows in a face, and appearances aren't deceiving,
    I suspect there is some god in you two.
But if some god were the source of your existence,
    in such a crisis, he would bring help.   400
He would surely bring help, if your mother didn't need it herself,
    having and losing her children on a single day.
Twins in death as twins at birth, sink below the waves
    as a pair." He grew silent and set them down.
They both wailed alike: you'd have thought they understood.   405
    The servants went home with tear-stained cheeks.
The hollow ark kept the twins afloat atop the waves.
    What a destiny was riding on such a little plank!
Driven toward a shadowy forest, gradually the ark
    sank in the mud as the river receded.   410
There was a tree; bits of it remain, and today's
    Ruminal fig used to be the Romulan fig.
A she-wolf newly whelped came to the outcast twins—a miracle!
    Who'd believe the beast didn't harm the boys!
Didn't harm them? She even helped. A she-wolf fostered   415
    those whom kin had tried to kill.
She stood and wagged her tail at her delicate charges,
    and licked their bodies into shape with her tongue.
You'd have known they were sons of Mars, fearlessly pulling from her teats,
    fed with milk not intended for them.   420
The wolf gave her lupine name to the place, which gives the Luperci theirs.
    The nurse got a handsome reward for her milk.

What's to prove the Luperci weren't named after Mount Lycaeus
    in Arcadia where Faunus has a temple?

Bride, what are you waiting for? Strong drugs won't make you   425
    a mother, nor prayer nor incantation.
Put up with blows from a fertilizing hand and "father-in-law"
    will soon be "grandfather," as he longs to be.

Once upon a time harsh fate kept wives from scarcely
    ever redeeming their pledges of love.   430
"What was the good of carrying off the Sabine women?"
    Romulus cried (this happened during his reign),
"if that assault has brought me war instead of strength?
    Better to have had no daughters-in-law."
At the foot of the Esquiline Hill was a grove, uncut   435
    for many years, named after mighty Juno.
When they had come there, both brides and husbands alike
    humbly went down on bended knees.
The tree tops suddenly stirred and shook in the grove, and
    an amazing revelation came from the goddess.   440
"Let a sacred billy-goat mount Italian matrons."
    The weird pronouncement appalled the frightened crowd.
An exiled diviner, whose name has been lost with the passage of time,
    had recently arrived from Etruscan soil.
He slaughtered a goat. As instructed, the girls offered   445
    their backs to be struck by strips of its hide.
For the tenth time a crescent moon was waxing,
    when suddenly the couples all became parents.
Thanks be to the goddess Lucina. You got this name from the grove
    or from bringing us into the light.[5]   450
Kindly Lucina, be gentle, I pray, with pregnant girls,
    and ease their delivery when it is due.

When this day has dawned, stop trusting the winds. You can't
    count on the breezes during this period.
There are variable gales, and for six days the door of Aeolus'   455
    prison lies open wide and unbolted.

Aquarius and his tilted urn have already set. Pisces,
    the horses of the sun will enter you next.
They say that you and your brother (together your stars
    shine brightly) supported two gods on your backs.   460
Once, when Jupiter waged war in heaven's defense,
    Venus was escaping the dreadful Typhon.
She reached the Euphrates with her little companion, Cupid,
    and sat at the edge of that Syrian river.
Poplar trees and reeds overarched the top of the banks   465

and willows provided more hope of concealment.
While Venus lay hidden, a wind whistled in the trees; pale
    with fear, she believed her enemy was near by.
She clutched her son to her breast and said, "Nymphs,
    come to the rescue, bring help for two gods!"   470
Without hesitation she jumped. Two fish surfaced beneath her.
    For that, you see, the sign of Pisces was named,
and wary Syrians consider it wrong to dine on that species,
    and won't let fish cross their lips.

17 February

The next day is nothing special, but the following one is Quirinus'.   475
    He got this name (it used to be Romulus)
because the ancient Sabines called a spear a "curis"
    (the warlike god got to heaven by this weapon),
or maybe his Quirites gave their name to their king,
    or else from his union of Cures with Rome.   480
When Mars, the patron of war, had seen the new walls rising
    and the many campaigns that Romulus waged,
"Jupiter," he said, "the power of Rome is flourishing.
    She no longer requires my scion's services.
Return my son to his father. Although the other one died,   485
    the survivor will be both himself and Remus to me.
'There will be one for you to elevate to heaven's azure,'
    you said to me. Let Jupiter's words come true."
When Jupiter nodded assent, his nod shook both of the poles,
    and Atlas felt the weight of heaven.   490
There's a place the ancients called the She-Goat's Marsh,
    where Romulus happened to be giving verdicts.
The sun fled the scene. Clouds moved in and blocked out the sky,
    and heavy rain poured down in showers.
There's a clap of thunder and lightning bolts split the sky. The people   495
    take flight; the king ascended in his father's chariot.
Amid the grief, allegations arose of a patrician conspiracy.
    That suspicion might have stuck in people's minds.
But Julius Proculus was returning from Alba Longa.
    The moon was bright, so he didn't need a torch.   500
The hedges on his left suddenly rustled and shook.
    He drew back and his hair stood on end.

Handsome and larger than life in fine royal robes,
　　Romulus appeared in the middle of the road
and seemed to say, "Forbid my Quirites to grieve. 505
　　They shouldn't spoil my godhead with tears.
Have the devoted crowd bring incense to appease the new Quirinus,
　　and have them maintain their fathers' skill in war."
He gave these orders, and into thin air he vanished from sight.
　　Proculus assembled the people and reported the orders. 510
A temple was built for the god, and a hill was named after him.
　　Our fathers' cult is renewed every year.

Here's why the same day is also the "Feast of Fools."
　　Listen. The reason is trivial but it fits.
In olden days the land lacked expert cultivators. 515
　　Fierce wars exhausted the able-bodied men.
There was more glory in the sword than in the plough.
　　Neglected fields bore little for their owners.
But the men of old did sow spelt and did reap spelt,
　　and gave Ceres first-fruits of harvested spelt. 520
From experience they learned to parch it on open fires,
　　and suffered great losses from their own mistakes.
Sometimes they swept up sooty ashes instead of the spelt;
　　at other times their huts caught fire.
The oven became a goddess. Overjoyed, the cultivators 525
　　pray that Oven would cure their grain.
Nowadays the chief warden uses a prescribed formula to announce
　　the Oven Festival,⁶ because it's a moveable feast.
Around the forum lots of billboards hang, and each ward
　　is indicated by its particular mark. 530
The foolish folks who don't know which ward is theirs
　　postpone their sacrifice to the last day possible.

21 February

Tombs get tribute too. Appease your ancestral spirits
　　and bring⁷ small gifts to the pyres you've built.
The dead make small demands. Devotion counts as much 535
　　as a lavish gift; the spirits below aren't greedy.
It's enough to cover a tile with an arrangement of wreathes,
　　a sprinkling of grain and a bit of salt,

bread soaked in wine and violets scattered about.
    Set these on a tile in the middle of the road.   540
More is all right, but one can appease a ghost with just these.
    Set up a hearth and say the right prayers.
Aeneas, appropriate paragon of devotion, brought
    your country this custom, fair-minded Latinus.
That hero used to bring annual gifts to his father's spirit.   545
    From this his people learned devoted rites.
But once, in the course of a long hard-fought campaign,
    they neglected the days of the Parentalia.[8]
They paid for that! After that slip, the story goes
    the pyres on Rome's outskirts grew hot.   550
I can hardly believe it. They say the resentful ancestors
    left their tombs, in the dead of night,
and howled through the streets of city and countryside,
    shapeless spirits, they say, a shadowy horde.
After this the tombs were paid their neglected tribute   555
    and those ghastly hauntings came to an end.
During this period, bide your time, unmarried girls,
    and save the wedding torch for better days.
In the eyes of your eager mother you may be of age,
    but don't fix your hair for your wedding just yet.   560
God of marriage, hide your torches and stay away.
    Mournful tombs need gloomy torches.
Even the gods should be hidden behind closed temple doors;
    no incense on the altar, no fire on the hearth.
Ethereal spririts are now afoot, bodies already buried.   565
    The ghosts now nibble food set out for them.
This only lasts 'til eleven days are left in the month,
    as many days as my couplets have feet.
They called this day Feralia because they do what's fair.
    That's the last day for appeasing the dead.   570

Look at the aged crone, sitting in a circle of girls, performing
    rites for the Silent One (far from silent herself).
With three fingers she puts three bits of incense under
    a threshold where a mouse has burrowed in secret.
Then she fastens enchanted threads with dark-colored lead   575
    and rolls seven black beans around in her mouth.
She smears a fish head with pitch, sticks a bronze needle

through it, and roasts it in the fire.
She also drips in wine. What's left of the wine, either she
    or her companions drink; but she drinks more.   580
"I have gagged spiteful tongues and muzzled unfriendly mouths,"
    says the crone as she tipsily departs.
Right away you're going to ask me, who's the Mute Goddess.
    Hear what I learned from ancient old men.
Smitten with boundless passion for Juturna, Jupiter   585
    put up with a lot such a god shouldn't have to.
The nymph would now hide in the hazelwood forest,
    now she would dive into her sisters' waters.
The god assembled all the nymphs who inhabited Latium
    and hurled these words into their midst: 590
"Your sister is spiting herself by shunning her own advantage,
    an entanglement with the highest god.
Look out for us both. What will be a great pleasure for me
    will be in your sister's great interest.
Block her as she flees at the bank of the river   595
    to keep her from jumping into its waters."
He had had his say. All the nymphs of the Tiber consented
    and those of the Almo, the chambers of Ilia.
There happened to be a Naiad, Lara, whose original name
    was the first syllable repeated again.   600
It suited her babbling. Almo had often said to her,
    "Daughter, hold your tongue." But she didn't.
As soon as she reached her sister Juturna's pool she said,
    "Flee the banks" and repeated Jupiter's words.
She even went to Juno, and feeling sorry for wives,   605
    had said, "Your husband loves the Naiad Juturna."
Jupiter exploded. He ripped out the tongue she'd used
    with no restraint, and then summoned Mercury.
"Guide her to the dead. That's the right place for the silent.
    She'll be a nymph—of the pool down there."   610
Jupiter's will was done. En route the two entered a grove.
    They say she caught her divine guide's eye.
He got ready to rape her. She pleaded with a look in place of words,
    her mute mouth struggled vainly to speak.
She conceived and delivered twins, who guard intersections,   615
    the Lares, always on watch in our city.

22 February

Caring kin have named the next day Caristia
    and relatives meet at the gods they share.
Of course it's a comfort to turn one's gaze from the tombs
    and departed kin right back to the living,   620
and after seeing so many gone, to survey what's left
    of the line and count the generations.
Let the guiltless come, let the wicked stay far, far away:
    the disloyal brother, the mother cruel to her own,
the one whose father's too spry, who counts up his mother's age,   625
    the mother who wrongs her son's hated wife.
Away with Tantalus' feuding family, and Medea who murdered
    her sons, and the wicked stepmother, Ino.
Away with Procne and her sister and Tereus who wronged them both,
    and anyone who increases his wealth by crime.   630
Good people, give incense to your family's gods. Gentle Concord
    is supposed to be a very strong presence today.
Offer a bit of food, a token of welcome tribute,
    on a plate to feed the dancing Lares.[9]
At last when dewy night induces peaceful slumbers,   635
    raise a large glass of wine for the toast:
"To your health, and to yours, Father of His Country, excellent Augustus."
    Pour the wine after these good wishes.

23 February

When night has passed, let the usual tribute be paid
    to the god whose symbol divides the fields.   640
Terminus, whether you are a stone or a post set up in the field,
    your divine power goes back a long way.
Two landowners wreathe you from their opposite sides,
    each one bringing a wreath and a cake.
They set up an altar. The farmer's wife brings fire to it   645
    taken from her warm hearth in a broken pot.
The old man chops firewood and piles on the fuel with skill,
    and struggles to stick branches in the ground.
Then he coaxes the first flames from the dry bark kindling;
    a boy stands by holding big baskets.   650
From them a little girl tosses three handfuls of grain

on the fire, and reaches out honeycomb bits.
    The others have wine; the flames get a sample of everything.
      The crowd in white looks on in reverent silence.
The common Terminus is also sprinkled with the blood of a lamb,   655
      but the god doesn't mind if it's only a suckling pig.
The simple neighborhood assembles to attend the feast
      and hymns your praises, holy Terminus.
"You bound nations and cities and mighty kingdoms; without you,
      every field's title would be in dispute.   660
You don't play favorites, and you don't take bribes.
      You faithfully guard the fields in your trust.
If you had marked the Cynurian border of Sparta and Argos,
      the Three Hundred wouldn't have met their death,
and we wouldn't read the name of the Spartan sole survivor   665
      on the mound of weapons from the battlefield.[10]
What happened when Jupiter's new temple was going up? Of course
      the whole crowd of gods ceded him the place.
Terminus, legend tells, stayed put in the shrine he was found in,
      and occupies the temple along with great Jupiter.[11]   670
Even today, so that he may see nothing but stars overhead,
      the temple roof has a tiny hole.
After that, Terminus, you can't be free to roam.
      Remain on alert where you've been posted.
Don't budge an inch if a neighbor should make that request.   675
      You didn't for Jupiter, so why for a mortal?
And if you are struck by a plough or a hoe, shout,
      'This field is yours, that one, his.'"
A highway carries traffic into the Laurentian district,
      once the kingdom sought by Aeneas of Troy.   680
Six miles from the city it beholds the sacrifice to you,
      Terminus, of a woolly sheep's insides.
To other races territory is granted with a fixed border.
      The world's the limit for the city of Rome.

24 February

Now I must tell about the flight of the king. The sixth day   685
      from the end of the month got its name from that.
Tarquin the Proud was the last to reign over the Roman race,
      a wicked man, but a good general.

He had captured some cities, had demolished some others,
    and made Gabii his by a shameful scheme. 690
His third and youngest son, a proud man like his father,
    went behind the lines in the dead of night.
The enemy bared their swords. "Go on," he said, "kill an unarmed man.
    My brothers would like that and so would Tarquin,
my father, who cut up my back with a savage flogging" 695
    (to be able to say that, he'd taken a flogging).
By moonlight they regarded the young man and sheathed their swords.
    He stripped and they saw the welts on his back.
They were moved to tears and begged him to join in their mutual defense.
    He cunningly consented to their naive request. 700
Once in command, he sent a friend to contact his father,
    to find out the way to destroy Gabii.
There was a carefully tended garden with fragrant flowers.
    Through it ran a purling stream.
There Tarquin listens to the secret dispatch from his son, 705
    and mows down tall lilies with a stick.
When the agent returned and mentioned the lilies he mowed down,
    the son responded, "I see my father's plan."
The leading men of Gabii were cut down at once.
    Stripped of its chieftains, the city surrenders. 710
Here's a horrible sight—a snake coming out of the altar
    to snatch the innards from the dying flames. The Roman princes and their
cousin consulted Apollo. The response:
    "The first man to kiss his mother, will triumph."
Each of them hurried to give his mother a kiss, 715
    quick to believe what they misunderstood.
Brutus had wisely been playing the fool, to keep safe
    from your traps, cruel Tarquin the Proud.
Lying on his belly, he kissed our mother the Earth.
    The others believed he had tripped and fallen. 720
Meanwhile Ardea was surrounded by Roman standards
    and suffered a long drawnout siege.
During the lull while the enemy wouldn't come out and fight,
    the idle troops fooled around in camp.
Young Tarquin treated his comrades to food and drink. 725
    From their midst, the king's son said,
"While Ardea keeps us tied up with this tedious war,
    and doesn't let us decamp and go home,

do you think the marriage vow is still respected, and do
    our wives still share our love for them?"   730
Each man spoke up for his wife, and the debate grew heated,
    as tempers flared from lots to drink.
Collatinus, named for his famous birthplace, got up and said,
    "No need for words; rely on the facts.
The night is yet young. Let's mount up and head for the city."   735
    They liked his proposal; horses were saddled.
They got their riders through. The men headed straight for
    the palace. No watchman was at the door.
Here's how they found the princes' wives—wearing garlands on their necks,
    with drinks set out for staying up late.   740
From there they quickly headed for Lucretia. Beside
    her couch were baskets of fluffy wool.
By a dim light her maidservants were spinning their quota.
    In their midst she said in a gentle voice,
"Hurry now, hurry, girls. I must send this homemade cloak   745
    to your master as soon as it's finished.
But what do you hear (since you get to hear the word on the street)?
    How much longer is the war supposed to last?
Ardea, you'll fall in defeat at last. You're resisting your betters,
    you wicked city, to keep our men away.   750
Just let them come back. That man of mine is so impulsive,
    rushing all over with his sword at the ready.
I grow faint and almost die when I imagine him fighting,
    and a cold chill grips my heart."
In tears she stopped and let go the thread she'd begun,   755
    and looked modestly down in her lap.
That in itself was charming. Her modest tears were charming,
    and her features were her spirit's worthy match.
"Don't be afraid. I've come," says her spouse. She recovered,
    and hung, a sweet armful, from her husband's neck.   760
Meanwhile a raging fire ignites the young prince, and
    he is blindly in the grip of mad passion.
Her beauty is attractive, her snowy complexion and golden hair,
    and a charm which is completely uncontrived.
Her speech is attractive, and her voice, and her unavailability.   765
    The smaller his chances, the greater his desire.
The harbinger of daylight had already crowed
    when the young men got back to camp.

Tarquin's dazed senses were tormented by fantasies of her.
    Her attraction grew with his recollections.   770
The way she sat, the way she was dressed, the way she spun,
    the way her hair fell down her back.
She had worn this expression, these were her words,
    this complexion, these features, these charming lips.
As the sea grows calmer after a gale, but the waves   775
    still swell although the wind has passed,
likewise, although that attractive beauty was no longer present,
    there remained the passion that beauty's presence had caused.
He burned, and aroused by wicked passion's goading, he planned
    rape and coercion against that innocent bed.   780
"The outcome is uncertain. I will dare the utmost," he said.
    "She'd better watch out! Luck and the gods help
the daring. By daring I took Gabii too." So saying,
    he buckled on his sword and mounted his horse.
Collatia admitted the young man through its bronze gate   785
    as the sun was ready to hide its face.
As a visitor the villain entered the home of Collatinus.
    He was warmly received, as a relative by blood.
How mistaken minds can be! Unaware of his real motive,
    the hapless young woman served the villain a meal.   790
He was finished with the meal. The time for sleep had come.
    It was night and the house was completely dark.
He got up and freed his gilded sword from its scabbard,
    and came, modest wife, to your chamber.
As he got on the bed, the king's son spoke: "Lucretia,   795
    I've got my sword. It's Tarquin speaking."
No reply. She'd lost her voice, the strength to speak
    was gone and with it all composure.
She trembled like a lamb caught away from the fold,
    lying beneath a predatory wolf.   800
What to do? Resist? A woman who resists will be overpowered.
    Cry out? The sword in his hand prevented that.
Escape? His hands on her breasts were forcing her down,
    breasts only her husband had ever touched.
Her fervent foe persisted with prayers and bribes and threats.   805
    Prayers, bribes, and threats had no effect.
"No use," he said. "I'll take your life and spread suspicion.
    Your rapist will bear false witness to adultery.

I'll kill a slave and say I caught you together."
    Fear for her honor triumphed and the girl gave in.   810
Why gloat triumphantly? This conquest will be the end of you.
    A single night has cost you your kingdom!
At last day dawned. She sat with her hair in disarray,
    like a mother going to her son's funeral,
and summoned her aged father and faithful spouse   815
    from camp. Each of them came at once.
When they saw her condition, they asked the reason for her grief,
    who had died, what trouble had struck.
She kept still a long time, modestly veiling her face.
    Her tears poured down in a constant stream.   820
Father and spouse both comforted her tears, and begged her to speak.
    They wept and grew pale from vague unease.
Three times she tried to speak and failed. On the fourth attempt
    she still didn't look them in the face.
"Do I have Tarquin to thank for this too, that I, that I   825
    must unhappily speak of my own disgrace?"
She told what she could, but not the last part. She wept
    and her wifely cheeks turned scarlet.
Father and spouse pardon what she had been forced to do.
    "The pardon you grant, I myself refuse."   830
At once she stabbed her breast with a concealed weapon
    and fell bleeding at her father's feet.
Even then, on the point of death, she made sure her collapse
    was not unseemly—her last concern as she fell.
On top of the body, there, groaning for their mutual loss,   835
    heedless of propriety, father and husband lay.
Brutus "the dolt" was there. At last his spirit belied his name;[12]
    he seized the weapon from the half-dead body.
He holds up the dagger dripping with noble blood
    and fearlessly utters this threat: 840
"I swear to you by this blood, brave and untainted,
    and by your ghost, like a god to me,
Tarquin and his line will be banished to pay for this.
    I've had enough now of disguising my courage."
As she lay, she turned her glazed eyes toward his voice,   845
    and seemed to shake her head in assent.
The wife with the courage of a man was borne to her funeral.
    Tears and resentment followed her cortege.

The gaping wound lay exposed. With a shout, Brutus roused the Romans
    and reported the king's unspeakable acts.   850
Tarquin fled with his sons. The consuls began their year-long term.
    That was the monarchy's final hour.

Am I wrong, or has spring's harbinger, the swallow, come
    without care for the return of winter weather?
But, Procne, you'll often complain that you came too soon,   855
    and your husband Tereus will be pleased that you're cold.

27 February

Now two more days are left of the second month,
    and Mars whips up his speedy equine team.
Equirria has kept its accurate designation, for the races
    which the god beholds in his very own Field.   860
You're right to come, Marcher; your days demand their place
    and the month that bears your stamp is here.

I have come into port at the end of the month and the book.
    Let my skiff soon sail through other waters.

Book
3

March

War-like Mars, put down your shield and spear a while,
    remove your helmet, and be with me.
Perhaps even you may ask what's a poet's business with Mars.
    The month of which I sing was named for you.
You can see for yourself that Minerva puts her hand to fierce wars.   5
    But she has time to spare the arts, doesn't she?
Follow her example, and take time to put down your spear.
    Unarmed, you'll still find something to do.
You were unarmed then too, when the Roman priestess caught
    your eye, and you sowed the great seeds of this city.   10
The Vestal Silvia (what's to keep me from starting here?)
    was fetching water to wash the sacred utensils.
She had come by a footpath gently sloping down to the bank.
    She set down the clay jug from on top of her head.
Wearily she sat on the ground, welcomed the breeze on her   15
    uncovered breast, and tidied her tousled hair.
While she sat, shady willows and winged songsters
    and the gently purling water lulled her to sleep;
repose stole seductively over her heavy lids

and her hand slipped faintly from her chin.   20
Mars saw her, wanted what he saw, and took what he wanted.
    With a god's resources he concealed what he stole.
Sleep departed and she lay sluggish. Of course, by now
    within her womb was the founder of Rome.
She got up faint, without knowing why she got up faint,   25
    and went over these words as she leaned on a tree:
"I pray that what I saw in the guise of a dream may be
    a good omen. Or was that too vivid for a dream?
I was at Trojan Vesta's fire, when the woolen headband
    fell from my head in front of the sacred hearth.   30
From there sprang up—an amazing sight—two palm trees
    together. One of the two was bigger,
and had spread its heavy fronds over the whole world
    and its top had touched the stars above.
Look, uncle is wielding an ax against them; I am frightened   35
    by the memory and my heart leaps with fear.
Mars' bird, the woodpecker, is defending the twin trunks
    along with a wolf. They kept each palm safe."
She finished speaking, and lifted the full jug unsteadily.
    She had filled it while recounting her vision.   40
Meanwhile as Remus was growing and Romulus was growing,
    her belly was swollen with a heavenly weight.
At last the shining sun god had two signs of the zodiac left
    before the year completed its appointed rounds.
Silvia became a mother. They say that Vesta's image   45
    covered its eyes with its virginal hands.
The goddess' altar surely did shake as her servant gave birth
    and the flame withdrew in alarm beneath its ashes.
When her uncle Amulius found out, a man who scorned what was right
    (he held in triumph a kingdom usurped from his brother),   50
he ordered the twins drowned in the river. The water shrank
    from the crime, so the boys were abandoned on dry land.
Who doesn't know that the foundlings grew on wolf's milk
    and a woodpecker often brought them food?
I won't keep still about you, Larentia, nurse of so great   55
    a race, nor about your help, poor Faustulus.
Your tribute will come when I tell about the Larentalia,
    in December, merry month of the Saturnalia.
In eighteen years the scions of Mars had grown to manhood

and their first golden beards had come in.   60
The farmers and herders of cattle all would bring lawsuits
    for the brothers, Silvia's sons, to adjudicate.
They often came home exulting in the blood of rustlers
    and driving cattle back to their own fields.
When they learned their descent, their father's identity increased their spirit 65
    and they were ashamed to be famous among a few huts.
The sword of Romulus brought down Amulius and the kingdom
    was restored to their elderly grandfather.
Walls were founded, over which, small as they were,
    no good came of Remus' jumping.   70
Now there, where woods and pastoral retreats had recently been,
    was a city, when the eternal city's founder said:
"Ruler of arms, from whom I am believed to have be born—
    and I will give plenty of proof to support that belief—
I am going to call the beginning of the Roman year after you.   75
    The first month will take my father's name."
He kept his word and called the month by his father's name.
    They say this act of devotion pleased the god.
And besides, our ancestors worshipped Mars above all.
    The warlike crowd followed its disposition   80
Athena is worshipped by Athenians, Diana, by Minos' Crete,
    the island of Lemnos worships Vulcan.
Sparta worships Juno, and so does Atreus' Mycenae,
    Arcadia worships pine-garlanded Faunus.
Mars had to be revered by Latins, since he is in charge of arms.   85
    Arms brought this fierce race power and glory.
If you have the time, take a look at neighboring Italian calendars.
    In these there's also a month named for Mars.
It was the Albans' third month, the Faliscans' fifth,
    and sixth among the people of the Hernician land.   90
The calendars of Aricia and Tusculum (high walls built
    by Telegonus, Ulysses' son) match the Albans'.
Laurentians have it fifth, the fierce Aequiculi, tenth,
    and the crowd of Sabine Cures, fourth.
Paelignian warriors agree with their Sabine forefathers.   95
    The god's month is fourth for both these races.
To surpass all these, in pride of place at least, Romulus
    assigned the first period to the source of his bloodline.
The ancients didn't have as many Kalends as there are now.

The year was two months shorter then.   100
The Greeks, an eloquent race, but a cowardly one, hadn't yet
    surrendered their conquered science to their conquerors.
Science for the Romans was knowing how to fight well.
    Eloquence came from a javelin throw.
Who then had noticed the Hyades and Pleiades, daughters of Atlas,   105
    or knew there were twin poles under the sky?
Who then had noticed the two Bears that sailors steer by,
    Cynosura for Phoenicians, Helice, for Greeks,
or knew that the sun travels through the zodiac in a year's span,
    while his sister's horses do that in a single month?   110
The stars used to run free and uncharted throughout the year,
    but people agreed that they were gods.
They didn't stand by the constellations gliding through the sky,
    but by their standards[1] (a great disgrace to lose).
Those standards were made of hay, but that hay got as much respect   115
    as you see your legionary eagles get today.
A long pole used to troop bundles of hay attached.
    Hence we speak of troops attached to their unit.[2]
And so untutored minds still ignorant of natural laws
    spent decades that were twenty months short.[3]   120
A year had passed when the moon's disk had waxed ten times.
    That number was highly regarded then,
either from the ten fingers which we use for counting,
    or because a woman gives birth in the tenth month,
or because we count by tens, starting all over again   125
    each time we reach a multiple of ten.
Accordingly Romulus subdivided his hundred senators
    into ten circles, and established the lines
of battle formation, ten companies of spearmen, and as many
    of front liners, javelin throwers, and cavalry.   130
And yes, he also assigned as many wards to his three tribes,
    the Titienses, Ramnenses, and Luceres.
And so he preserved the familiar number in his year.
    For this period a wife sadly mourns her husband.
To convince yourself that the Kalends of March once was New Year's Day,   135
    you can turn your attention to the following evidence.
The laurel which has stayed a whole year by the flamens' houses
    is removed, and new foliage is highly regarded.
Then the king-priest's door is green when Apollo's tree is replaced.

The same happens at the door of the old ward-hall.   140
So that Vesta too may shine decked with fresh leaves,
    the gray laurel withdraws from her Trojan hearth.
Besides, they say a new fire is made in that secret shrine
    and the flame gains strength from this renewal.
This month's festival of Anna Perenna makes me believe   145
    that the annual cycle used to start here.
Further, we recall that today officials used to be inaugurated
    until the period of wars with deceitful Carthage.
Lastly, the fifth month after this is Quintilis; from then on
    each month gets its name from a number.   150
Numa, brought to Rome from olive-bearing Sabine fields,
    was the first to notice that two months were missing,
whether he learned this from Pythagoras, who believed in reincarnation,
    or from the advice of his own wife Egeria.
But still the calendar continued to be off, until this too   155
    became one of Caesar's many concerns.
That god and father of our great Augustus didn't believe
    such matters were beneath his attention.
He wanted to get to know heaven before his apotheosis,
    so he'd know his way around his new home.   160
With exact notations they report he arranged the time it takes
    the sun to retrace the signs of the zodiac.
To three score⁴ five and three hundred days he joined
    one-fifth of another whole day.
This is the length of a year; every fifth year we have to   165
    add one day, made up of those fractions.

1 March

"If poets may receive privileged information from the gods,
    as common opinion certainly thinks we may,
tell me, Mars, why do matrons celebrate the holiday
    of a god connected with a masculine occupation?"   170
That's what I said. Here's what Mars said. He'd removed his helmet
    but there still was a spear in his right hand.
"Now's the first time this god of war has been recruited
    for peaceful pursuits, a novel campaign for me.
The project doesn't displease me. I'm glad to spend time in this   175
    sphere too, so Minerva won't think it's hers alone.

Industrious poet of the Latin calendar, learn what you want,[5]
    and stamp my words in your retentive mind.
Rome was small, if you want to go back to the very beginning,
    but that small city held great expectations.   180
Walls were already standing, too cramped for the future population,
    but then considered excessively spacious.
If you want to know what my son's palace was like,
    take a look at a house of reeds and straw.
He used to reap the rewards of peaceful sleep on straw,   185
    and yet from such a bed he reached the stars.
The Romans' reputation had already extended beyond their territory,
    but they had neither wives nor fathers-in-law.
Their wealthy neighbors looked down on poor sons-in-law
    and didn't believe I was the source of the bloodline.   190
It hurt their cause that they lived in stables, grazed sheep,
    and possessed meager acres of untilled land.
The birds and the beasts all find their match to mate with.
    Even the snake has a female to bear his young.
Foreign nations are granted the right of intermarriage,   195
    but no woman was willing to marry a Roman.
This irked me, so I gave my son Romulus his father's spirit.
    'Forget prayers; arms will provide what you want.'
He prepared a festival for Consus. Consus will tell you the rest
    when you sing of his ritual on that date.   200
Cures and the other Sabine towns exploded with their grievance.
    That was the first time for war between in-laws.[6]
Only recently abducted, the women had already become mothers,
    as the war between neighbors dragged on a long time.
The wives assembled in the temple dedicated to Juno. Among them   205
    my son's wife dared to speak this way:
'Women abducted like me (we have this common bond),
    no longer can we postpone our duty.
The battle lines are drawn. Choose which side you want to pray for.
    Here a spouse, there a father is bearing arms.   210
The question is, do you prefer to be widows or orphans.
    I'll tell you a plan both brave and dutiful.'
She told them the plan. They complied, undid their hair,
    and sadly dressed in mourning clothes.
Now the battle lines had been drawn, ready for the sword and death,   215
    now the bugle was about to sound the attack,

when the abducted women came between their fathers and husbands,
    bearing their sons, dear tokens of love.
When they reached midfield with their hair torn in grief,
    they went down on the ground on bended knees.   220
With a winsome shout, as if they understood, the grandsons
    reached out their little arms to their grandfathers.
The ones who could, cried out to grandfathers seen at long last,
    and the ones who barely could were prompted.
The men dropped their weapons and their grievance. Fathers sheathed   225
    their swords and shook hands with their sons-in-law.
They praised and embraced their daughters, and each grandfather carried
    a grandson on his shield, a sweeter use for a shield.
Therefore Roman matrons have no slight obligation
    to pack the festival on my Kalends.   230
Either because they dared to confront drawn swords
    and end the martial struggle with their tears,
or because it was Silvia's luck that I made her a mother,
    mothers duly celebrate the rites on my day.
Not to mention that frost-covered winter withdraws at long last,   235
    and the snow melts away in the warmth of the sun.
The leaves which cold had shorn away return to the trees
    and the moist bud swells on the delicate vine.
The fruitful sprout, hidden so long, now finds secret
    passages to raise itself to the air.   240
Now the fields are productive, now is the season for breeding,
    now birds prepare sheltering homes in the branches.
Latin mothers rightly celebrate the productive season,
    when childbirth gets active duty and answered prayers.
And besides, where the Roman king used to post his watch,   245
    which now is called the Esquiline Hill,[7]
Latin daughters-in-law dedicated a temple to Juno
    for the city on this date, if I remember right.
Why am I dawdling, loading your mind with all sorts of reasons?
    What you want is right in front of your face.   250
My mother loves wives; my mother's crowd packs my temple.
    This very dutiful reason especially becomes me."
Bring flowers to the goddess: in flowering plants this goddess delights.
    Garland your heads with delicate flowers.
Say, "Lucina, you have brought us all to light."   255
    Say, "Come answer the prayers of a woman in labor."

But if any of you is pregnant, let her loosen her hair and pray
    that the goddess gently ease her delivery.

Who now will tell me why the Leaping Priests carry
    shields from heaven and sing "Mamurius"?   260
Advise me, nymph, busy at Diana's grove and pool.
    Numa's consort, attend events of your doing.
In the valley of Aricia is a lake encircled by a dark wood.
    Ancient awe has made it holy.
Here Hippolytus hides, tangled and torn in his horses' traces,   265
    the reason why no horse may enter that grove.
Threads hang veiling the long hedge where many a tablet
    has been put up in thanks for the goddess' help.
Often a woman whose prayer has been answered garlands her forehead
    and carries burning torches from the city   270
The "king of the grove" is a powerful runaway slave, who kills
    his predecessor and later meets the same fate.
A rocky stream flows down purling indistinctly.
    I have drunk from here often, but in tiny sips.
Egeria supplies the water, a goddess dear to the Muses.   275
    She was Numa's consort and counsellor.
Because the Romans at first were too ready for war, he decided
    to tame them with law and with fear of the gods.
So he made laws to keep the stronger from always getting his way
    and introduced the scrupulous observance of rituals.   280
They shed their savagery, right was stronger than might,
    the citizens were ashamed to fight among themselves,
and a man once bloodthirsty now turned at the sight of an altar
    to give the warm hearth wine and salted meal.
But look how the father of the gods sows the clouds with ruddy   285
    flames and drains heaven dry with showers of water!
Never before had lightning fallen so thick and fast.
    The king was frightened and alarm gripped the masses.
"Control your alarm," Egeria told him. "The lightning can be
    appeased and the wrath of harsh Jupiter averted.   290
Picus and Faunus can impart the ritual of appeasement,
    each one a spirit native to Roman soil.
They will only impart it under duress. Catch them and tie them up."
    And so she revealed the trick for catching them.

There was a grove at the foot of the Aventine, dark with shady oaks.   295
    At the sight you would say, "Some spirit dwells here."
In the middle there was grass, and a stream of water constantly
    trickled on the green, moss-covered rocks.
Faunus and Picus were almost the only ones who drank from it.
    King Numa came here and slaughtered a sheep for the spring,   300
and set out cups full of wine with a fragrant aroma,
    and hid with his men out of sight in a cave.
The woodland spirits came as usual to the spring
    and slaked their dry throats with a lot of wine.
After the wine they rested. Numa came out of the chilly cave   305
    and put tight bonds on the sleepers' hands.
When sleep departed, they tried to break the bonds by struggling.
    The bonds held faster the more they struggled.
Then Numa spoke: "Gods of groves, forgive what I've done,
    if you know that criminal intent is not in my nature,   310
and show the way to appease the lightning." That's what Numa said.
    Here's what Faunus said, shaking his horns:
"You want a great deal and something not right for you to learn
    from our instruction. Our power has its limits.
We are gods of the forest, whose domain is the high mountains.   315
    Jupiter's realm is his own jurisdiction.
You won't be able to entice him from heaven by yourself,
    but perhaps you will with our assistance."
Faunus had had his say. Picus gave the same response.
    "But let us out of these bonds," said Picus.   320
"Jupiter will come here, enticed by a powerful trick.
    The cloudy Styx will guarantee my promise."
What they did when released from their ropes, the spells they recited,
    and the trick that drew Jupiter from his abode on high,
is wrong for a mortal to know. I'll tell what's allowed   325
    and what may issue from the mouth of a devout poet.
They elicited you from heaven, Jupiter, and so posterity
    even today worships you with the epithet "Elicius."
Everyone knows how the treetops shook in the Aventine wood
    and the earth sank under Jupiter's heavy tread.   330
The king's heart leaped, the blood left his entire body,
    and his shaggy hair stood on end.
When his wits returned, he said, "Give reliable means of appeasement

for the lightning, king and father of the gods on high,
if I have touched your altar with scrupulous hands, and if   335
    I make this request too with a dutiful tongue."
The god assented to his prayer, but concealed the truth in a roundabout
    riddle and alarmed the man with ambiguous responses.
"Cut off a head," he said. The king replies, "I will.
    I'll have to cut a cabbage[8] from my garden."   340
He added, "A man's." Numa says, "You'll get some hair."
    He demands a life. Numa says "a fish's."
Jupiter laughed and said, "Be sure to appease my weapons with these;
    you're a man not to be barred from parley with the gods.
But when tomorrow's Sun has displayed its entire disk,   345
    I will give you reliable guarantees of empire."
He spoke and ascended above the sky shaken by a great
    thunderclap, and left Numa at prayer.
The king joyfully returned and told the Romans what had happened.
    They were slow to believe and hard to convince.   350
"But surely you'll believe me," he said, "if things turn out as I say.
    Listen now, everyone here, about tomorrow.
When the Sun has displayed its entire disk to the world,
    Jupiter will give reliable guarantees of empire."
They departed in doubt. The promise seemed a long time off,   355
    and belief depended on events of the following day.
The soft ground was dewed with frost in the morning.
    The people were on hand in front of their king's door.
He came out and sat in their midst on his maple throne.
    Countless men stood around in silence.   360
Only the very edge of the Sun had risen. Their troubled
    minds trembled with hope and fear.
Numa stood up, covered his head with a snow-white mantle,
    raised his hands, already well-known to the gods,
and spoke in this way: "The time is at hand for the gift you promised.   365
    Jupiter, give credence to the words of your promise."
While he was speaking, the sun had already pushed up its entire disk,
    and a heavy crash came from the vault of heaven.
The god thundered three times from a cloudless sky and loosed three bolts.
    Believe what I say. It's amazing but it happened.   370
The sky began to gape in the area at the center.
    The crowd and their leader lifted their eyes.

Here comes a shield tumbling gently end over end in the breeze.
    A shout from the people reached the stars.
Numa picked up the gift from the ground, after slaughtering   375
    a heifer which had never been broken to the yoke,
and he called the shield "ancile," because no angle is visible
    to the eye, since it was cut away on both sides.
Then, recalling that the fate of the empire rested on this,
    he hit on a plan of considerable cunning.   380
He ordered others to be made, stamped in the same shape,
    to confuse anyone with designs against it.
Mamurius concluded the work, a man as conscientious
    in character as in the craft of working metal.
Generous Numa told him, "Name the reward for your work.   385
    If my word is good, you'll get whatever you ask for."
The king had already named the Leaping Priests for their leaping dance,
    and had given them the shields and words for their hymn.
Here's what Mamurius said then: "Let fame be my wages,
    and let my name resound at the end of the hymn."   390
And so the priests pay the promised reward for the ancient
    workmanship, and call out "Mamurius."

If any of you girls wants to marry, even if you're both in a hurry,
    put it off. A little wait has great advantages.
Weapons stir up battles; battles are unsuitable for couples.   395
    Better to wait 'til the shields have been put put of sight.
On these days even the girded wife of Jupiter's
    pointy-capped flamen must keep her hair uncombed.

3 March

When the third night of the month has changed the position of the stars,
    one of the two Fishes will be put out of sight.   400
Indeed there are two. One is closer to the South Wind,
    the other to the North Wind. Each gets it name from the winds.

5 March

When Tithonus' saffron-cheeked spouse begins to bring dew
    and ushers in the hours of the fifth day,
whether you call it the Bear Keeper or lazy Bootes,   405

that sign will sink and flee your sight.
But the Grape Picker will not flee. It won't take long
    to teach the origin of this star too.
They say that Bacchus loved adolescent Ampelos, son of a nymph
    and a satyr, on the ridges of Thracian Ismarus.   410
To him was entrusted the vine hanging on the elm's leafy branches.
    The vine now gets its Greek name from the boy's.
While recklessly picking ripened grapes on a branch, he fell.
    Bacchus brought his lost love to the stars.

6 March

When the sixth Sun scales steep Olympus from Ocean, and picks   415
    his way through heaven with his winged horses,
everyone here who worships the sanctuary of chaste Vesta,
    rejoice with her and put incense on the Trojan hearth.
To Augustus' countless honors (which did he prefer to earn?)
    has been added the office of chief high-priest.   420
Over the flames eternal the eternal divinity of Augustus has charge.
    You see two guarantees of empire combined.
Gods of ancient Troy, booty most fitting for the one who carried you,
    by whose weight Aeneas was kept safe from the foe,
a priest from the line of Aeneas handles a kindred divinity.   425
    Vesta, safeguard your kinsman's life.
The flames which he keeps alive with his hallowed hand are flourishing.
    Live on unquenched, both fire and leader, I pray.

7 March

There's one thing of note on the Nones. They think that's the date the temple
    of Vejovis between the two groves was consecrated.   430
When Romulus surrounded the grove with a stone wall, he said,
    "Seek refuge here, whoever you are; you'll be safe."
Oh how the Romans grew from their humble beginnings!
    How ungrudging its ancient population was!
So the oddness of the name doesn't stump you in your ignorance, learn   435
    who that god is and why he's called like that.
The statue portrays a youthful Jove. Look at his youthful face;
    then look at his hand: no thunderbolts.
Jove didn't take up his thunderbolts until after the Giants

made designs on heaven. At first he was unarmed.   440
Ossa blazed with his new fires, and Pelion higher than Ossa,
    and Olympus planted on solid ground.
A she-goat is part of the statue. They say when Cretan nymphs
    were afraid to feed baby Jove, she gave him milk.
Now I'm called to account for the name. Peasants call spelt   445
    which has grown poorly "vegrandia," and small things "vesca."
If that's the meaning of the prefix, why shouldn't I surmise
    the temple of Vejovis is the temple of little Jove?

Now when the stars have spangled sky-blue heaven,
    look up. You'll see the neck of Pegasus.   450
When Perseus beheaded pregnant Medusa, they say this horse
    sprang up with a blood-spattered mane.
Gliding above the clouds and beneath the stars, he used
    the sky in place of earth, and wings for feet.
Bellerophon had just bridled his skittish neck when his hoof   455
    lightly gouged out the Boeotian spring Hippocrene.
Now he enjoys the sky, where he headed before with his wings,
    and he shines and twinkles with fifteen stars.

8 March

Right away on the following night you'll see Ariadne's Crown.
    Wronged by Theseus, she became immortal.   460
She had already done well to exchange a lying husband for Bacchus,
    she who gave an ingrate the key to the Labyrinth.
Delighted with her lucky new marriage, she said, "Why did I weep
    like a hick? That man was a cheat to my advantage."
In the meantime Bacchus conquered the long-haired Indians   465
    and came back with riches from the Eastern world.
Among the outstandingly beautiful captive girls
    was the princess, much too attractive to Bacchus.
His loving wife was weeping as she paced the curving shore,
    and uttered these words with her hair unkempt: 470
"Come on, waves, once again listen to the same complaints.
    Come on, sand, once again soak up my tears.
I recall I used to say, 'Theseus, you liar and cheat!'
    He went away, but Bacchus commits the same wrong.

Now again I will cry aloud, 'Let no woman trust a man.'   475
    The defendant has changed, but my grievance is the same.
How I wish my luck had continued as it first began,
    and I existed no longer right now.
Liber, why did you save me from death on abandoned sands?
    I could've put an end to my grief once and for all.   480
Bacchus, you lightweight, lighter than the leaves which frame your brow,
    Bacchus whose acquaintance has brought me to tears,
how could you dare bring a rival before my very eyes
    and put our well-matched marriage in turmoil?
Where is your good faith commitment? Where are the oaths you swore?   485
    Poor me, how often must I speak these words?
You used to reproach Theseus and call him deceitful yourself.
    You sin the more shamefully by your own indictment.
Let no one find out, and let me burn with grief in silence,
    so people don't think I deserve to be deceived so often.   490
Most of all I want this kept from Theseus, so he doesn't
    rejoice to have you as his fellow-sinner.
But you, I suppose, prefer my fair rival to my swarthy self.
    May all my enemies have a complexion like that.
But what's the use? That very blemish makes her more attractive to you.   495
    What are you doing? She pollutes your embraces.
Bacchus, be faithful, and don't prefer another to the love
    of your wife. It's my habit to love a man forever.
The horns of a handsome bull won over my mother, and yours
    won me. But this love is laudable, that was taboo.   500
Don't let it hurt me that I love you. It didn't used to hurt you
    that you confessed your burning desire to me.
No wonder you make me burn. They say you had a fiery conception
    and your father snatched you out of that fire.
I am the woman to whom you used to promise heaven.   505
    Alas, this is what I get instead of heaven."
She finished speaking. Liber had long been listening to her complaint,
    since he happened to have followed behind her.
He took her in an embrace, kissed away her tears, and said,
    "Let's head for the heights of heaven together.   510
Connected to me by marriage, you'll get a name connected to mine,
    for your name will be Libera when you've been transformed,
and I will make a memorial of you and the crown
    which Vulcan gave to Venus, and she to you."

He did as he said, and turned the nine jewels into fires,   515
  and now it twinkles like gold with nine stars.

14 March

When the sun with rosy day in his swift chariot has six times
  lifted up his disk and set it down as often,
you'll see the second Equirria on grassy Mars' Field
  which the Tiber threatens at the bend in the river.   520
But if it happens to be flooded with water spilling over the banks,
  the race will be run on the dusty Caelian Hill.

15 March

On the Ides the merry festival of Anna Perenna takes place,
  not far from the banks of the wandering Tiber.
The common people come and drink scattered about on the grass,   525
  each man stretched out with his partner.
Some rough it out in the open, a few pitch tents;
  some have leafy lean-to's made of branches;
some set up cane poles instead of sturdy pillars,
  and spread their togas out on top.   530
But they still warm up from the sun and the wine, and pray for
  as many years as they drink toasts.
There you'll find a man who drinks up Nestor's years
  and a woman whose cups have made her a Sibyl.
There they sing whatever they've learned at the shows   535
  and wave their hands nimbly along with the words.
They set the punchbowl aside and perform crude reels, and a stylish
  girlfriend lets down her hair and dances.
They come back home staggering, a spectacle for the masses,
  and the crowd they run into calls them lucky.   540
A procession recently took place (it seems to be worth reporting),
  a drunken old woman dragging a drunken old man.
Since opinion varies about the identity of the goddess,
  I don't intend to cover up any story.
Pitiful Dido had carried a torch for Aeneas and   545
  had torched the pyre built for her death.
Her ashes were collected and this short epitaph, which she left
  when she died, was put on her marble tombstone:
AENEAS FURNISHED BOTH THE MOTIVE AND THE MEANS;

DIDO USED HIS SWORD ON HERSELF.   550
The Numidians immediately attacked the defenseless kingdom,
 and Iarbas the Moor took over the captured palace.
Recalling her refusals, he said, "But now look who's
 in Dido's bed—the one she rejected so often."
The Carthaginians flee wherever their wandering takes them,   555
 like bees sometimes swarm when they've lost their queen.
A third harvest had gone to the threshing floor,
 and a third vintage to the hollow vats:
Anna was driven from home and left her sister's walls
 in tears. First she paid her last respects.   560
The soft ashes soaked up perfume mixed with tears,
 and got a lock of hair from her head.
Three times she said "Farewell," and three times pressed the ashes
 to her lips, and sensed her sister's presence.
After she found a ship and fellow refugees, she sailed   565
 full speed ahead, looking back at her sister's dear walls.
Near barren Cosyra is the bountiful island of Malta,
 pounded by the waves of the Libyan strait.
Anna headed there, counting on ancient ties of hospitality.
 Her host was Battus, the king and a wealthy man.   570
After he had learned the fate of each of the sisters, he said,
 "This land, tiny as it is, is yours."
And he would have dutifully offered hospitality to the end,
 but he feared the great power of Anna's brother Pygmalion.
The sun had reviewed the zodiac twice, a third year was passing, 575
 and Anna had to find a new land for exile.
Her brother threatened to attack. Detesting warfare, the king
 told Anna, "We are not warlike, you flee to safety."
She fled as ordered and entrusted her ship to wind and waves:
 her brother was rougher than any sea.   580
Near the fish-filled waters of the rocky Crathis river
 is a small territory the locals call Camere.
This was Anna's destination. She was no farther away
 than nine times the range of a slingshot.
First the sails went slack and were kept up by an unsteady breeze. 585
 The crew said: "Part the waves with rowing."
While they prepare to haul in the canvas with the ropes,
 the curved prow was struck by a violent storm
and carried out to the open sea, despite the captain's

futile struggle, and land disappeared from sight. 590
The waves leapt up and the sea was churned from its very depth,
    and the vessel shipped water white with foam.
Seamanship was vanquished by the wind and the helmsman could no longer
    steer the rudder, but he too prayed for help.
The Carthaginian exile was tossed on the swollen waves 595
    and covered her tear-filled eyes with her dress.
That was the first time her sister called Dido lucky, her
    and any other woman dead on dry land anywhere.
The ship was guided to the Laurentian shore by a huge gale,
    then swamped and lost after all hands had disembarked. 600
Dutiful Aeneas had already been strengthened by Latinus' kingdom
    and his daughter, and had united Trojans and Latins. On the shore he'd got
as a dowry, accompanied by Achates alone,
    while making his way barefooted on a secluded path,
he saw Anna wandering, and couldn't believe it was she. 605
    Why would she have come to Latin territory?
While Aeneas was thinking to himself, Achates shouted, "It's Anna!"
    She looked up at the sound of her name.
Oh, what to do? Flee? Hope the earth would swallow her?
    Before her eyes was her wretched sister's fate. 610
The hero, Venus' son, noticed her reaction and addressed her
    as she trembled (but he wept, disturbed by Dido's memory):
"Anna, I swear by this land, which you once used to hear
    was given to me by a luckier destiny,
and by the gods that accompanied me, recently settled here, 615
    that they often rebuked me for wasting time.
But I wasn't afraid for her life. Anxiety about that was remote.
    Oh, she was braver than I could have believed.
No need to tell me. I saw the wounds, an outrage to that body,
    when I dared to enter the realm of the Underworld. 620
But you, whether some purpose has driven you to our shores,
    or a god, enjoy my kingdom's bounty.
I haven't forgotten how much I owe to you, how much to Dido:
    you will be welcome for your sake and for hers."
She trusted what he said (for he was her last hope) 625
    and told the story of her own wanderings.
When she entered his home, garbed in Carthaginian fashion,
    Aeneas began (the rest of the crowd was silent):
"Duty is the reason, Lavinia my wife, for bringing this woman

to you; I made use of her help when I was shipwrecked.   630
    She was born in Tyre and had a kingdom on the Libyan coast.
        I pray that you love her like a dear sister."
Lavinia agrees completely, but conceals an imagined injury
        in her heart and silently masks her anxiety.
When she saw Anna given many gifts in her presence,   635
        still she thought many more were sent in secret.
She didn't know just what to do. Her hatred was fiendish
        as she planned a trap and longed to die avenged.
It was night. At the foot of her sister's bed Dido appeared
        to stand, bloodstained, with matted hair,   640
and to say, "Flee, don't hesitate, flee this gloomy house."
        Just then the wind slammed the groaning door.
Anna jumped up and quickly threw herself out a low window
        (fear itself had emboldened her)
and stole away anxiously, wrapped in a hitched-up chemise,   645
        and ran like a deer frightened by wolves it has heard.
People think the horned river Numicius stole her away
        in his passionate waves and hid her in his waters.
There was meanwhile a loud search in the fields for the Carthaginian:
        traces and marks of her feet appeared.   650
They had come to the bank: on the bank there were footprints.
        Her river accomplice kept his waters quiet.
She seemed to speak: "I'm the nymph of the peaceful Numicius,
        called Anna Perenna for hiding in a perennial river."
At once they feasted happily in the fields they had wandered,   655
        and filled themselves and the day with much wine.

To some, Anna is the Moon, filling the annual cycle with months.
        Some think she's Themis, others, Isis.
You'll find those who say she's the Arcadian nymph
        Azanis, who gave Jupiter his first food.   660
This story too, which I'm going to tell, has reached
        my ears, and isn't far from the truth.
The common people of old, still not safeguarded by tribunes,
        seceded[9] to the top of the Sacred Mount.
Already the provisions they brought along had run out,   665
        including grain fit for human consumption.
A certain Anna came from Bovillae, a town near the city,
        a poor old woman, but very industrious.

With her white hair tucked up in a light babushka she would knead
    country-style loaves with her palsied hand.   670
Come morning she used to distribute them, still hot from the oven,
    to the people. The people were grateful for these supplies.
When peace was settled at home, they erected a statue to Perenna
    because she brought them help when they'd run out.

Now it remains to tell why girls sing indecent songs,   675
    for they get together and sing some shocking stuff.
Anna had recently become a goddess. Mars came to her,
    drew her aside, and said the following:
"Your festival takes place in my month, I have shared my days with you.
    A great hope of mine depends on a favor from you.   680
A god in arms, swept away with desire for a goddess in arms,
    I burn for Minerva, and I've nursed this wound a long time.
Fix it so two gods with similar interests can get together.
    This role suits you, affable old woman."
She duped the god with an empty promise and continually prolonged   685
    his foolish hope with hesitation and delay.
When he kept pestering her, she said, "I've carried out your commission.
    She's been won over. She surrendered—just barely—to prayers."
The lover believed her and got his bedroom ready. In came
    Anna, covering her face, like a new bride.   690
On the verge of stealing a kiss, Mars suddenly recognized Anna.
    First shame, then anger came over the divine dupe.
The new goddess laughed at dear Minerva's suitor, and nothing
    pleased Mars' former lover Venus more.
And so old jokes are made and indecent things are sung   695
    and it is a pleasure to have tricked a mighty god.

I was going to pass over the swords thrust into Julius Caesar,
    when Vesta said this from her chaste hearth:
"Don't hesitate to mention it. That man was my priest.
    Sacrilegious hands aimed their weapons at me.   700
I stole the man away and left a mere likeness.
    What fell to the sword was a phantom of Caesar."
Installed in heaven indeed that man sees the halls of Jupiter
    and has a temple dedicated in the great Forum.
But whoever dared such wickedness, forbidden by the power of the gods,   705
    and violated the person of the chief high-priest,

lies dead as he deserves. Bear witness, Philippi,
    and the battlefield white with their scattered bones.
This was the task, this the duty, this the foundation
    of Augustus avenging his father in a righteous war.   710

16 March

When the next Dawn has refreshed the delicate grass,
    the front half of Scorpio will be there to see.

17 March

The third day after the Ides is full of honor for Bacchus.
    Bacchus, indulge this poet's discussion of your festival.
I'm not going to tell about Semele. If Jupiter had come to her   715
    without his thunderbolts, you'd have been born a mere mortal.
Nor about how your father's body performed a mother's
    function so you could be born in due time.
Your Thracian and Scythian victories would make a long story,
    as would the defeat of incense-bearing India.   720
I'll also keep quiet about Pentheus, his mother's ill-gotten trophy,
    and Lycurgus, who turned on his own family in a frenzy.
Look, I'd like to tell about the Tyrrhenian sailors, suddenly
    dolphins, but that's not the function of this passage.
The function of this passage is to set down the reasons why   725
    the Vine Planter summons people to his libation cakes.
Before your birth, Liber, altars went without tribute,
    and one could find grass on the cold hearths.
They report that after you subdued the Ganges and the whole East,
    you set aside the first-fruits for great Jupiter.   730
You were the first to give cinnamon and captured incense
    and the roasted innards of a cow led in triumph.
"Libations" are named for their originator, as are "libation" cakes,
    part of which is given to hallowed hearths.
Libation cakes are made for the god because he loves   735
    sweet liquids and reportedly he discovered honey.
He was going from the sandy Hebrus River accompanied
    by satyrs (my story has an amusing twist).
They had already come to Rhodope and flowery Mount Pangaeum.
    His companions clashed the bronze cymbals in their hands.   740
Look, strange flocks come winging, attracted by the jingling,

and bees are following the sounds of the bronze.
Liber rounded up the swarm, confined it in a hollow tree,
    and got the rewards of the honey he found.
When the satyrs and bald old Silenus tasted the flavor, they went   745
    looking for golden combs throughout the grove.
Old Silenus hears a swarm buzzing in a rotten elm
    and doesn't let on that he's seen the waxy combs,
and as he was lazily sitting on a sway-backed ass, he rode
    it up to the elm and its hollow bark.   750
He stood on the ass, and leaning on the branching trunk,
    greedily searched for the honey hidden in the tree.
Thousands of hornets came swarming and buried their stingers
    in his bald head and marked his snub-nosed face.
As he fell head over heels, he got a kick from the ass,   755
    and he shouted for his comrades to come and help.
The satyrs came running and laughed at their father's swollen
    face. He was limping from the kick to his knee.
Bacchus laughed too and showed him how to smear on mud.
    He took the advice and smeared his face with mud.   760
Father Bacchus enjoys honey, so we duly offer its discoverer
    shining honey drizzled over a warm libation cake.
There's no arcane reason why a woman takes charge of this.
    He incites troops of women with his thyrsus rod.
Why an old woman does this, you may ask. That age is fonder   765
    of wine and loves the gifts of the loaded vine.
Why is she garlanded with ivy? Ivy is precious to Bacchus.
    Why this is so, you can learn in no time.
They say the nymphs of Nysa camouflaged his cradle with its leaves
    when Juno was hunting for her infant stepson.   770

It remains for me to find out why the liberal[10] toga is given
    to boys on your day, splendid Bacchus.
Either because you always seem both boy and young man,
    and yours is the age in between the two;
or because you are father Bacchus and fathers entrust   775
    their beloved sons to your care and power;
or because you're the Liberator, the liberal garment is assumed
    en route to a more liberal stage of life.
Or in the days when the ancients tilled their fields more diligently—
    a senator did the work on his ancestral estate,   780

a consul went into office directly from his curved plough,
    and it was no sin to have calloused hands—
then the country folk would come to town for the public shows,
    but they paid that tribute to the gods, not to the pastimes.
The inventor of the grape used to have shows on his day.   785
    Now he shares them with torch-bearing Ceres.
So, in order that the crowd on hand could honor the neophytes,
    did that day seem appropriate for giving the toga?
Father, turn your head and peaceful horns over here
    and grant billowing sails to my talent.   790

The procession to the Argei (turn some pages to learn who they are)
    takes place, as I recall, today or yesterday.

Down toward the Arcadian Bear, formerly Callisto, turns
    the Kite Star.[11] Tonight it becomes visible.
If you want to know what won that bird its place in heaven,   795
    it happened when Jupiter drove Saturn from his kingdom.
Enraged, Saturn incited the mighty Titans to arms
    and tried the help which was owed by the Fates.
There was a spawn of Mother Earth, an amazing monster,
    a bull in front, and a snake behind.   800
On advice of the Fates, the raging Styx had shut him up
    in a dark grove surrounded by a triple wall.
Whoever sacrificed that bull's innards to the flames
    was destined to conquer the everlasting gods.
Briareus the hundred-handed slaughtered it with an ax of adamant,   805
    and was just about to sacrifice the innards to the flames.
Jupiter ordered the birds to steal them away. The kite
    brought them to him and came to the stars for this service.

19–22 March

There's a one-day interval before Minerva's festival, which gets
    its name—Quinquatrus—from its five consecutive days.   810
The first day is bloodless and gladiators may not engage in swordplay.
    The reason? That's Minerva's birthday.
The next four days are celebrated on the arena's smoothed sand.
    The warlike goddess delights in drawn swords.
To Pallas now pray, boys and delicate girls.   815

Whoever appeases Pallas will be skilled in his craft.
When Pallas has been appeased, girls will learn
    to card wool and unload full distaffs.
She also teaches how to run the shuttle through the warp
    and she packs the loose work with the reed.   820
Worship her, you who remove spots from soiled clothing.
    Worship her, whoever prepares dye-vats for wool.
No one will be a good cobbler against the will of Pallas,
    be he cleverer than Tychius who made Ajax his shield.
And be his hands a match for Epeus of the Trojan Horse,   825
    if Pallas is angry, a carpenter will be all thumbs.
You too, who drive off diseases with Apollo's skill,
    bring the goddess a few gifts from your fees.
Teachers, don't you despise her either, despite your lost income
    on this school holiday (she recruits new pupils),   830
and you who employ the burin, or paint encaustic pictures,
    or make stones plastic with your skillful hands.
The goddess of a thousand crafts, she is surely a goddess of poetry.
    If I deserve it, may she befriend my endeavors.

Where the Caelian Hill slopes down from its height to the plain,   835
    here where the road is almost, but not quite, flat,
you can see the little temple of Capta Minerva,
    where the goddess began to reside on her birthday.
The origin of the name isn't certain. We call a clever
    talent "capital"; she is a goddess of talent.   840
Or is it because they say she sprang forth with her shield
    from her father's occipital region, without a mother?
Or because she came to us Romans as a captive when Falerii was defeated?
    There's an old inscription to this effect.
Or because there's a law which demands capital punishment   845
    for thefts recovered from that place?
For whatever reason you derive that epithet, Pallas,
    may you always protect our generals with your shield.

23 March

The last of her five days requires us to purify the tuneful
    trumpets and sacrifice to the valiant goddess.   850

Now if you lift your face toward the sun, you can say,

"Yesterday it left the sign of Phrixus' Ram."
When the seeds had been parched by wicked stepmother Ino's deceit,
    the grain had not put forth its usual sprouts.
Someone was dispatched to Delphi to bring back in a reliable response   855
    what remedy Apollo would declare for the barren earth.
Like the seed, the messenger had been tampered with, and so he reported
    that the response called for the death of the king's children.
Despite the king's continued refusals, his subjects, the crisis,
    and Ino compelled him to submit to the atrocious order.   860
With fillets around their temples, Phrixus and Helle stood together
    before the altar and bewailed their common fate.
Their mother beheld them as she happened to float through the sky,
    and she beat her bare breast in dismay,
and jumped with her fellow clouds into Thebes, city born   865
    of a dragon, and snatched her children from there.
For their escape, she supplied a ram of brightest gold.
    He carried the two over the wide sea.
They say that the girl had hung on weakly to one horn
    until she fell and gave the Hellespont her name.   870
Her brother was almost lost too. He wanted to help her
    as she fell, and kept on stretching out his hands.
He was weeping for the lost partner of their twin danger, unaware
    that she'd been united with sea-blue Neptune.
After they made landfall, the ram became a constellation,   875
    but his golden fleece reached the realms of Colchis.

26 March

When three more dawns have sent the Morning Star ahead,
    you'll say the day's length equals the night's.

30 March

When the shepherd has penned his well-fed kids four more times,
    and the grass has been rimed with fresh dew four more times,   880
we will have to worship Janus and with him, gentle Concord,
    and Roman Security and the Altar of Peace.

31 March

The Moon regulates the months. The length of this month, too,
    is ended by the Moon, worshipped on the Aventine ridge.

Book 4

April

"Kindly mother of love, requited or slighted, indulge me."
    She turned her face in this poet's direction.
"What do you want with me? Surely you were singing a grander song.
    Have you got that old wound in your sensitive heart?"
"You know, goddess," I replied, "about the wound." She smiled,   5
    and at once that region of the sky was cloudless.
"In sickness or in health, have I ever deserted your service?
    You were my only subject, my only work.
In my early years, as was proper, I dallied innocently;
    now my horses are running on a bigger track.   10
The dates—and their origins—dug up in ancient chronicles,
    stars rising and setting—of that I sing.
I have come to the fourth month, full of honor for you;
    Venus, you know both the poet and the month are yours."
Stirred by this, she gently touched my temples with her myrtle   15
    from Cythera, and said, "Complete the work you've begun."
I felt it, and suddenly the origin of the days was revealed:
    while I may and the winds are fresh, let my ship proceed.

If any portion of the calendar ought to concern you,
    Augustus, in April you have something to safeguard.   20

Your heritage bequeaths this month to you; it becomes yours
    through your adopted father's noble rank.
Father Romulus noticed this, when he was drafting the calender,
    and made a record of the founders of your family.
Just as he gave fierce Mars his share as first in the series,   25
    because he was the immediate reason for his birth,
so he wanted Venus, who was more distantly related,
    to take her place in the second month.
Unrolling the centuries to trace his family's beginnings,
    he went all the way back to divine kin.   30
How could he fail to know that Dardanus was the son of Atlas'
    daughter Electra, and that Electra had bedded Jupiter?
Dardanus' son was Ericthonius, who begat Tros;
    Tros sired Assaracus, and Assaracus, Capys.
Next came Anchises; Venus did not disdain   35
    to share with him the honors of parentage.
From him was born Aeneas, whose devotion was seen by the flames of Troy
    as he shouldered his venerable father and his venerable gods.
We have come at last to the lucky name of Julus, through whom
    the Julian family reaches its Trojan ancestors.   40
Postumus was his son; because he was born on sylvan heights,
    he was called Silvius by the Latin race.
This was your father, Latinus; Alba succeeded Latinus:
    next to inherit Alba's title was Epytus.
That man gave to Capys a name that went back to Troy,   45
    and became in turn Calpetus' grandfather.
When Tiberinus succeeded to his father's throne, he supposedly
    drowned in the swirling eddies of a Tuscan stream.
But he lived to see his son Agrippa and his grandson Remulus;
    Remulus, they say, was struck by lightning.   50
After them came Aventinus, for whom the district is named,
    and the hill; after him the throne went to Proca;
he was followed by Numitor, the brother of hard-hearted Amulius;
    Silvia and Lausus were Numitor's children.
Lausus fell by his uncle's sword; Silvia attracted Mars   55
    and bore you, Romulus, with Remus your twin.
Romulus always said that Venus and Mars were his ancestors
    and he deserved to have his word believed:
in order that his later descendants could not fail to know them, he gave
    successive months to the gods in his family.   60

I interpet April as designated by Venus' name in Greek,
    Aphrodite, from the word for "sea foam."
Don't be surprised that it's called by a Greek word,
    since the land of Italy was a greater Greece.[1]
Evander had come with a ship full of his people, and Hercules   65
    had come, both of them Greek by birth
(the stranger with the club grazed his herd on Aventine grass
    and the Tiber was drunk by the great god himself).
Plus the Ithacan captain. Witness the Laestrygonian colony
    Formiae, and the promontory still called Circe's;   70
and now his son Telegonus' walls, the walls of Tivoli,
    were standing because Greek hands had erected them.
Harassed after the death of Agamemnon, Halaesus had come,
    for whom Falerii thinks it was named.
Add Antenor, Trojan proponent of peace (and Padua's founder),   75
    and Diomedes, Apulian Daunus' son-in-law.
After Antenor, long after the Trojan conflagration,
    Aeneas brought his gods to our area.
One of his companions was Solimus from Phrygian Ida;
    from him the walls of Sulmo get their name,   80
of cool Sulmo, Germanicus, where I was born.
    Alas, how far that is from Scythian soil!
And I, so far away—but stifle your complaints, my Muse,
    you mustn't treat religion in a mournful key.

Does envy spare no one? Some begrudge you the tribute   85
    of your month, Venus, and want to rob you of it.
Because all things appear in spring and the freezing sharpness
    of the cold departs and the fertile earth relaxes,
they say April was named for this season of appearance,[2]
    but kindly Venus formally claims it as hers.   90
She indeed quite rightfully regulates the entire world,
    no god has greater jurisdiction than she,
she lays down the law for heaven, earth and her native sea;
    her approach perpetuates every species.
She produced all the gods (too numerous to mention),   95
    she provided crops and trees with their origin,
she brought together the hearts of primitive men
    and taught each to be joined with his partner.
What but seductive pleasure produces every species of bird?

Cattle would not mate, in the absence of gentle love. 100
The belligerent ram locks horns with other males, but refrains
    from hurting his beloved ewe's forehead.
In pursuit of a heifer the bull sheds his ferocity, the bull,
    terror of every glade and every grove.
The same drive preserves everything living beneath broad ocean 105
    and fills the waters with countless fish.
Venus was the first to rid man of his savage customs;
    from her came elegance and concern for style.
They say a lover denied admission sang the first song
    while keeping watch at the barred door, 110
and rhetoric arose to plead with a hard-hearted girl,
    and everyone was eloquent on his own behalf.
She inspired a thousand skills; eagerness to be attractive
    supposedly discovered many things hidden before.
Who would dare plunder her of the distinction of the second month? 115
    Keep that crazy idea far away from me!
And while she's powerful everywhere, glorified in crowded temples,
    in Rome the goddess holds still greater sway.
Romans, Venus took up arms in defense of your Troy, and groaned
    when a spear injured her delicate hand. 120
When Trojan Paris was judge, she defeated two heavenly goddesses
    (how I wish the defeated goddesses had forgotten this).
She became the mother of a Trojan son, plainly in order
    that one day great Augustus might have Julian ancestors.
No other season is better suited to Venus than spring: 125
    in spring the land glistens and the fields are thawed;
now the grasses break through the ground and push up their blades,
    now the vine forces buds through the swollen bark.
Lovely Venus deserves a lovely season, and now,
    as usual, she comes right after her beloved Mars. 130
In spring she advises curved ships to cross her native seas,
    and no longer fear the threats of winter.

1 April

Duly you worship the goddess, Latin wives, old and young,
    and you who may not dress like respectable women.
Remove the golden necklace from the goddess' marble neck, 135
    remove her ornaments: she must be thoroughly bathed.

Replace the golden necklace on her neck when it is dry:
    now you must give her new flowers, new roses.
She further demands that you be bathed beneath green myrtle:
    learn the specific reason for this demand.   140
Naked on the shore she was drying her dripping hair:
    a randy bunch of satyrs saw the goddess.
Noticing them, she covered her body with a screen of myrtle:
    this kept her safe, so she demands you repeat it.
Now learn why you give incense to Manly Fortune[3]   145
    where the baths are damp with cold water.
That place admits all women with their clothing removed
    and sees a naked body's every blemish.
Manly Fortune takes care of covering these and hiding them from men,
    and does so on request for a little incense.   150
Don't be reluctant to take a dose of poppy crushed
    in snow-white milk with honey drained from the comb.
When her passionate husband first took Venus home,
    she drank this; from then on she was a wife.
Appease her with humble words; under her sway abide   155
    beauty, character, and good reputation.
Sexual morality at Rome once slipped from ancestral standards;
    the ancients consulted the Sibylline Books,
which demanded a temple for Venus. When it was duly built,
    from that Venus got the epithet "Changer of Hearts."[4]   160
Always smile, goddess most fair, on Aeneas' descendants
    and safeguard your many daughters-in-law.

As I write, the Scorpion with the fearsome stinger in his
    uplifted tail plunges into the green waters.

2 April

When night has passed, and the sky first begins to redden,   165
    and the birds, damp with dew, are twittering plaintively,
and the wayfarer sets down his half-burned torch after a night
    awake, and the peasant goes to his daily work,
the Pleiades will begin to unburden their father Atlas' shoulders.
    Called the "Seven Sisters," but usually six appear,   170
either because six were taken in a god's embrace
    (they say that Sterope bedded with Mars,

Alcyone and lovely Celaeno both with Neptune,
    Maia, Electra, and Taygete with Jupiter),
but Merope, the seventh, wedded the mortal Sisyphus;   175
    she's sorry she did, and hides alone in shame.
Or else because Electra couldn't bear to watch the fall
    of Troy, and covered her eyes with her hands.

4 April

Let the heavens revolve three times on their eternal axis,
    let the Sun hitch and unhitch his horses three times,   180
and at once the curved Berecyntian flute will blow and the festival
    of the Great Mother of Ida will commence.
The eunuchs will parade and strike their hollow tambourines,
    and cymbal clashing on cymbal will jingle.
Riding on the soft necks of her followers she will be carried   185
    through the city's streets amid their howling.
The theater is noisy, the shows are calling: citizens, attend,
    and empty the quarrelsome courts of their warfare.
I'd like to ask about many things, but I'm frightened by the shrill
    noise of the cymbals and the flute's spine-chilling noise.   190
"Goddess, give me someone to interview." Cybele sighted her learned
    granddaughters and ordered them to attend to my concern.
"Keep your charge in mind, fosterlings of Helicon, and disclose
    why the great goddess delights in incessant noise."
That's what I said. Here's what Erato said (Venus' month   195
    was allotted to her because of her erotic name):
"Saturn once got the following oracle: 'Best of kings,
    you will be knocked from your throne by your son.'
Fearing his own offspring, he swallowed each when it
    was born, and kept it in the depths of his belly.   200
Rhea frequently complained, so often pregnant but never
    a mother, and grieved at her own fertility.
Jupiter had been born (trust tradition's testimony
    and don't disturb received opinion).
A rock concealed in swaddling settled in the divine gullet: 205
    the father was fated to be tricked like that.
For a long time steep Mount Ida echoed with jingling
    so the baby boy could wail in safety.
Some struck shields with pikes, others struck hollow helmets:

the Curetes performed this task, the Corybantes, too.   210
The truth was concealed, and imitations of the ancient deed survive:
    followers of the goddess shake cymbals and rumbling hides.
They beat cymbals instead of helmets, tambourines instead of shields:
    as before, the flute produces Phrygian tunes."
She was finished. I began. "Why does the fierce lion species   215
    serve the goddess as unusual beasts of burden?"
I was finished. She began. "People believe their ferocity
    is gentled by her, as her chariot attests."
"But why is her head loaded down with a crown bearing towers?
    Because she gave towers to the earliest cities?"   220
She nodded. "Where," I asked, "does the impulse for self-castration
    come from?" When I was silent, she began to speak:
"In the woods, a remarkably handsome Phrygian boy, Attis,
    held the tower-bearing goddess in chains of pure love.
She wanted to keep him for herself, to safeguard her temple, and said,   225
    'Make sure that you want to be a boy forever.'
He gave his word at her behest and said, 'If I am untrue,
    let the love I cheat you with be my last.'
He cheated her with the nymph Sagaritis, and ceased to be what he'd been.
    The goddess' wrath exacted a price from the girl: 230
she cut down the Naiad with blows inflicted on a tree, and that one
    was done for; the tree was the Naiad's talisman.
Attis went mad, and believing his bedroom ceiling was collapsing,
    he took off and headed for the heights of Dindymus.
Now he shouted, 'Take away the torches,' now, 'Take away   235
    the whips,' often swearing the Furies were after him.
He even hacked at his body with a sharp rock,
    and dragged his long hair in the filthy dust.
He cried, 'I deserved it, I'll pay the deserved price in blood.
    I wish that these parts which harmed me were done for.   240
I wish they were done for,' he repeated: he removed the burden of his groin,
    and suddenly there wasn't a trace of his manhood left.
This madness set an example and the soft acolytes toss
    their hair and cut off their worthless organs."
Such was the eloquent response of the Muse from Boeotia   245
    to my question about the reason for that madness.
"Advise me, please, on this, my guide. Where did we go to get
    her from? Or has she always been in our city?"
"The Mother always loved Dindymus, and Cybele, and Ida

with its delightful springs, and the wealth of Troy.   250
When Aeneas was carrying Troy to the fields of Italy, the goddess
    almost followed the ships that bore his gods,
but she realized that Fate did not yet require her power for Latium,
    so she stayed behind in familiar places.
Later when Rome, powerful and mighty, had seen five   255
    centuries and towered over the mastered world,
the priests examined the fateful words of the Sibylline Books;
    here's what they say the examination yielded:
'Your mother is missing: I bid you, Roman, find your mother.
    When she comes, chaste hands must receive her.'   260
The senators were bewildered by the opaque response's riddle.
    What mother was missing? Where should they look for her?
They consulted Apollo who said, 'Send for the Mother of the gods.
    She can be found on the ridges of Ida.'
Leading men were dispatched. Attalus then held the throne   265
    of Phrygian Pergamum; he refused the men from Italy.
I'll tell you a miracle; the earth shook with a long rumble,
    and from her sanctuary the goddess said this:
'It was my wish to be looked for. Don't delay. Dispatch me as I wish.
    Rome is a worthy destination for any god.'   270
Shaking with fear at the sound, the king said, 'Be on your way.
    You'll still be ours, since Rome has Phrygian ancestors.'
At once countless axes were felling those forests of pine
    which dutiful Aeneas had used for his escape.
A thousand hands assembled, and the hollow ship, painted   275
    with encaustic colors, held the Mother of the gods.
She was carried in complete safety over her son Neptune's waters,
    and approached the long strait of the Hellespont,
then crossed the wide promontory of Rhoeteum and the Sigean coast
    and Tenedos and Andromache's birthplace in Mysia.   280
The Cyclades received her, after Lesbos had been left in her wake,
    and the waves which break on southern Euboea.
She also crossed the Icarian sea where Icarus lost his wings
    and gave his name to the vast expanse.
Then she left Crete to port and the Peloponnese to starboard   285
    and made for Cythera, Venus' sacred island.
From here she wended her way to the Sicilian sea where the three
    Cyclopes regularly temper white-hot metal,
and the African ocean, and looked back at the realm of Sardinia

from the port side oars, and reached Italy.   290
She had entered the mouth where the Tiber branches into the deep
    and flows in a less confining area.
All the knights, the respected senate, and the common people
    came to meet her at the mouth of the Tuscan river.
Likewise, the women, old and young, married and single,   295
    advanced with the virgins who tend the sacred hearth.
The men busily exhaust their arms on the straining towrope,
    but the foreign ship barely makes headway upstream.
The earth had long been dry, drought had singed the grass:
    the ship ran aground and settled in the muddy shallows.   300
Everyone on the job did more than his share and helped
    by shouting encouragement to the strong laborers.
But she settled like a steadfast island in mid-ocean; dumbstruck
    by the portent the men stood and quaked.
Claudia Quinta traced her descent to noble Clausus   305
    (her beauty was a match for her high birth).
She was chaste but no one believed it; unfair gossip had hurt her
    and she stood indicted on a false charge.
Her elegance and the way she appeared in a variety of hairstyles prejudiced
    the inflexible old men, as did her quick retorts.   310
Her clear conscience laughed off rumor's falsehoods, but we
    are a bunch ready to believe the worst.
When she advanced from the ranks of the chaste matrons
    and scooped pure river water up in her hands,
she sprinkled her head three times, raised her hands three times   315
    to heaven (the onlookers thought she was out of her senses),
and on bended knees she fixed her gaze upon the image
    of the goddess, undid her hair and said:
'Fertile mother of the gods, kindly heed the prayers
    of your petitioner with this stipulation.   320
They say I'm not chaste: if you condemn me, I'll admit I deserved it;
    I'll pay with my life if convicted with a goddess as my judge.
But if the charge doesn't stick, give proof of my honorable life
    by action, and chastely follow my chaste hands.'
She spoke and pulled on the towrope with a slight effort: 325
    It's a miracle, but one the stage attests to:
the goddess was stirred, followed her guide and vouched for her
    by following; a cry of joy rose to the stars.
They came to the bend in the river (the ancients called it

Tiber's Courtyard) where it veers to the left.   330
Night came on: they tied up the rope to the trunk of an oak,
    enjoyed a meal and fell into a light sleep.
Day came on: they untied the rope from the trunk of the oak,
    but first they set up an altar for an offering of incense,
first they garlanded the ship and sacrificed a flawless   335
    heifer, innocent of both work and mating.
There's a place where the gliding Almo flows into the Tiber
    and the smaller river loses its name in the big one.
A white-haired priest in a purple robe came there and bathed
    our lady and her holy things in the Almo's waters.   340
Her followers howled, the maddening flute was blown
    and soft hands struck the cowhide drumskins.
With joy on her face Claudia advanced before the crowd, at last
    believed respectable on the word of a goddess.
The goddess herself, riding in a wagon, was conveyed to Capena Gate: 345
    fresh flowers were scattered on the ox-team.
Nasica received her; her temple founder's name has not survived:
    Augustus is the present builder, Metellus, a former one."
Erato stopped here and paused in case I had other questions.
    "Tell me," I said, "why she wants small change."   350
"The people contributed pennies, from which Metellus built
    her temple," she says; "the custom survives from that."
Why, I ask, do people attend and put on banquets,
    flocking to dinner invitations more often then?
"The Berecyntian did well by going to another home," she said,   355
    "so they try for the same luck by changing homes."
I had started to ask why the Megalensia were the first shows
    in our city, when the goddess (anticipating me) said:
"She gave birth to the gods, so they deferred to their parent
    and the Great Mother got the first tribute offered."   360
"So why do we call the self-castrated priests 'Galli,'
    when Gallic soil is so far away from Phrygia?"
"Between verdant Cybele," she says, "and the high town of Celaenae,
    runs a river with unhealthy water, Gallus by name.
Whoever drinks it, goes mad. Keep a long way off, if you care   365
    for your sanity: whoever drinks it, goes mad."
"Isn't it a disgrace," I said, "to set a green salad before
    our lady? Or is there some reason for this?"
"The men of old supposedly lived on pure milk," she says, "and

whatever greens the earth produced on its own.   370
Now they tear up greens and combine them with white cheese,
    so the primitive goddess may recognize primitive food."

5 April

When Dawn next shines after the stars have left the sky
    and the Moon has unhitched her snow-white horses,
whoever says, "Once on this date the temple of Public Fortune   375
    was consecrated on the Quirinal Hill," will be right.

6 April

It was the third day of the shows (as I recollect)
    and the old man next to me said as we watched,
"This is that famous date when Caesar crushed proud Juba's
    treacherous forces at Thapsus in North Africa.   380
Caesar was my commander. I'm proud to have served under him
    as a colonel: that man bestowed my rank.
I earned this seat in the service, you, in civilian life,
    holding office as one of ten commissioners."
A sudden downpour interrupted and concluded our conversation.   385
    The scales of Libra, balancing in the sky, made it rain.

9 April

But before the last day of the festival brings the shows
    to an end, Orion with his sword will sink in the ocean.

10 April

When the next Dawn has looked upon Rome the conqueror,
    and the stars disperse to make room for the Sun,   390
the Circus will be packed when the gods' statues are paraded,
    and horses will race like the wind for first prize.

11–12 April

Next come Ceres' shows. The reason doesn't require an informant;
    the beneficial service of the goddess is self-evident.
The daily bread of earliest man was leafy greens   395
    which the earth produced when nobody bothered it.

Sometimes they used to crop grass fresh from the turf,
    and sometimes the forest canopy supplied their banquets.
Later the acorn became known. The acorn's discovery was a boon,
    and the sturdy oak held sumptuous treasure.   400
Ceres was the first to invite mankind to better nourishment
    by replacing acorns with more nutritious food.
It was she who compelled oxen to offer their necks to the yoke:
    that's when the uprooted ground first saw daylight.
Bronze was prized, since iron nuggets still lay buried;   405
    oh, they should have stayed covered forever.
Ceres delights in peace, and you, farmers, pray for
    everlasting peace and the leader who brings peace.
You may give the goddess spelt and the tribute of spurting salt
    and a grain of incense on ancient hearths;   410
or if you don't have incense, light torches smeared with pitch:
    little things, if pure, appeal to the good Ceres.
Vested priests, take your knives away from the ox:
    the ox ploughs; sacrifice the lazy pig.
A neck suited for the yoke should not be struck by an ax: 415
    let it live to work the hard ground again.

This section of my work demands an account of the Rape of Proserpina:
    much will be familiar, but you'll learn a few things.
Sicily juts out into the vast sea with three cliffs,
    also called "Trinacris" from its triangular shape,   420
a home dear to Ceres, where she occupies many cities,
    among them Henna, fertile with its tilled soil.
Arethusa had invited the divine matrons to her chilly spring;
    the amber-haired goddess was one of the guests.
Her daughter, accompanied as she usually was by her girlfriends,   425
    was wandering barefooted through her meadows.
There's a place at the bottom of a shady valley, damp
    with much spray from a high waterfall.
All the colors of nature's palette were there, and the ground
    was brightly dappled with a variety of flowers.   430
As soon as she saw it, Proserpina said, "Companions, come
    with me and bring back skirts full of flowers."
The trifling booty attracted their girlish attention
    and they were too absorbed to notice the effort.
This one fills up baskets woven out of pliant wicker,   435

this one loads her lap, that one, her loose skirt;
that one picks marigolds, violets are this one's concern,
    that one clips poppy blossoms with her nail;
hyacinths occupy these, amaranths slow those down;
    some love thyme, others, wild-poppy and clover.   440
A great many roses are picked, and nameless flowers as well:
    she is picking delicate saffron and white lilies.
In her zeal for plucking she gradually goes further afield;
    by chance no companion followed her lady.
Her uncle Dis saw her, and swiftly abducted what he saw,   445
    and carried her to his realm with his dark blue horses.
Of course she was calling out, "Quick, mother dearest, I'm being
    abducted!" and had torn open her own skirt.
Meanwhile the path opened up for Dis, when his horses
    could barely stand the unfamiliar daylight.   450
But her band of peers, attendants heaped with flowers, called out,
    "Persephone, come see what we've got for you."
When there's no response to their call, they fill the mountains with howling,
    and mournfully beat their bare breasts with their hands.
Ceres was stunned by their lamentation (she had just come to Henna)   455
    and said without pausing, "Oh no, daughter, where are you?"
Bereft of her senses, she was swept away, as convention tells us
    Thracian maenads rush with streaming hair.
The way its mother bellows for the calf taken from her udder
    and searches for her offspring in every grove,   460
that's how the goddess didn't hold back her moans and was spurred
    to run full speed, beginning from the fields of Henna.
There she found the prints of a girlish foot and saw
    the ground stamped by the weight she knew so well.
That day could perhaps have been the end of her wanderings   465
    if pigs hadn't disturbed the trail she found.
And now as she ran she passed Leontini and the Amenanus
    and the grassy banks of the Acis river,
and she passed Cyane and the spring of the gentle Anapus
    and the Gela, inaccessible because of its whirlpools.   470
She had left behind the island Ortygia and Megara and the Pantagias,
    and the spot where the Symaethus reaches the sea,
and caves which are scorched from the heat of the Cyclopes' forges,
    and the place named Zancle for its sickle shape,
and Himera and Dindyme, Agrigento and Taormina, and Mylae,   475

lush pasture for the cattle of the Sun.
From here she went to Camerina and Thapsus and the vale of Helorus
    and the spot where Mount Eryx faces the West Wind.
And now she had circled Pelorus, Lilybaeum and now Pachynus,
    the promontories at the corners of her land.   480
Wherever she went, she filled the whole place with pitiful complaints,
    as the nightingale moans for her lost son Itys.
By turns she calls, sometimes "Persephone," sometimes "daughter";
    she calls and cries out each name in turn:
but Persephone doesn't hear Ceres, nor the daughter   485
    her mother, and each name dies out in turn.
Always the same question, if she saw a shepherd or someone tilling
    his fields: "Has any girl passed this way?"
Now everything was the same color, and all was covered
    in shadows, now the watchdogs were silent.   490
Tall Mount Etna lies on top of the giant Typhoeus' face
    and the ground is ablaze from his fiery gasps.
There the goddess lights two pine-branch torches;
    to this day a torch plays a role in her mysteries.
There is a cave, a rough structure of eroded pumice,   495
    an area inaccessible to man and beast.
As soon as she got there, she harnessed serpents and hitched them up
    to her chariot and wandered the surface of the sea.
She avoided the Syrtes sandbar and Charybdis near Zancle
    and doggy Scylla, the shipwrecking menace,   500
and the wide open Adriatic and the Isthmus of Corinth:
    that's how she got to the harbor of Athens.
Here for the first time she sat, grief-stricken, on a cold rock:
    even today the Athenians call it "sad."
Out in the open she roughed it motionless for many days,   505
    enduring moonlit nights and rainy weather.
Every place has its own destiny: what today is called
    Ceres' Eleusis was old man Celeus' farm.
That fellow was carrying home acorns and berries shaken
    from brambles and dry wood to burn on his hearth.   510
His little daughter was driving two she-goats back from the hills,
    and his delicate son was sick in his cradle.
"Mother," says the maiden (the goddess was touched by the name "mother"),
    "what are you doing by yourself in this lonely place?"
The old man stopped, despite his heavy load, and asked her   515

to take shelter in his cottage, tiny as it was.
She declined (she'd disguised herself as an old woman with a head-scarf);
    when he insisted, she replied as follows:
"May you always stay safely a parent; my daughter has been abducted.
    Oh, how much better your lot is than mine!"   520
She spoke, and a shining drop like a tear (for the gods
    may not shed tears) fell to her warm lap.
Maiden and old man wept together with tender hearts.
    Here's what the righteous old man had to say:
"May you find your abducted daughter safe and sound; get up   525
    and don't reject the shelter of a tiny cottage."
The goddess replied, "Lead on; you have found what I can't resist,"
    and she rose from the rock and followed the old man.
Her escort told his companion how his son was sick
    and didn't sleep, kept awake by his pains.   530
Before entering the little house, she picked a gently
    sleep-inducing poppy from the rustic soil.
In the act of picking, they say she absentmindedly tasted it
    and unintentionally broke her long fast.
Because Ceres cast off her hunger in the early evening,   535
    her initiates take food when the stars appear.[5]
When she crossed the threshold, she found everything full of woe;
    already hope for the boy's recovery was gone.
After greeting his mother (his mother was called Metanira),
    she saw fit to kiss the boy on the lips.   540
His pallor went away, and suddenly strength appeared in his body:
    such vitality came from the heavenly lips.
The entire household rejoiced, that is, mother and father
    and daughter: those three were the entire household.
Soon they set out a meal, rennet dissolved in milk,   545
    apples, and golden honey still in the comb. Kindly Ceres
abstained and gave the boy a drink
    of warm milk with poppy to make him sleep.
Late at night, amid the stillness of peaceful sleep,
    she held little Triptolemus up to her breast,   550
stroked him three times with her hand, said three spells,
    spells that mortal speech should not repeat,
and covered the boy's body with live ashes on the hearth,
    so the fire might cleanse away his human dross.
His mother woke up, cried out frantically with inept devotion,   555

"What are you doing?" and snatched his body from the fire.
The goddess told her, "Your intentions were good, your action was criminal:
    a mother's anxiety has undone my blessing.
That boy will remain a mortal, of course: but he'll be the first
    to plough and plant and reap the rewards of tillage."   560
Ceres spoke, and wrapped in cloud she left to find her serpents,
    and was carried off by her winged chariot.
She left behind windswept Sunion and Piraeus safe
    in its harbor and the coast which lies to the right.
From here she entered the Aegean with all the Cyclades in sight,   565
    navigated the greedy Ionian Sea and the Icarian,
headed past the cities of Asia Minor for the long Hellespont,
    and wandered aloft on a route over various places.
Now Arabs gathering incense, now Indians were visible below,
    here Libya, and there the Egyptian desert.   570
Now she approached the Western rivers—Rhine, Rhone, and Po,
    and the Tiber destined to father a mighty stream.
What tangent is this, to tell the countless lands she wandered?
    No place on earth did Ceres bypass.
She wandered in the heavens as well, and addressed the never-setting   575
    constellations closest to the chilly North Pole:
"Starry Bears, you never sink beneath the sea,
    and so can find out everything.
Point out my daughter Persephone to her pitiful mother."
    When she finished, Helice replied as follows: 580
"The night is blameless. For news about the abducted maiden,
    consult the Sun, who sees the events of the day."
The Sun responded, "Don't waste more effort; the one you seek
    is wed to Jupiter's brother and reigns below."
After long rehearsing her grievance, she addressed the Thunderer like this   585
    (her face gave signs that showed how great her grief):
"If you remember by whom I conceived Proserpina,
    half of this worry should be yours.
After wandering the world over, I have only discovered the outrageous act;
    the abductor still has the rewards of his crime.   590
But Persephone doesn't deserve a pirate for a husband,
    and we shouldn't have been presented with a son-in-law that way.
If the Titans had triumphed, what worse might I have borne as a prisoner
    than I have now with you on heaven's throne?
But let him go unpunished, I will endure this unavenged;   595

let him return her and amend his former act."
Jupiter calmed her down, offering love as the act's excuse,
    and said, "We shouldn't be ashamed of that son-in-law:
I don't outrank him: my palace is in heaven, another brother
    possesses the waters, another, the empty pit.   600
But if it happens that your mind is set and you are resolved
    to break the bonds of the marriage just joined,
let's make a test to see if she has abstained from food.
    If not, she'll be the wife of a spouse down below."
Mercury put on his wings as ordered, and returned from Tartarus   605
    quicker than expected to report precisely what he saw:
"The abducted girl broke her fast with three seeds
    which a tough pomegranate rind had covered."
Sadly, her mother grieved as if the girl had just been abducted
    and took a long while to recover somewhat.   610
And so she said, "Heaven is no place for me to live either.
    Have the Underworld's entrance admit me too."
And she would have done it, if Jupiter hadn't promised
    that Persephone would be in heaven six months a year.
Then at last Ceres' expression and spirits brightened   615
    and she put a garland of grain on her head.
An abundant harvest came forth in fields that had been idle,
    and the threshers could scarcely handle the heaps of bounty.
White is becoming to Ceres: put on white clothes for Ceres'
    festival; now there's no use for somber wool.   620

13 April

Jupiter, titled "Victorious," lays claim to the Ides of April:
    on this date he was given a temple.
Also today, unless I'm mistaken, Liberty, so right for our
    people, began to have a hall of her own.[6]

14 April

On the following day, sailors, head for a safe haven: 625
    the wind from the west will be mixed with hail.
Although that was so, nonetheless in the hail on this date
    Augustus broke Antony's siege of Modena.

15 April

When the third day after Venus' Ides has dawned,
    the high-priests will sacrifice a brood cow.   630
A "brood" cow is one that bears, called bountiful from bearing.
    From this they also think "birth" is derived.[7]
Now the stock is pregnant, the earth too is pregnant with seed.
    To the teeming Earth a teeming victim is given.
One cow falls on Jupiter's stronghold, and the thirty wards each   635
    get one and drip with copiously spattered blood.
But when the acolytes have ripped the calves from the wombs and offered
    the carved-up innards to the smoking hearths,
the eldest Vestal burns up the calves in the fire,
    for the ashes that purify on Pales' day.[8]   640
When Numa was king, toil bore no fruits in return,
    and the frustrated farmer's prayers were in vain.
Sometimes the year was dry with chilly winds from the North,
    sometimes the fields were rank from constant rain;
often the grain would fail the landowner right after sprouting   645
    and weeds would stand in the beleaguered ground.
The cattle would give untimely birth to premature young,
    and the birth of a lamb would often kill the ewe.
An ancient forest stood, long unspoiled by any ax,
    left untouched as holy to Arcadian Faunus.   650
He used to give oracles in the dead of night to a mind asleep.
    Here King Numa slaughtered two sheep.
The first fell to Faunus, the second to gentle Sleep;
    the fleeces of both were spread on the hard ground.
Twice he sprinkled his unshorn head with water from a spring,   655
    twice he set beech leaves on his temples.
He abstained from love's enjoyment, he couldn't put meat
    on his table, there wasn't a ring on his fingers.
Clothed in a coarse garment, he lay his body on the new
    fleeces after the right prayer to the god.   660
Meanwhile Night came on, her peaceful brow garlanded with poppies,
    bringing along dark dreams in her train.
Faunus appeared, and treading the fleeces with his hard hooves,
    uttered the following from the right of the bed:
"With the death of two cows, o king, you must appease the Earth.   665
    Let one heifer offer two lives in sacrifice."

Shaken from sleep by alarm, Numa pondered what he'd seen,
    recalling the riddle of the opaque command.
His wife, very dear to the grove, resolved his confusion:
    "The demand is for a pregnant cow's innards."   670
He offers a pregnant cow's innards. The year turns out
    more bountiful, and the earth and stock bear fruit.

16 April

Once Venus ordered this day to make haste and plunged
    the Sun's horses down at breakneck speed,
so that the next day's successful battle might more quickly   675
    acclaim the young Augustus "Imperator."

17 April

But already the fourth dawn looks back on the Ides just passed;
    tonight the Hyades enter the Ocean.

19 April

When the third day has dawned after the Hyades' retreat,
    the Circus will have horses at their post positions.   680
So I have to explain the reason why foxes are turned loose
    with burning torches tied to their backs.
The land at Carseoli is cold and unfit for raising olives,
    but the fields are naturally suited for crops of grain.
I was heading this way for Paelignian territory, fields of my birth,   685
    small, but ever exposed to constant rain.
I entered the house where I usually stayed with an elderly host;
    the Sun's horses had already earned their rest.
Many of his stories have informed my current work,
    including this one he used to tell: 690
"In this plain," he said (pointing to the plain), "a thrifty farm wife
    and her sturdy husband had a small plot of land.
He would work his ground, whether he had to use a plow
    or a curved sickle or a two-pronged hoe.
She would sweep the farmhouse with its ramshackle shoring,   695
    or give a mother hen eggs to hatch.
She would gather green mallows or white mushrooms,
    or warm the low hearth with a welcome fire,

and yet she also kept her hands constantly busy at the loom,
    preparing defenses against the menacing cold.   700
This woman's son was a mischievous young child,
    two years more than ten years old.
He caught a fox in a valley at the end of a willow thicket:
    it had stolen many chickens from the flock.
He wrapped his captive in straw and hay and set it on fire: 705
    it ran from the hands that were burning it.
Wherever it ran, it torched the fields that were harvest-clad.
    A breeze gave strength to the destructive fires.
This deed is past but a memorial remains: even today
    a law at Carseoli makes the fox taboo,   710
and to punish it, these people burn it at Ceres' festival, and it dies
    itself in the way it destroyed the crops of grain."

20 April

When Memnon's saffron mother next comes on her rosy horses
    to see the world stretching out below,
the sun will leave the Ram, leader of the woolly flock,   715
    who let Helle fall: a larger beast lies in his path.
Whether it's heifer or bull is no easy matter to tell:
    the front is visible, the hindquarters are hidden.
But whether the sign is Europa's bull or Io the cow,
    it rewards Jupiter's love in spite of Juno.   720

21 April

Night has left and dawn is breaking. I am summoned for the Parilia,
    and not in vain, with kindly Pales' indulgence.
Kindly Pales, indulge me as I sing of your pastoral rites,
    if I accompany your festival with my dutiful service.
Of course I have often carried a handful of the burned means   725
    of atonement, ashes from a calf and from bean stalks.
Of course I have jumped over three bonfires set in a row,
    and sprinkled water from a wet laurel branch.
The goddess has taken heed and indulges my work. My ship
    is leaving the dock and now the wind fills my sails.   730
People, go and ask for fumigant from the virgins' altar.
    Vesta will give it, with Vesta's gift you'll be pure.
The fumigant will be blood of horse and ash of calf;

the third ingredient is a tough bean's empty stalk.
Shepherd, sprinkle water and sweep the ground with twigs,   735
    then purify your well-fed sheep at first twilight.
Hang up leaves and boughs to deck the sheepfolds
    and wreathe the doors with a long garland.
Make smoke rise blue from pure sulphur, and let the sheep
    bleat at the touch of smoking sulphur.   740
Burn olive, pine, and Sabine juniper, and let the laurel
    crackle as it burns in the middle of the hearth.
Follow this with millet cakes and baskets of millet:
    the country goddess likes this food especially.
Bring her food and a pail of milk. Cut up the food,   745
    then pray with warm milk to Pales of the woods:
"Look after the flock and the keepers of the flock alike:
    ward off harm and keep it from my stalls.
If on sacred ground I've pastured or sat beneath a sacred tree,
    or a sheep has unwittingly browsed from a tomb;   750
if I've entered a forbidden grove, or the nymphs or Pan
    the half-goat god have fled my sight;
if my sickle has robbed a grove of a shady branch
    to give a sick sheep a basket of leaves,
pardon my offense: don't hold it against me that I sheltered   755
    my flock from a hailstorm in a rustic shrine.
Don't let harm come from disturbing ponds: nymphs, forgive
    the hoof that stirred and clouded your waters.
Goddess, appease for us the springs and spirits in them,
    appease the gods dispersed through every grove.   760
Let us not catch sight of the Dryads nor Diana at her bath,
    nor Faunus when he rests in the fields at noon.
Drive off diseases. Keep sound both men and herds,
    and keep sound the watchful pack of guard dogs.
May I never drive home fewer than there were in the morning, nor groan   765
    as I bring back fleeces retrieved from a wolf.
Avert unwarranted hunger: let grass and leaves abound,
    and water for bathing, and water for drinking.
May I milk full udders, may I make a profit on cheese,
    and may the strainer let the clear whey pass through.   770
May the ram be randy and his mate conceive and breed,
    and may there be many a lamb in my stalls.
May the wool turn out so it doesn't irritate a single girl,

soft and fit for hands however delicate.
Let my prayers come to pass and let us next year offer 775
    big cakes to Pales, our lady of shepherds."
Like this you must appease Pales: facing east, say this
    four times and wash your hands with running water.
Then you may set up a bowl like one for mixing wine
    and drink white milk and purple must, 780
and next your nimble limbs should swiftly vault across
    the blazing piles of crackling straw.
I've described the custom; the origin of the custom is next:
    the flock of theories makes me hesitate.
Consuming fire purifies everything and tempers flaws in metal. 785
    Does it therefore purify the sheep and the herder?
Or, because the opposing seeds of all matter are
    two conflicting powers, fire and water,
did our ancestors join these elements and consider it appropriate
    to treat the body with fire and sprinkles of water? 790
Or, because these are the source of life, denied to an exile,
    presented to a bride, are these considered so potent?
I can hardly believe there are some who believe that this is related
    to Phaethon's fiery ride and Deucalion's flood.
And others say that when shepherds used to strike stones 795
    together, suddenly sparks would jump out.
The first one went out, of course; the second was caught in straw.
    Is this the basis for the Parilia flame?
Or was it instead the devotion of Aeneas which produced this custom,
    since the flames of Troy let him pass unscathed? 800
But isn't it nearer the truth that when Rome was founded and the settlers
    were told to convey their households to new dwellings,
before they moved they set fire to their rustic dwellings
    and the cottages they were going to leave behind,
and over the flames the flock and the farmers both jumped? 805
    Even today that happens on the birthday of Rome.
The event itself gives a poet scope: I've come to the City's origin.
    Be present, great Quirinus, for these deeds of yours.
Numitor's brother had already been punished, and the whole mob
    of shepherds was under the twins' leadership. 810
Each was fit to unite the rustics and erect the walls.
    Which would erect the walls was open to question.
"No need for a quarrel," Romulus said. "Augury is quite

reliable, so let's resort to augury."
The idea was attractive. One of them ascended the well-wooded Palatine,   815
    the other climbed the Aventine peak in the morning.
Remus spotted six birds, Romulus, twice six in a row;
    the bargain was kept and Romulus got control of the city.
A suitable day was chosen for outlining the walls with a plough:
    the Parilia was approaching; the work was started then.   820
A trench was made to the subsoil, into the bottom were cast
    fruits of the earth and clods from the ground nearby.
The trench was refilled with dirt, an altar was set up on the fill,
    and the hearth enjoyed its newly kindled flame.
Guiding the plough, Romulus outlined the walls with a furrow.   825
    A white cow and a snowy bull bore the yoke.
These were the words of the king: "As I found the city, Jupiter,
    be present with father Mars and mother Vesta.
And all you gods whom it's right for me to invoke, give heed:
    under your auspices let this work of mine arise.   830
Long may this city live and be mistress of the world,
    holding both east and west under her sway."
As he prayed, Jupiter gave a sign with thunder on the left,
    and loosed lightning from the left quadrant.
Delighted by the portent, the citizens laid the foundations,   835
    and shortly there was the new wall.
Celer was supervising. Romulus himself had called him over
    and said, "Celer, make it your business
that no one crosses the walls or the trench I ploughed.
    Put to death whoever presumes such a thing."   840
Unaware of this, Remus began to scorn the lowly walls
    and say, "Are these going to keep the people safe?"
Without pausing, he jumped across. Celer met this presumption
    with a shovel and Remus lay bloodied on the hard ground.
When the king found out, he choked back the tears welling up inside,   845
    and kept the hurt locked in his heart.
He didn't want to weep openly and he kept up a brave front,
    saying, "So may all enemies cross my walls."
But as he conducted the funeral, no longer able to hold back
    the tears, he revealed his hidden devotion.   850
He pressed the last kisses on the body placed on its bier
    and said, "Farewell, brother taken against my will."
He anointed the body for cremation. Faustulus did the same,

and Acca, with her hair loosened in grief.
  Then the Quirites, not yet so called, wept for the young man.   855
    At last they set fire to the lamentable pyre.
A city arose (who could then have believed this prediction?)
    destined to trample the world in conquest.
May you rule everything and always be under great Caesar's
    sway, and often have others from his line;   860
and for as long as you tower over the globe you have mastered,
    may everything be head and shoulders beneath you.

23 April

I have treated Pales; I will likewise treat Vinalia.
    A single day comes between the two.
Girls of the street, worship the power of Venus Erycina;   865
    Venus helps business for licensed working girls.
With a gift of incense ask for beauty and your public's patronage.
    Ask for sweet-talk and spicy jokes.
Give our lady pleasing mint along with her myrtle,
    and a basket covered with an arrangement of roses.   870
Now you should pack the temple right next to the Colline Gate,
    which gets its name from a mountain in Sicily.
When Marcellus looted Syracuse, site of Arethusa's spring,
    and also took Mount Eryx by force of arms,
Venus was moved from there to comply with the aged Sibyl's prophecy,   875
    and preferred to be worshipped in the city of her son Aeneas.
So why, do you ask, is a festival of Venus called Vinalia,
    and for what reason is that day Jupiter's?
Turnus and Aeneas were at war for the hand of the Latin princess;
    Turnus appealed for Etruscan assistance.   880
Mezentius was illustrious and fierce in taking up arms,
    a great fighter on horseback, greater still on foot.
Turnus and the Rutulians tried to ally him to their side.
    In reply the Etruscan general said this:
"My valor does not come cheap. Witness my wounds and   885
    my weapons, often splashed with my own blood.
If you want my help, share with me a slight reward,
    next year's must from your wine vats.
No need for delay. Yours is to give, to conquer, is mine.
    How Aeneas would like for me to refuse!"   890

128

The Rutulians agreed and Mezentius buckled on his weapons.
    Aeneas buckled on his and addressed Jupiter:
"The enemy's vintage has been promised to the Etruscan king.
    You'll get the must from Latin vines."
The better promise prevailed. Mighty Mezentius fell   895
    and struck the ground with his resentful breast. Autumn arrived,
soiled with the juice of trampled grapes, and
    the debt of wine was paid for Jupiter's services.
Hence the day has been called the Vinalia. Jupiter claims it,
    and is glad to include it among his festivals.   900

25 April

When April has but six days left to go, the season
    of spring will have run half its course,
and in vain will you look for the ram of Athamas' daughter Helle.
    The weather signs bring rain and the Dog Star rises.
As I was returning to Rome from Nomentum on this date,   905
    a crowd in white stood blocking the road.
A flamen was entering the grove of ancient Rust,
    to offer dog guts and sheep guts to the flame.
I approached at once, to learn about the rites.
    The flamen of Quirinus uttered these words: 910
"Rough Rust, may you spare the blades of grain and may
    their still smooth blades rustle above the ground.
Allow the crops to grow, nourished by the weather of a favorable
    sky, until they are ready for the scythes.
Your power is not slight: the grain which bears your mark,   915
    the farmer mournfully regards as a loss.
Neither winds nor rains do the grain so much harm, nor does
    it turn so pale when blighted by marble frost,
as when the Sun has warmed the damp stalks. Then,
    dreaded goddess, your wrath gets its chance.   920
Be sparing, I pray, and keep your scruffy hands off the harvest.
    Don't harm the crops; the power to harm is enough.
Don't get in your clutches the delicate grain, but hard steel,
    and first destroy what can destroy others.
Better you should eat away swords and harmful spears: 925
    no need for them; the world is at peace.
Let the hoe gleam now, the hard mattock and the curved ploughshare,

the countryside's ordnance. Let neglect spoil weapons,
and if someone tries to draw his sword from its scabbard,
    let him feel it stick after the long lull.   930
But don't you ravage the grain, and let the farmer always
    be able to pay his vow to you in your absence."
He had finished; on his right hand was a smooth-napped towel,
    a saucer of wine and an incense box.
He offered incense and wine on the hearth, a sheep's entrails, and—   935
    I saw them—a nasty dog's disgusting guts.
The flamen then said: "You ask why a strange victim is offered
    in sacrifice?" (I had asked.) "Here's the reason.
There's a Dog they call 'Icarian.' When that star has risen,
    the earth is parched and the grain gets ripe too soon.   940
In place of the starry Dog, this dog is put on the altar,
    for no other reason aside from the name."

28 April

When Dawn has left Phrygian Assaracus' cousin Tithonus,
    and three times shone above the immense globe,
a goddess comes with multi-colored garlands of thousands of flowers and   945
    the stage has a custom of greater licentiousness.
The rites of Flora extend past the Kalends of May: I'll return
    to them then, now a grander subject is pressing.
Take your day, Vesta: Vesta has been welcomed in the palace
    of her kinsman Augustus, as the righteous senators decreed.   950
Apollo has a share; a second share has gone to Vesta;
    the third that remains he occupies himself.
Endure, laurels of the Palatine. May the house with the oak-leaf cluster
    endure, a single house for three immortals.

Book
5

❧

May

You want to know where I think the month of May got its name?
　　I haven't found out the reason clearly enough.
Like a traveller who hesitates and doesn't know where he should go
　　when he sees a path in every direction,
I don't know where to proceed either, because various reasons　　　　5
　　are at hand, and their very abundance is a nuisance.
You tell me, you who frequent the spring of Boeotian Hippocrene,
　　the darling tracks of Pegasus, sprung from Medusa.
The Muses gave differing opinions. Polyhymnia was first to begin
　　(the rest were silent and mentally marked her words):　　　　10
"After Chaos, as soon as the three elements were given to the universe,
　　and the whole structure separated into new forms,
the earth sank of its own weight and pulled the waters along,
　　but heaven's lightness carried it up high.
Neither did any heaviness keep back the Sun and the stars,　　　　15
　　and up sprang the horses of the Moon.
But for quite a while the earth did not defer to heaven,
　　nor the other stars to the sun. All rank was the same.
Often some god from the lower class[1] would dare
　　to sit on the throne which Saturn occupied.　　　　20
None of the recent arrivals would offer his arm to Ocean,

and Themis often got the very worst seat,[2]
until there were joined in legal wedlock Honor and Respect,
    she of the charmingly peaceful expression.
To them was born the goddess Majesty, who chose her parents well.   25
    On the day of her birth she was a major divinity.[3]
Without hesitation she settled up high in the midst of Olympus,
    all golden and lovely in a purple robe.
Inhibition and Shame settled there too. You could see
    every god had wiped the old look off his face.   30
At once regard for the honors of rank got into their heads.
    Merit was rewarded and no one was self-complacent.
This situation in heaven endured for many a year,
    until Saturn fell as fated from his stronghold.
Earth spawned unruly offspring, enormous monsters, the Giants,   35
    destined to dare attack the home of Jupiter.
She gave them a thousand hands and snakes for legs, and said,
    'Wield your weapons against the mighty gods.'
They were getting ready to pile up mountains to the stars
    above and harass mighty Jupiter with war.   40
Hurling thunderbolts from heaven's stronghold, Jupiter turned
    those tremendous weights against the perpetrators.
Well-defended by these divine weapons, Majesty held out,
    and continued to be worshipped from then on.
She sits at Jove's side, she is Jove's most loyal guardian,   45
    and she keeps Jove's awesome sovereignty unchallenged.
She came to earth as well. Romulus worshipped her, and Numa,
    and others soon, each in his own time.
She preserves fathers and mothers in devoted honor;
    she comes as an escort for boys and girls;   50
she assigns the emblems of supreme political authority;
    she rides in triumph atop garlanded horses."
Polyhymnia had finished her speech. Clio endorsed her words
    and so did Thalia, expert on the curved lyre.
Urania took over. The others maintained silence   55
    and not a voice but hers could be heard.
"Once there was great respect for a head of white hair,
    and the wrinkles of age got their due.
Young men conducted the military business of stouthearted wars
    and were at their post in defense of their gods.   60
The weaker age, no longer fit for bearing arms,

often assisted its country with advice.
The senate-house then was open only to advanced years,
    and the senate was named for its mellow seniors.
The elders prescribed laws for the people, and specific statutes   65
    established the age at which office could be sought.
An elder was flanked by his juniors without their resentment,
    and the younger of two men walked on the outside.
Who would've dared use indecent language in an old man's presence?
    Advanced old age prescribed morality.   70
Romulus noticed this, named his chosen stalwarts "fathers,"
    and referred the new city's welfare to them.
From this I'm led to believe that the elders had their age
    of majority in mind when they named May.[4]
Or maybe Numitor said, 'Romulus, give the elders   75
    this month,' and his grandson couldn't resist.
No slight assurance of the honor intended is the following
    month of June, named for the juniors."[5]
With a wreath of ivy in dishevelled hair, Calliope
    then began like this as leader of her chorus: 80
"Ocean, whose clear waters encircle the ends of the earth,
    one day married the Titaness Tethys.
Their daughter Pleione was joined, the story goes, with Atlas,
    heaven's upholder, and she bore the Pleiades.
Of these, Maia reportedly topped her sisters in beauty   85
    and went to bed with Jupiter most high.
On the ridge of cypress-clad Mount Cyllene she delivered the god
    who picks his heavenly way on winged feet.
The raging Ladon river and mighty Mount Maenalus duly worship him
    in Arcadia, a land believed to predate the moon.   90
An exile from Arcadia, Evander had arrived in Latin territory,
    bringing his gods along on board.
Where Rome is now, capital of the world, were trees and grass,
    a few livestock and an occasional cottage.
Upon arrival here, his visionary mother said, 'Stop!   95
    That countryside will be the seat of power.'
The Arcadian hero obeyed her, mother and prophet combined,
    and halted as a stranger on foreign soil.
He taught the natives here a great many rituals, but first the ones
    of two-horned Faunus and wing-footed Mercury.   100
Faunus, half-goat, you are worshipped by Luperci in loincloths,

when their leather straps purify the crowded streets.
But you, inventor of the curved lyre, associate of thieves,
    have presented this month with your mother's name.
That wasn't your first act of devotion. You reputedly gave the lyre   105
    seven strings, as many in number as the Pleiades."
This Muse too had stopped. Her adherents praised her. What to do?
    Each faction has the same number of votes.
May the favor of all the Muses alike be with me,
    and may I praise none of them more than the others.   110

1 May

Let this work take off from Jupiter. On the first night of May
    the star that tended Jupiter's cradle can be seen.
The rainy constellation of the Olenian She-Goat rises.
    Heaven's her reward for the milk she gave.
They say that Amalthaea, a famous Cretan Naiad,   115
    hid Jupiter away in the woods of Mount Ida.
To her belonged the lovely mother of two kids,
    a sight to see among the herds on Mount Dicte,
with horns that arched up high in the air over her back,
    and an udder fit for nursing Jupiter.   120
She was giving milk to the god, but she broke her horn on a tree,
    and half of her glory was shorn away.
The nymph picked it up, wreathed it with fresh grasses,
    filled it with apples and brought it to Jove.
When he controlled the affairs of heaven from his father's throne,   125
    nothing was greater than unvanquished Jove,
so he made stars of his nurse and her horn of plenty,
    which even today is called Amalthaea's Horn.

The Kalends of May witnessed the founding of the Standby Lares'[6]
    altar and the little statues of those gods.   130
Curius vowed them, but great antiquity has turned them to ruins;
    advanced old age has damaged the stone.
The reason for the epithet given to them is the fact that
    they stand by vigilantly guarding everything.
They also stand up for us and stand by the City's walls   135
    and stand at the ready to bring us help.
A dog fashioned from the same stone used to stand at their feet.
    What was the reason for its standing with the Lares?

Both watch over the house, and both are loyal to their master;
    these gods frequent crossroads, and so do dogs. 140
Both the Lares and the pack of hounds drive thieves away.
    Lares are night watchmen, and dogs are too.
I was trying to find the two statues of the twin gods
    which the might of the passing years has collapsed.
The City has a thousand shrines to the Lares and the spirit of the leader 145
    who restored them. Every parish worships those three.
But, whoa! The month of August will give me the right to this subject.

    Meanwhile, the Good Goddess must be my theme.
There's a natural outcrop which has given its name to the place
    they call the Rock; it's a good part of the Aventine. 150
Here Remus had stood in vain, that time when the birds
    of the Palatine gave his brother the first omen.
There on the gently sloping ridge, the senate decreed
    a temple which loathes the gaze of men.
It was dedicated by a descendant of the ancient Crassus family, 155
    a maiden who had never submitted to a man's embrace.
Livia has restored it, in order to imitate her husband
    and follow his lead in every respect.

2 May

After the stars have been banished and Dawn has next raised
    her rosy lamp on the horses of early morning, 160
a chilly Northwest Wind will brush the ears of grain
    and white sails will be spread from Calabrian waters.
But as soon as the evening shadows have brought on the night,
    the whole flock of the Hyades is visible.
The face of Taurus twinkles and shines with seven fires, 165
    which Greek sailors call Hyades from their word for rain.
Some think they wet-nursed Bacchus, others believe they were
    the granddaughters of Tethys and old man Ocean.
Atlas was not yet standing with his shoulders burdened by Olympus
    when Hyas was born, a handsome sight to see. 170
Ocean's daughter Aethra bore him and his seven sisters
    in timely deliveries, but Hyas was her first-born.
While his beard was just coming in, he frightened stags that trembled
    in terror, and also preyed liberally on hares.
But after his prowess had come of age, he dared 175

to tangle with boars and shaggy lions,
and while he was tracking a pregnant lioness to her lair and cubs,
    the hunter became that African beast's bloody prey.
His mother wept for Hyas, for Hyas his mournful sisters wept,
    and Atlas, yet to submit his neck to the sky.   180
But both of his parents were outdone by his sisters' devotion.
    That got them heaven, Hyas gave them their name.

"Be with us, mother of flowers, honored with bawdy shows:
    I've postponed your turn from the previous month.
Your holiday begins in April and runs into the month of May: 185
    one has you on its way out, the other upon arrival.
Since the boundary between these months is yours and belongs to you,
    your praise can fit in either one of the two.
The races and the cheers from the theater extend into this one.
    Let this poem keep pace with the race-track's tribute.   190
Teach me yourself who you are: human opinion is fallible;
    you'll be the best source for your own name."
That's what I said. Here's what the goddess replied to my questions
    (as she spoke, she gave off essence of spring roses):
"I used to be Chloris, who am now called Flora. The Greek letters   195
    of my name were corrupted by Latin pronunciation.
I used to be Chloris, nymph of the happy fields where tradition
    puts the former abode of the blessed.
What my beauty was like goes against my modesty to tell,
    but it found my mother a divine son-in-law.   200
It was spring, I was strolling; the West Wind saw me, I started to leave;
    he followed, I fled; he was stronger.
The North Wind had given his brother complete sanction for kidnapping
    by boldly carrying off a similar prize from Athens.[7]
But the West Wind made up for the rape by giving me the title of wife,   205
    and I can't complain about my marriage.
[I enjoy constant spring: the year constantly glistens,
    trees have leaves and the ground has constant fodder.][8]
Among the estates of my dowry, I have a bountiful garden,
    caressed by the breeze, watered by a clear spring.   210
My husband filled it with flowers of the best stock
    and said, 'Goddess, take charge of the flowers.'
I often wanted to count the colors of the plants he'd set out,
    but I couldn't: the profusion was beyond counting.

As soon as the leaves shake off their dewy frost,   215
 and the dappled blossoms grow warm in the sun,
the Seasons hitch up their colorful dresses and assemble
 to gather my bounty into light baskets.
Right away the Graces join in, by weaving wreaths
 and garlands to entwine the heads in heaven.   220
I was the first to sprinkle new seeds through countless nations.
 Before that the earth was a single color.
I was the first to make a flower from Spartan Hyacinthus' blood,
 and his lament is still inscribed on its leaves.
Narcissus, you too are famous in well-tended gardens,   225
 unhappy because you weren't your own alter ego.
Why should I mention Crocus, or Attis, or Cinyras' grandson Adonis,
 from whose wounds tribute springs up through me?
In case you don't know, I also contrived the birth of Mars.
 I pray that Jupiter continues not to know.   230
When Minerva was born without a mother, blessed Juno
 was annoyed that Jupiter had not needed her services.
She was going to complain to Ocean about what her husband had done.
 Worn out from the effort she lingered at my door.
As soon as I saw her, I said, 'What brings you here,   235
 daughter of Saturn?' She revealed her objective
and added the reason. I was trying to comfort her with friendly words.
 'No words,' she said, 'are going to relieve my distress.
Jupiter became a father without benefit of spousal relations,
 and gets the credit for both roles in one,   240
so why should I give up hope of motherhood without a spouse
 and of chastely giving birth without touching a man.
I am going to try every drug the wide world over,
 and I'll shake up the seas and the Underworld's valleys.'
While this speech was in progress, I wore a hesitant expression.   245
 'Nymph, you look like you could do something.'
Three times I wanted to promise help, but my tongue stayed stuck.
 Jupiter's anger was a cause of great fear.
'Bring help, I pray; the source will remain concealed,' she said,
 swearing by the power of Stygian water.   250
'Your object,' I said, 'will be supplied by a flower sent me
 from the fields of Olenus, the only one in my garden.
My supplier said, "Touch a barren heifer with this
 and she'll be a mother." I did and at once she was.'

Right away I plucked the resisting flower with my thumb.   255
    I touched her belly and she conceived at the touch.
Pregnant now she entered Thrace and Marmara's western shore.
    She got her wish and Mars was born.
Remembering that his birthday was a gift from me, he said,
    'Thou too shalt have a place in the city of Romulus.'   260
Perhaps you think my realm is restricted to delicate wreaths.
    My power affects the fields as well.
If the stalks have flowered well, the threshing floor will be rich.
    If the vine has flowered well, there'll be wine.
If the olive has flowered well, the year will glisten.   265
    Fruit gets its growth from this period too.
Once the bloom is damaged, both vetch and beans are a loss,
    and lentils from the wandering Nile are a loss.
Wine laboriously stored in great cellars also blooms
    with a film that covers the top of the vats.   270
Honey is my gift: I invite the winged producers
    of honey to violets and clover and thyme.
[People do the same thing too, when youthful spirits are high
    and bodies themselves are in their prime.]"
I silently marveled at the words she was speaking, but she said,   275
    "You have permission to learn whatever you ask."
"Tell me, goddess," I replied, "the origin of your shows."
    I had barely finished, when she responded:
"That was before the other accessories of luxury flourished—
    the wealthy owned cattle or broad acres   280
(whence the financial terms 'stock' and 'holdings')[9]—
    but everyone now profited from posted land.
The practice had arisen of grazing down the public pastures.
    This had long been permitted with no penalty.
The masses were without a champion to protect the public reserves   285
    and now only lazy men grazed on private land.
These liberties were brought before two plebeian aediles
    named Publicius; courage had failed before.
The people recovered their property, the violators were fined.
    The champions were praised for their public spirit.[10]   290
A share of the fine was given to me, and with great approval
    the triumphant officials established new shows.
They used the rest to contract for a slope, a steep cliff then,
    today the convenient Publician route."

I had thought the shows were always held annually. She said no,   295
    and added some more to what she had said:
"Honor affects us too. We delight in festivals and altars,
    we gods are a status-seeking bunch.
Often someone has prejudiced the gods by doing wrong,
    but then a sacrifice has attoned for the offense.   300
Often have I seen Jupiter, already intending to loose
    his lightning, stay his hand for a gift of incense.
But if we are slighted, it takes severe penalties to pay
    for the insult, and our anger exceeds reasonable bounds.
Look at Meleager: he burned with flames that weren't there;   305
    the reason was the lack of fire on Diana's altar.
Look at Agamemnon: the same goddess held back his fleet,
    and a second time avenged the scorn to her hearth.
Unlucky Hippolytus, you wished you'd worshipped Aphrodite
    when your bolting horses tore you to pieces.   310
It's a long story, all the oversights penalties have mended.
    I too was once overlooked by the Roman senators.
What to do? How to give clear signs of my dismay?
    What kind of penalties to demand for this slur?
Grief made my duties slip my mind: I didn't watch over   315
    any fields, nor value my bountiful garden.
The lilies had fallen, you'd have seen the violets dry up
    and the scarlet saffron's pistils go limp.
Often the West Wind said to me, 'Don't spoil your dowry,'
    but my dowry was worth very little to me.   320
The olive trees were in bloom, but violent winds damaged them.
    The stalks were in bloom, but the grain was injured by hail.
There were high hopes for the vines, but the sky grew dark from the South
    and a sudden shower knocked off the leaves.
I didn't mean to be merciless in my anger—I'm not like that;   325
    I just had no interest in fending off harm.
The senators met and vowed my divinity a yearly festival,
    providing the year was a blooming one.
I agreed to their vow. The consul Laenas with Postumius
    his colleague conducted the shows for me."   330

I was getting ready to ask why there's greater lewdness
    and more permissive bawdiness in these shows,
but it came to me that this divinity isn't a stern one

and that she brings gifts connected with pleasure.
At parties every brow is wreathed with chains of flowers   335
    and the polished table is piled with roses.
A drunken reveller dances with a wreath of bast in his hair,
    inspired by wine to indiscretion.
A drunken lover serenades his girlfriend's callous door
    with pliant garlands in his perfumed hair.   340
No serious business is conducted by the brow that wears a wreath,
    and waterdrinkers don't wear flower chains.
So long as the grape wasn't mixed with branch water,
    there was no charm in picking roses.
Bacchus loves flowers: you can tell that Bacchus approves of wreaths   345
    from the constellation of Ariadne's Crown.
Light drama suits Flora. She shouldn't, believe me, she shouldn't
    be considered a goddess of the tragic stage.
Of course the reason why the crowd of streetwalkers honors
    these shows isn't hard to figure out.   350
Flora isn't one of the bluenoses, isn't one of the uppercrust.
    She wants her rites open to a lower-class crowd,
and advises exploiting the beauty of youth while it blooms;
    the thorn is despised when the roses have fallen.

But why, when people dress in white for Ceres' festival,   355
    do multi-colored fashions suit this goddess?
Is it because the harvest turns white when the ears are ripe,
    while flowers have every beautiful color?
She nodded yes and flowers fell from hair she had shaken
    like rose petals scattered on tables.   360
Her festival's lights, whose reason eluded me, were left,
    when she removed my confusion like this:
"Maybe because the fields are bright with purple flowers,
    lights seem to suit the days of my festival;
or because neither flower nor flame has a dull color   365
    and the brightness of both attracts our attention;
or because the liberties taken at night befit my pleasures.
    The third reason best fits the truth."
"There's a little besides I have left to ask about,
    if I may," I said, and she said, "You may."   370
Why are there netted at your shows, not African lions,
    but harmless roe deer and twitching hares?

She replied that forests don't belong to her, but gardens
    and fields not haunted by aggressive beasts.
Completely finished, she withdrew in thin air, but her perfume lingered.   375
    One just knew that a goddess had been there.
To insure that Ovid's poem blooms in every age,
    sprinkle my heart, I pray, with your gifts.

3 May

On the fourth night but one, Chiron displays his stars,
    a body compounded of man and chestnut horse.   380
Pelion is a Thracian mountain which faces to the south,
    pine-green on top, the rest is oak,
the haunt of Philyra's son, where they say the righteous old man
    inhabited a cave of ancient stone.
He supposedly kept Achilles' hands busy with melodies on the lyre,   385
    the hands which would one day send Hector to his death.
Hercules turned up there after carrying out most of his labors,
    when that man was almost at the end of his tasks.
You'd have seen Troy's two banes standing together by chance,
    Aeacus' grandson as a boy, and the son of Jupiter.   390
Philyra's noble son gave the young man a warm welcome.
    He asked, and was told, the reason for his coming.
Meanwhile he glanced at the club and the lion trophy, saying,
    "That man and his weapons are right for each other."
Achilles' hands couldn't keep themselves from venturing   395
    to touch the bristles of the shaggy pelt.
And while the old man was handling the arrows crusted with poison,
    one of them slipped and stuck in his left foot.
Chiron groaned and pulled the metal point from his flesh;
    Hercules and the boy from Thrace groaned in sympathy.   400
But he himself blends herbs gathered on the hills of Thessaly
    and soothes his wound with various treatments.
The virulent poison was beyond treatment and the bane
    had riddled his bones and all his flesh.
The blood of the Hydra from Lerna compounded with the Centaur's blood   405
    allowed no time for an antidote to take effect.
Achilles stood drenched with tears, as if beside his father:
    if Peleus were dying, he would've wept like that.
He frequently stroked the afflicted hands with his loving ones:

the tutor profits from the character he had shaped.   410
He kissed him frequently, and frequently said to him lying there,
    "Live, oh please, don't leave me, dear father."
When the ninth day had come, Chiron most righteous, you got
    your body outlined with twice seven stars.

5 May

The curving Lyre would like to follow him, but its course   415
    won't be right for three nights yet.

6 May

Half of Scorpio will be there to see in the sky
    when we say that the Nones will dawn tomorrow.

9 May

When the Evening Star has three times shown his lovely face
    and the routed stars have three times yielded to Phoebus,   420
the ancient ritual of the Lemuria will be observed by night,
    when offerings are given to the silent spirits.
When the year was shorter, and the means of atonement still unknown,
    and two-headed Janus didn't lead off the months,
people already used to bring bring gifts when a pyre had cooled   425
    and grandson appeased the tomb where grandfather was buried,
in the month of May, named for the elders' age of majority,
    which even today has its share in the archaic practice.
When night is half over and furnishes quiet for sleep,
    and dogs and colorful birds have grown silent,   430
a god-fearing man who remembers the ancient observances gets up
    (both his feet are unconfined by shoes)
and makes the sign of the fig with his thumb and adjacent fingers
    to keep from meeting a shadowy ghost in the silence.
And when he has washed his hands clean with spring water,   435
    he turns and starts by taking black beans,
then tosses them over his shoulder, and says as he does, "These
    I let fall, with these I ransom me and mine."
He says this nine times without looking back. The ghost is thought
    to pick up the beans and follow behind unseen.   440
Again he washes and bangs bronze pots and pans together

142

and asks the ghost to be gone from his dwelling.
When he's said, "Be gone, ancestral spirits," nine times,
    he looks back and regards the ritual as rightly done.
What the day is called for and the origin of its name   445
    elude me. I have to find out from some god.
Son of Maia, revered for your powerful wand, advise me:
    you've often seen the palace of the Jupiter below.
The Caduceus-bearer came as invoked. Here's the reason
    for the name: I learned the reason from the god himself.   450
When Romulus had laid his brother's ghost to rest in a tomb
    and over-agile Remus was paid his due,
unhappy Faustulus and Acca who let down her hair
    were sprinkling the burned up bones with their tears.
From there they sadly went home at early twilight   455
    and collapsed on their hard bed just as it was.
Remus' bloodstained ghost seemed to be standing by the bed
    and saying these words in a feeble whisper:
"Here I am, the other half of your hopes and dreams.
    Look at the terrible shape I'm in now.   460
Just now if I had obtained the birds that dispatched the kingdom,
    I could have been the mightiest of my people,
but now I'm an idle phantom that's slipped from the pyre's flame.
    This is what's left of the Remus you knew.
Oh where is my father Mars? If you told the truth, he provided   465
    a wild creature's teats when we were exposed.
One whom a she-wolf rescued has been destroyed by a citizen's
    impetuous hand. How much gentler she was!
I hope that brutal Celer loses his life to violence,
    and goes to the Underworld bloodied, like me.   470
My brother didn't want this, his devotion is a match for mine;
    he gave what he could—tears for my death.
By your tears and by your charity for us, ask him
    to mark a festival day in honor of me."
Longing to embrace as he gave this charge, they reached out their arms;   475
    his ghost slithered away from their grasp.
When the phantom had fled and taken sleep along with it,
    they both reported his brother's words to the king.
Romulus complied and called that day the Remuria on which
    buried ancestors are brought their due.   480
The very first letter of the name has changed from rough

to smooth with the passage of much time.
Soon the silent ghosts were also called "lemurs."
  This is the meaning and force of the word.
Well, anyhow, the ancients closed the temples on those days,   485
  as today you see them shut in the season of All Souls.[11]
That same season was fit for neither marriage nor remarriage:
  the woman who wed was not long for this world.
For this reason too, if you pay attention to proverbs,
  folks say wicked women wed in May.   490
Well, these three days are observed within the same period,
  but none of them falls on consecutive days.

10–11 May

If you look for Boeotian Orion in the meantime, you'll be mistaken.
  Now I must tell that constellation's origin.
Jupiter and his brother who rules over the wide ocean   495
  were making their way in Mercury's company.
It was the time when teams bring back upended ploughs
  and lambs gulp the milk of well-fed ewes.
Old Hyrieus, who tilled a cramped little plot, happened to see them
  as he stood in front of his tiny cottage, and said,   500
"Your way is long, but remaining daylight isn't,
  and my door is open to guests."
He accompanied his words with a smile and asked again.
  They obeyed his behest, but hid their godhead.
They entered the old man's dwelling, blackened with filthy smoke;   505
  the fire from yesterday's log was low.
He got down on his knees and blew the flame to life,
  brought out kindling and broke it finer.
Pots were set up. The smaller one held beans, the other, greens,
  and each one bubbled under its potsherd lid.   510
While they waited, he offered red wine with a shaky hand.
  The god of the ocean took the first cup,
and said as soon as he drained it, "Now offer the next drink
  to Jupiter." Hyrieus turned white at the sound of that name.
When his wits returned, he sacrificed the ox who tilled   515
  his poor field and roasted it on a big fire,
and he brought out wine he had stored in a smoky jug
  from a vintage dating to his early boyhood.

They couldn't wait to stretch out on linen cushions that were stuffed
    with river grass, but still not very thick. 520
The table was resplendent now with the feast, now with the wine.
    The punchbowl was earthenware, the cups were beech.
Jupiter's words were these, "If you fancy something, just ask:
    it's yours." The kindly old man's words were these:
"I had a dear wife whom I met in the spring of my early youth. 525
    Where is she now, you ask? In an urn.
I swore to her in words which you were called to witness,
    'Only you will get to be my wife.'
I'm keeping my word, but in fact I want something else:
    I want to be, not a husband, but still a father. 530
They all agreed, they all stood over the ox's hide—
    I'm embarrassed to tell what happened next.
Then they dusted over the damp spot with dirt,
    and ten months later a boy was born.
Hyrieus calls him Urion, from the manner of his conception. 535
    The initial letter lost its original sound.
He had grown enormously, when Diana took him as her companion.
    He was the goddess' bodyguard, he was her escort.
Unguarded words provoke the wrath of the gods. He said,
    "There isn't a beast that I can't take." 540
Earth turned loose a scorpion. When it got the urge to strike
    Apollo and Diana's mother with its curving stinger,
Orion blocked it. Latona put him with the shining stars
    and said, "Have this reward for your service."

12 May

But why are Orion and the other stars hurrying to withdraw 545
    from the sky, and night is cutting its journey short?
Why does the shining day, with the Morning Star in advance,
    raise its radiance so early from the clear ocean?
Am I wrong, or are weapons clanking? I'm not wrong, they were clanking.
    Mars has come, giving a warlike signal. 550
The Avenger himself is descending from heaven for his own festivities
    to his eye-catching temple in the Forum of Augustus.[12]
The god and the structure are both impressive, just the way
    Mars should dwell in his son's city.
This shrine is fit for housing spoils taken from the Giants. 555

From here it suits the Marcher to start fierce wars,
whether someone from the Eastern world treacherously provokes us,
    or someone from the land of sunset must be subdued.
The patron of war surveys the gables of his tall structure
    and approves the presence of Victories at the top.   560
He surveys the weapons of various shapes on the doors
    and armor of the world which his troops have won.
From here he sees Aeneas loaded with a priceless burden
    and so many ancestors of the noble Julian line.
From here he sees Romulus shouldering spoils from a general,   565
    and exploits inscribed beneath a row of statues.
He examines the name of Augustus bordering the temple. From reading
    "Caesar," he thinks the structure even greater.
The young man vowed this temple when he dutifully took up arms:
    he had to make such a start as our leading citizen.   570
Gesturing to the loyalist forces standing on one side,
    the conspirators on the other, he made this vow:
"If my father, Vesta's priest, is my inspiration for going to war,
    and if I intend to avenge the divinity of them both,
be with me, Mars, glut my sword with the criminals' blood,   575
    and back the better cause with your support.
If I am victorious, you'll get a temple and be called the Avenger."
    After this vow, he returned exultant from the rout.
It wasn't enough for Mars to have earned that epithet just once:
    he pursued the standards held captive in Parthian hands.   580
That was a people defended by deserts and cavalry and archery
    and made impregnable by rivers on all sides.
The death of Crassus and his son had increased the people's arrogance,
    when troops, standards, and general were all lost at once.
Roman standards, the glory of war, were held by the Parthians,   585
    an enemy was trooping the Roman eagles.
This disgrace would still have continued, if the western world
    were not defended by Augustus' valiant arms.
That man removed the old blot and the long-standing infamy:
    the recaptured standards recognized their own.   590
What good did your usual parting shots do you Parthians then,
    or geography or reliance on speedy horses?
You returned the eagles and also surrendered your vanquished bows:
    you no longer have the tokens of our disgrace.
Temple and epithet are rightly given to the twice avenging god   595

and this well-earned tribute discharges the vow.
Citizens, pack the commemorative races in the Circus:
    the stage didn't seem right for that brawny god.

13 May

You'll see all the Pleiades, the whole troop of sisters,
    when there's one night left before the Ides: 600
then summer begins, reliable sources tell me,
    and the mild spring season comes to an end.

14 May

The eve of the Ides reveals Taurus lifting his starry face.
    There's a famous story behind this sign.
When Jupiter, as a bull, offered his back to Phoenician Europa,   605
    wearing phony horns on his forehead,
she hung on, mane in her right hand, dress in her left,
    and her very fright was a fresh source of charm.
The breeze made her robe billow, and made her blond hair stream—
    nice for Jupiter to behold the Phoenician like that.   610
Often she drew up her girlish feet from the sea's surface
    for fear of the touch of the cresting waves.
Often the god intentionally dipped his back in the water
    to make her cling more tightly to his neck.
At landfall Jupiter stood there with no horns at all;   615
    he had been transformed from cow into god.
The bull entered heaven while Jupiter entered the Phoenician,[13]
    and one of the continents now bears her name.
In another version Taurus is Isis, the Egyptian heifer,
    who turned cow from human, from cow, divine.   620

On this date it's also the custom for the Vestals to toss straw dummies
    of the men of yore from the wooden bridge.[14]
Whoever believes that carcasses were tossed to death at age sixty,
    condemns our ancestors of a wicked crime.
An ancient story has it that when this land was called Saturn's,   625
    the oracle of Jupiter spoke like this:
"For the Old Man with the Sickle, pick out and toss in two
    of your people's carcasses for the Tiber to take."
Until the hero from Tiryns came to these fields, the grim

ritual was annually conducted like a lovers' leap, 630
but Hercules tossed citizens of straw into the water.
 From that example we throw in fake carcasses.
Others think the young men pitched the feeble old ones
 off the gangways in order to monopolize the voting.
Tiber, teach me the truth. Your banks are older than the City; 635
 you must know the ritual's origin well.
Tiber lifted his reed-covered head from mid-channel
 and hoarsely parted his lips in the following:
"I have seen this place forlorn and unwalled pastureland.
 Cattle once grazed here and there on my banks. 640
Even the livestock looked down on me then, the Tiber,
 which now the world's people both know and fear.
You've often heard mention of Arcadian Evander's name:
 that immigrant rippled my stream with his oars.
Hercules came too, accompanied by a crowd of Greeks. 645
 My name was Albula then, as I recall.
The Arcadian hero gave the young man a warm welcome,
 and Cacus finally got what he had coming.
The conqueror departed, hauling his cattle with him, his booty
 from Spain, but his companions refused to go further. 650
The majority of them had abandoned Argos when they came with him.
 They'd settled their hopes and hearths on these hills,
yet often they were stirred by sweet yearning for their homeland,
 and one on his deathbed assigned this little task:
'Toss me into the Tiber, so that Tiber's waves may carry 655
 my paltry dust to the shores of Argive Inachus.'
The burial chore, assigned like this, displeased his heir,
 so at death the foreigner was consigned to Italian soil.
Instead of himself, a likeness of rush was tossed to the Tiber,
 to return to its home in Greece overseas." 660
With this, Tiber descended to a wet grotto of natural stone.
 Swiftly his waves maintained their course.

15 May

Illustrious grandson of Atlas, be with me, you whom one of the
 Pleiades once bore to Jupiter in the mountains of Arcadia.
Umpire of war and peace for the gods above and below, 665

you who make your way on winged feet,
delighted by the lyre's strum and the sweat of the wrestling ring,
    you tutored tongues to talk with style,
for you the senators founded a temple facing the Circus,
    so today—the Ides—is a holiday for you.   670
Everyone whose line is selling merchandise offers incense
    to you and asks you for profits in return.
Close by Capena Gate is Mercury's spring. It pays
    to believe those who've tried it: it works.
Here comes a merchant with his clean sleeves rolled up to draw water   675
    in a fumigated pitcher to take along with him.
With this he wets a laurel spray, with the laurel he sprinkles
    all the stuff that's going to have new owners.
He evens sprinkles his hair with the dripping laurel, and presents
    his prayer in a voice that's used to fraud: 680
"Wash away the duplicities of times gone by," he says,
    "wash away the deceits of the day gone by.
Whether I invoked you or took in vain the name of Jupiter
    when I knew he wouldn't be listening,
or intentionally defrauded any other god or goddess, let the wind   685
    make swiftly off with the shameless things I've said.
Let me resort to duplicities on the day to come,
    and let the gods disregard whatever I say.
Just give me profits, give me joy in profit taken,
    and make it pay to have swindled the buyer."   690
Mercury smiles from on high at demands like that, remembering
    his theft of brother Apollo's cattle.

20 May

But because my request is for something so much better, reveal,
    I pray, the date when the sun enters Gemini.
"When you see as many days left in the month as the labors   695
    that Hercules did," Mercury replies.
"Tell me," I countered, "the origin of this sign of the zodiac."
    The god's eloquent lips supplied the origin.
The brothers of Helen, one a horseman and the other a boxer,
    had made off with Phoebe and Phoebe's sister.   700
Idas and his brother, each one betrothed to the girls by Leucippus

their father, mobilized to recover what was theirs.
Love prompts this pair to recover, that pair not to return them.
        Each side fights from the very same motive.
The Spartan boys could have outrun their pursuers,   705
        but it didn't seem right to win by escape.
There's a place devoid of trees, a suitable site for a skirmish.
        They took their stand at that place, named Aphidna.
Run through the chest by Lynceus' sword, Castor bit
        the dust because of a wound he hadn't seen coming.   710
Pollux was there to avenge him and drilled his spear through the spot
        where Lynceus' neck stretched into his shoulders.
Idas came at him, scarcely kept off by Jupiter's lightning,
        and yet they say he wasn't disarmed by the bolt.
Already high heaven was opening up to receive you, Pollux,   715
        when you said, "Father, take in my words.
Share with two the heaven you're giving to me alone;
        half that gift will be greater than the whole."
This said, he ransomed his brother by taking rotations.
        As stars they both help ships in distress.   720

21 May

See above under "Janus" to find out what the Agonalia is,
        but it also occupies this date on the calendar.

22 May

On the night which follows that day, Sirius comes out.
        I've explained its origin in another entry.[15]

23 May

The next day is Vulcan's. They call it the Trumpet Purification: 725
        the trumpets he makes are ritually purified.

24 May

The entry after that is marked with four letters, the acronym
        for a ritual custom or a king's expulsion.[16]

25 May

I won't pass over the public Fortune of a powerful people,
   whose temple was consecrated on the following day.   730
When bountiful Ocean has welcomed that day into its waters,
   you'll see the golden beak of Jove's favorite bird.

26–27 May

The coming dawn will take Bootes from your sight
   and the next day Hyas will be up.

Book
6

June

This month too has a name of uncertain origins.
    From the ones I present, take your pick.
What I'm telling you really happened, but some will say I've made it up.
    They think that gods by mortals are never seen.
There's a god in us, we get warmed up when that spirit moves us;   5
    this force has elements of holy intelligence.
For me in particular is it right to have seen gods face to face,
    because I'm inspired and because of my sacred themes.
There's a grove thick with trees, a place cut off
    from every sound, save a waterfall's din.   10
I was here researching the origin of the month just begun,
    giving serious attention to the name of it.
Look! I saw goddesses, not the ones the professor of ploughing[1]
    saw while tending his sheep on Boeotia's Mount Ascra,
nor the ones judged by Paris in the valley of well-watered Ida,   15
    and yet one of those was there.
One of those was there, her husband's sister. Her I knew
    from Jupiter's temple on the Capitoline.
I shuddered and my loss of color betrayed my state of mind.
    The goddess then removed the anxiety she had caused,   20

"Inspired composer of the Roman year, bold reporter
    of matters great in light-weight measures,
you have earned your right to see a power come down from heaven
    by choosing to compose poetry about the festivals.
But so you'll know and not be misled by popular folly,   25
    from my name the name of June derives.
It's no small thing being Jupiter's bride, being Jupiter's sister:
    I'm not sure which I'm prouder of.
If family is considered, I made Saturn a father first,
    I was the first child allotted to Saturn.   30
Rome was once called "Saturnian" after my father.
    He ranked this land second only to heaven.
If marriage counts for something, I am called the Thunderer's lady,
    and my temple is next to Jupiter's on the Capitoline.
Can it be that a hussy has given her name to the month of May,   35
    but you're going to begrudge me this token of esteem?
So why am I called the queen of heaven and its first lady?
    Why has a scepter been put in my hand?
Can it be that days light up the months but I whom they call
    the Lady, the Bringer to Light,[2] gets no month-name?   40
Then I should be sorry for dropping my resentment in good faith
    against Electra's line and Trojan Dardanus' house.
My resentment had a twofold motive. I was smarting over Ganymede's abduction,
    and then my beauty lost in the Judgment of Paris.
I should be sorry for not supporting the city of Carthage,   45
    although my chariot and armory were there.
I should be sorry for subjecting to Latium both Sparta and Argos,
    my very own Mycenae and ancient Samos,
plus old King Tatius and the Falernian cult of Juno,
    whose submission to Rome I tolerated.   50
But I shouldn't be sorry for that, and no nation is dearer to me.
    Let my cult be here, and a temple to share with my Jupiter.
Mars himself once told me, 'To you I entrust these walls:
    you will be powerful in your grandson's city.'
His promise came true. I am honored at hundreds of altars,   55
    but this month's distinction is just as important.
And yet not only Rome renders me this token of esteem.
    The neighboring towns pay me the same tribute.
Take a look at the calendars of Aricia, famed for its grove,
    the Laurentian people and my very own Lanuvium.   60

There too there's a month connected with Juno. Examine Tivoli
    and Palestrina with its temple of Fortune,
and you'll make out a period for Juno: Romulus didn't
    found these, but Rome was my grandson's city."
When Juno had finished, I looked around. There stood Hercules'   65
    wife, looking as youthful as she is.[3]
"If Mother tells me to get out of heaven entirely,
    I won't dawdle against Mother's will.
I won't wrangle about this period's name now either.
    I'll use charm and act like a virtual beggar.   70
I'd rather hold onto what's rightfully mine by pleading.
    Perhaps you yourself might support my claim.
The gilded Capitoline temple is community property:
    Mother shares it with Jupiter, as she should.
But my whole glory is connected with the origin of this month;   75
    my sole distinction is what's troubling me.
Doesn't it count that Romans and their grateful descendants
    credited the month to Hercules' wife?
Here too a country owes me something for the sake of my great
    husband; here he drove Geryon's cattle,   80
here, ill-served by his father Vulcan's fiery inheritance,
    Cacus stained Aventine soil with his blood.
I turn to more recent events: Romulus classified his people
    by age, divided into two categories.
The one is better equipped to advise, the other to fight,   85
    the one counsels war, the other conducts it.
So he decreed, and distinguished the months by the same token:
    June for the juniors, May for the majority."
She was finished. Those two would have hotly contested the issue,
    and phony deference would have turned to anger.   90
Enter Concord, her long hair wreathed with Apollo's laurel,
    our peaceful leader's patroness and handiwork.
She recounted how Tatius and brawny Romulus joined forces,
    two kingdoms with their two populations,
when the Sabine women welcomed fathers and husbands to a joint hearth,   95
    and "June," she said, "is named for their union."[4]
I have heard all three claims. But forgive me, goddesses:
    my verdict mustn't settle this matter.
It's a tie. Ilium was eliminated thanks to Paris' judgment.
    Two do more harm than one can do good.   100

1 June

The first is dedicated to Carna, a cardinal goddess,[5] whose power
    opens what's shut and shuts what's open.
Where she got that power is a story that time has dimmed,
    but my account will clear it up for you.
There's an ancient grove to Alernus beside the Tiber,   105
    where even today the high-priests bring sacrifices.
A nymph was born there (men of old called her Cranaë)
    whom many suitors pursued in vain.
She roamed the countryside, harrying wild creatures with her spears
    and spreading her nets of rope in the hollows.   110
She had no quiver, but people still thought that she was Diana
    (a sister like that would not have embarrassed Apollo).
Whenever some young man spoke words of love to her,
    at once she'd reply in strains like this:
"It's too bright right here, and too embarrassing. Lead   115
    the way to a cave further off, and I'll follow."
When the dupe had gone on ahead, she stayed put and hid
    in some bushes and was nowhere to be found.
Then Janus saw her. Overpowered with desire for what he'd seen,
    he tried to soft-soap the hard-hearted girl.   120
As usual the nymph told him to find a cave more secluded.
    Playing follow the leader, she left him in the lurch.
Silly girl! Janus can see what's happening behind his back.
    Nothing doing, he can also see back to your hideout.
Nothing doing, see, I told you so. He nabbed you from hiding   125
    beneath a cliff, got what he wanted, and said,
"In return for lying with me, have dominion over the hinge.
    Take this compensation for your lost virginity."
He said this, and gave her a thorn branch (it was white),
    with which to avert dreadful harm from doors.   130
There are some greedy birds, a species related to the Harpies
    that used to cheat Phineus' gullet of his food.
They have huge heads, popeyes, beaks well suited to plunder,
    white-hued plumage and claws like hooks.
At night they fly in search of children unweaned,   135
    plundering cradles and mutilating the bodies.
People say they pick at the milk-fed flesh with their beaks

and drink the blood 'til their gullets are full.
They have the name of screech owls, a name they get
    from the terrible way they screech at night.   140
Whether they're birds from birth, or whether that happens by magic
    when a gypsy spell turns crones into winged creatures,
they came to Proca's nursery. As a five-day-old newborn,
    Proca was fresh meat for these birds.
They were greedily sucking the life from the infant's chest,   145
    but the poor little boy was bawling for help.
Alarmed by the sound of her charge's voice, his nurse ran in
    to find his cheeks scratched by tough claws.
What to do? His face was the color of autumn leaves
    after the first frost has blighted them.   150
She went to Cranaë and told her story. "Put aside your fears,"
    she said, "your charge is going to be fine."
Cranaë got to the cradle where the mother and father were weeping.
    "Stop your tears," she said. "I'm going to restore him."
At once she dabbed the door-posts three times in a row with a branch   155
    of arbutus, and three times marked the threshold,
sprinkling the entrance with water (the water contained a restorative).
    Holding a two-month-old piglet's raw innards,
she said, "Birds of the night, leave the boy's innards alone:
    in a little one's place a little victim falls.   160
A heart for a heart, I pray you deliver, a liver for a liver.[6]
    We offer you this life in place of one better."
After this offering, she set the innards out in the open
    and enjoined those present from looking back at the rite.
She applied the wand of white thorn she had gotten from Janus   165
    where a little window was letting light into the nursery.
The story goes that the birds outraged the crib no more,
    and the child's color returned to what it had been.

You ask why the menu for June the first reads: fat bacon
    and a steaming mess of beans and barley?   170
Carna's an old-time goddess, sustained by familiar foods,
    and she doesn't indulge in exotic banquets.
Folks back then still left the fish to swim in peace
    and oysters were safe in their shells.
Latium wasn't acquainted with the bird from wealthy Ionia,   175
    nor the one that delights in Pygmy blood.

The peacock provided no pleasure except with its plumage,
    nor had earth sent beasts to be caught in traps.
The pig was prized, they would butcher a pig to keep their feasts.
    The earth gave only beans and hardy barley: 180
if you eat a mess of these combined on the first of June,
    you won't have stomach trouble, so they say.

The temple to our Lady of the Mint on top of the stronghold
    was built, as people recall, to keep Camillus' vow.
Earlier it was the house of Manlius, who once routed   185
    a Gallic force from Jupiter's Capitoline temple.
How much better, ye gods, had he fallen in that battle,
    defending the throne of Jupiter on high!
He lived, to die convicted of an attempted coup d'etat:
    that's the distinction longevity got him.   190

Today is also a festival for Mars. Capena Gate surveys
    his temple outside the walls by the Covered Way.

You too, Stormy Weather, we declare earned a shrine today,
    when our fleet nearly sank in waters off Corsica.
These human memorials are close at hand. As to the stars,   195
    you'll find Jupiter's eagle is rising today.

2 June

The following day calls in the Hyades that form the horns
    on Taurus' brow, and the earth is drenched with rain.

3 June

When it's morning once more and the sun has repeated his rising
    and the grain has been soaked once more with dew,   200
it's the date they say Bellona's temple was dedicated during war
    with Etruscans. She's ever gracious to Rome.
It was proposed by Appius, whose refusal of peace on Pyrrhus' terms
    showed a great deal of insight despite his blindness.
One can see the Circus Flaminius from the square in front of the temple.   205
    Of no little import is the little column there.
From there it's the custom to loose a spear, war's harbinger, when the Senate
    has decided to fight a foreign king and nation.

4 June

The other side of the Circus is kept safe by Hercules the Guardian,
    a tribute the hero got from the Sibylline books.   210
The date of that tribute is the day before the Nones. Check out
    the inscription: Sulla certified the project.

5 June

I was checking out whether to assign the Nones to Sancus or Fidius,
    or to father Semo. Then Sancus told me,
"Whichever of those you give it to, I'll get the tribute.   215
    I bear three names; that's what the Sabines wanted."
So the ancient Sabines bestowed a shrine on him
    and erected it on the Quirinal Hill.

6 June

I have a daughter—may she live to a riper age than I—
    if she is well, I'll always be happy.   220
When I was ready to give her away, I was checking out
    dates auspicious for the wedding and ones to avoid.
Then I was shown that after the holy Ides, June is
    expedient for brides and for husbands too,
but I found that this month's first half is inopportune for weddings,   225
    as the venerable wife of Jupiter's flamen told me:
"Until gentle Tiber's muddy waters have brought the scourings
    from Trojan Vesta's temple down to the sea,
I may not comb down my hair with a comb of boxwood,
    nor trim my nails with an iron utensil,   230
nor have contact with my husband no matter that he's Jupiter's priest,
    no matter that our vows were 'til death do us part.
Don't you be hasty either. Your daughter will do better to wed
    when Vesta's fire shines on a scoured floor."

7 June

The third night after the Nones gets rid of Lycaon's grandson,   235
    so the Great Bear can stop looking over her shoulder.
Then I recall I saw shows that day on the grass of Mars' Field
    and they were called yours, gently flowing Tiber.

It's a holiday for those who reel in dripping lines
    and conceal their bent hook with bits of food.   240

8 June

Good Sense has divine power too. We see that a shrine was promised
    to Good Sense from dread of war with shifty Carthage.
Carthage had renewed war and a consul's death in battle
    stunned everyone into terror of Moorish squadrons.
Dread had banished hope when the Senate undertook the promise   245
    to Good Sense and right away she got better.
That day on which the promise to the goddess was kept glimpses
    the Ides on its way after a six-day interval.

9 June

Vesta, be favorable. To you I now open my lips in devotions,
    if I am permitted to come to your ritual.   250
While absorbed in prayer I felt a divine presence
    and the floor shone joyously with purple light.
Of course I didn't see you—so long, poetic license—
    you are not a goddess for a man to behold,
but I've learned with no human teacher what I didn't know   255
    while confusion had me in its grip.
When Rome had passed forty anniversaries, people say
    that a shrine welcomed the goddess who keeps the flame,
the project of that peace-loving king, the most god-fearing soul
    ever produced by the Sabine territory.   260
The roofs of bronze you see today were then straw-thatched,
    and the walls were plaited from pliant wattles.
This tiny spot, the site of the Vestals' official residence,
    was then the palace of King Numa the long-beard.
But the shape of the temple, which survives to this day, was there before, 265
    they say, and a commendable reason is behind that shape.
Vesta and the Earth are the same; behind both is an unsleeping fire.
    The Earth and Vesta's hearth symbolize its dwelling.
The Earth is like a ball, completely unsupported,
    its heavy weight hanging in the air beneath it.   270
Rotation itself balances the sphere and holds it up:
    there are no corners to weigh down any side.

Situated as it is in the central region of the universe,
    so it doesn't touch any side more than another,
if it were not curved, it would be one side's closer neighbor,   275
    and the universe wouldn't have Earth as its weighty center.
There's a globe suspended in space by Archimedes' know-how,
    a tiny model of the measureless heavens,
where the Earth is equidistant from its top and its bottom.
    The spherical shape makes such a thing possible.   280
Vesta's temple looks the same. Not a single corner
    sticks out, and the dome protects it from the rain.
Why do virgin attendants minister to the goddess, you ask?
    For this too I'll find the proper explanation.
Juno and Ceres, they say, were sired on Rhea   285
    by Saturn; Vesta was the third daughter.
The first two wed, we hear that the first two gave birth.
    Of the three, only one remained inexperienced with men.
No wonder that a virgin is delighted by a virgin attendant
    and welcomes chaste hands to her rites.   290
Don't imagine that Vesta is anything but living flame;
    you won't see a single substance born from flame.
And so she's rightly a virgin, she doesn't produce nor receive
    any seeds, and she loves her virgin associates.
For quite a while I stupidly thought there were statues of Vesta.   295
    I soon learned there weren't any in the domed rotunda.
A fire that never goes out is hidden in that temple;
    neither Vesta nor the fire has a single likeness.
The earth is very stable. From being very stable, Vesta gets her name,
    as in Greek she's Hestia from her heavy resting.[7]   300
The hearth is named for its hearty warmth that heartens all,
    but it used to be at the front of the house.
From this I believe the "vestibule" derives, and praying
    with a preamble to Vesta, who occupies first place.

It once was the custom to sit before the hearth on benches   305
    and believe one's gods were present at the table.
Even today when the rites of ancient Vacuna take place,
    one stands and sits before Vacuna's hearth.
A bit of archaic custom has come down to the present age:
    a clean little dish brings the food offered to Vesta.   310

Look at the bread hanging down from garlanded asses,
    and wreaths of flowers festooning rough millstones.
The early peasants used ovens only for toasting barley
    (the goddess of ovens has rites of her own):
the hearth itself got the bread ready, buried in the ashes,   315
    with a broken roof-tile laid on the warm ground.
And so the baker honors the hearth and our Lady of Hearths
    and the ass that turns the volcanic millstones.
Ruddy Priapus, should I bypass your disgrace, or recount it?
    It's a little story with a lot of laughs.   320
With her turreted crown in place on her forehead, Cybele
    invited the immortal gods to her feast.
She invited both the satyrs and those rural spirits, the nymphs;
    Silenus was there without an invitation.
It's prohibited and would be protracted to describe divine banquets: 325
    they stayed up all night with lots of wine.
Some were roaming aimlessly in the hollows of shady Ida,
    others lay down and relaxed on the soft grass;
some made merry, some were asleep; others linked arms
    and stamped a quick three-step on the verdant ground.   330
Vesta lay down and took a peaceful nap without a care,
    just as she was, with her head pillowed on the turf.
But the ruddy garden scarecrow went prowling for nymphs and goddesses,
    directing his roaming steps back and forth.
He glimpsed Vesta: maybe he thought she was a nymph or maybe   335
    he knew she was Vesta, but he says he didn't.
He got a nasty notion, and tried to approach stealthily,
    making his way on tiptoe with pounding heart.
Old man Silenus had happened to leave the ass he had ridden
    by the banks of a gently babbling stream.   340
The god of the long Hellespont was making a move to get started
    when that creature brayed an untimely blast.
The deep sound frightened the goddess awake. The whole crowd flocked
    together, the villain escaped amidst threatening hands.
At Lampsacus it's the custom to slaughter this beast for Priapus, singing,   345
    "We fittingly offer a tattler's guts to the flames."
But Vesta, you gratefully deck it with necklaces of bread.
    Work stops, and the idle mills fall silent.

Now I'll tell the meaning of the altar on the Thunderer's stronghold
    for Jupiter the Baker, more notable for its name than its cost.   350
The Capitoline was hemmed in and hard-pressed by savage Gauls:
    a siege of long standing had caused starvation.
Jupiter summoned the celestials to his royal throne and said
    "Commence" to Mars, who reported at once:
"Of course the state of their distress is unknown to you   355
    and this heartache of mine needs to voice a complaint.
But if you demand a concise account of their shameful distress,
    the Alpine foe has brought Rome to her knees.
This is the city you promised control of the world, Jupiter?
    This the one you would put in command of the earth?   360
Just now she crushed the nearby towns and Etruscan forces;
    hope was full speed. Now she's been driven from her home.
I have witnessed old men in their bronze-fitted courtyards meet death
    decked in the regalia of their past triumphs.
I have witnessed the talismans of Trojan Vesta moved from her dwelling   365
    to safety. Romans of course suppose gods are somebodies.
But if they looked around at the stronghold where you reside
    and all your homes hard-pressed by the siege,
they would know that no help is left to repay concern for the gods
    and that incense offered with a careful hand is a waste.   370
If only a chance to fight would appear. Let them take up arms
    and if they can't prevail, let them fall.
But now, without food and afraid of inglorious death, cooped up
    on their hill they're hard-pressed by the barbarian horde."
Then Venus, and Quirinus splendid with augur's crook and kingly robe,   375
    and Vesta too said much for their Latium's sake.
Jupiter replied, "Those walls concern every one of us,
    and vanquished Gaul will pay the price.
Now Vesta, see that the enemy thinks the grain that's gone
    is still left, and don't abandon your dwelling.   380
Whatever grain is intact, let the hollow machinery grind
    and the hearth fire-harden what kneading has softened."
By the time Saturn's virgin daughter had given her assent
    to her brother's command, the hour was midnight.
Toil had brought sleep to the Roman leaders. Thundering at them,   385
    Jupiter revealed his will through holy lips:
"Get up and from the stronghold's heights into the enemy's midst

let loose the resource you are least willing to lose."
Sleep departed and the strange riddle drove them to seek
    to surrender the resource as ordered against their will.   390
It appeared to be bread, so they threw down the bounty of Ceres.
    What they threw clanged on helmets and long shields.
There went the hope of starving them out. When the enemy had been routed,
    a splendid altar was put up for Jupiter the Baker.

I happened to be heading home on Vesta's holiday by the staircase   395
    that has recently linked New Street to the Roman Forum.
I observed a lady climbing down this way barefooted.
    Unable to speak, I stopped in my tracks.
An old woman from the neighborhood noticed, told me to sit down,
    and said as her head shook and her voice trembled: 400
"This area where the fora are today was occupied by sodden swamps;
    the storm sewer[8] was soggy with the river's overflow.
Lake Curtius over there, the site of altars high and dry,
    now solid ground, was a lake before.
The regular route for the parade to the Circus through the Velabrum   405
    district was nothing but willows and hollow reeds.
Often a reveller heading home by the city's waterway
    would sing and make drunken remarks to the boatmen.
Yonder god Vertumnus hadn't yet taken a name from averting
    the stream, that also fits his versatile shapes.[9]   410
Here too there was a grove thick with canes and rushes,
    and a swamp you wouldn't approach with your shoes still on.
The pools have receded and the banks keep their waters in,
    and now it's dry ground, but that custom survives."
That explained that. "Goodbye, my dear old woman," I said.   415
    "May what's left of your life be entirely easy."

The rest of the story I learned long ago in the time of my boyhood,
    but I mustn't omit it on that account.
Ilus, great-grandson of Dardanus, had just constructed new walls
    (Ilus the rich still controlled the East).   420
People believe a heaven-sent statue of Minerva in arms
    landed on the slopes of the city of Ilium.
I was anxious to see it: I saw the temple and its environs;
    that's still over there, but Rome has the Palladium.
When the Trojans consulted Apollo, from his shady grove darkly   425

he gave this response with lips that do not lie:
"Keep safe the goddess from heaven, and you'll keep your city safe.
 Authority over this area goes where she does."
Ilus kept her safe by shutting her away atop his stronghold,
 and this concern passed on to his heir Laomedon.   430
In Priam's reign she was not kept safe enough, as was her will
 after her beauty lost out in that contest.
They say she was stolen. Maybe Adrastus' grandson did it,
 or Ulysses, the proficient trickster, or Aeneas.
The culprit is uncertain, the object is at Rome, safeguarded by Vesta 435
 because she sees everything by her constant light.

Oh how frightened the senators were, when Vesta's temple caught
 fire, and she almost was buried by her very own roof!
It was a blaze of hallowed fires and fires accursed,
 a blend of flames profane and sacred.   440
The dumbstruck Vestals undid their hair and wept:
 fright itself had taken their strength.
Into their midst flew Metellus, who said at the top of his voice,
 "Come help; weeping won't do any good.
Pick up the talismans of destiny in your virgin fingers.   445
 Not your prayers but your hands must carry them off.
Woe is me! Why hesitate?" He saw them hesitate
 and go down in terror on bended knee.
He scooped up holy water, raised his hands, and said, "Forgive me,
 as a man I shall enter where a man must not go.   450
If this be a sin, let punishment for the offense fall on me.
 Let Rome be absolved by the loss of my life."
He spoke and burst in: the goddess he carried off approved his deed,
 and was kept safe by her chief priest's service.
Now, holy flames, in Augustus' reign you shine as you should: 455
 the fire on the hearth from Troy is here to stay.
There won't be any record in this leader's reign of a priestess
 sullying her vows, nor buried alive in the ground.
That's how an unchaste one dies, buried in what she's profaned:
 the Earth and Vesta are the same divinity.   460

This is the day a Brutus earned his title by staining
 Spanish soil with the blood of Callaican foes.
As the saying goes, joy is sometimes alloyed with sorrow

to keep the people from whole-hearted celebration.
At the Euphrates Crassus lost standards, son, and troops,   465
    and was himself the last to die.
"Parthian, why gloat?" said Nemesis. "You are going to return the standards
    and an avenger will make Crassus' murderers pay."

10 June

Well, as soon as the violets are taken from the asses' long ears
    and rough millstones grind the crops of grain,   470
a sailor sitting at the stern remarks, "We'll see the Dolphin
    when day is banished and damp night has risen."

11 June

Trojan Tithonus now complains that his wife is forsaking him
    as the watchful Day Star leaves the Eastern waters.
Go, good matrons—Matralia is your festival—and offer   475
    golden cakes to the goddess from Thebes.
Next to the bridges and the Circus is a very famous district
    named for the bull's statue erected there.
This is the place and date that King Servius' besceptered hands
    founded Mother Matuta's holy temple.   480
Who is the goddess, why does she bar slavegirls from the doorstep
    of her temple (for she does) and demand roasted cakes?
You, Bacchus, distinctive with ivy in your beclustered locks,
    if she is your kin, guide this poet's work.
After Jupiter's indulgence had incinerated Semele, Ino took in   485
    baby Bacchus, and nursed him as attentively as she could.
Juno exploded at her for raising the son who'd been snatched
    from a slut; but he was her sister's flesh and blood.
For this her husband Athamas was driven by a mad delusion
    and tiny Learchus died by his father's hand.   490
His grieving mother had laid Learchus' ghost to rest in a tomb
    and had given all that was due to the pitiful pyre.
With her hair still torn in mourning, she too, crazed like her husband,
    rushed and snatched her son Melicertes from his crib.
There's a narrow isthmus that beats back the waves from two seas,   495
    a single land battered by two bodies of water.
Here Ino came, hugging her son in the arms of a madwoman,
    and launched him with her into the deep from a cliff.

The Nereid Panope and her hundred sisters caught them unharmed
    and, gliding gently, carried them through their domain.   500
She wasn't yet called Leucothea, nor was the boy yet Palaemon,
    when they reached the shores of thickly eddying Tiber.
There was a grove, maybe called Semele's, maybe Stimula's,
    inhabited, they say, by Italian maenads.[10]
Ino asked them what nation this was. She was told they were   505
    Arcadians and Evander's scepter ruled the place.
Disguising her divinity, Saturn's daughter insidiously incited
    the Latin bacchants with lying words:
"You are too gullible, you are being completely taken in.
    She isn't coming to your band as a friendly stranger.   510
She is slyly pursuing her plan to learn your holy mysteries.
    Her son's the pawn to pay our price."
She had scarcely stopped talking, when the sisterhood filled the air
    with howls, as their hair streamed over their shoulders,
and they staked their claim to the boy, fighting to wrench him away.   515
    Ino called upon gods as yet unknown to her,
"Gods and men of this place, come help a pitiful mother."
    Her shout struck the nearby rocks of the Aventine.
Hercules had driven his Spanish cattle to the river bank.
    He heard the sound and hurried toward it.   520
At his arrival, those dames who were getting ready to use
    violence turned tail and fled in disgrace.
"What do *you* want here?" (for he'd recognized Bacchus' aunt).
    Does the same divinity harass us both?"
She told him part, but part the presence of her son suppressed,   525
    and the shame that madness had driven her to sin.
Rumor, swift as it is, flew on rapidly beating wings,
    and Ino's name was constantly on its lips.
It told that she'd entered good-hearted Carmenta's household
    as a guest, and put an end to her long fast.   530
The Arcadian priestess reportedly gave her cakes she herself
    had hastily fixed and baked in a freshly lit oven.
To this very day she is pleased by cakes at her festival of Matralia:
    old-fashioned attentiveness is more welcome than finesse.
"Now sibyl," she said, "disclose the destiny yet to come,   535
    if you may. Add this to your hospitality."
In a short while the sibyl assumed heavenly powers,
    and became completely filled by her god.

Suddenly you could barely recognize her, so much holier
    was she than just now, and so much bigger.   540
"Glad tidings I sing. Rejoice, Ino, you are done with your toils,"
    she said. "Be ever gracious to this people.
You'll be a spirit of the sea. The sea will also hold
    your son. Assume different names in your waters.
Among the Greeks you'll be Leucothea, but to us, Matuta;   545
    your son will have complete authority over ports;
he'll be called Portunus by us, Palaemon in his native tongue.
    Go, each of you, I pray, favorable to this place."
She nodded to guarantee good faith. They ended their toils and changed
    their names: he's a god, she's a goddess.   550

Why, you ask, does she forbid slavegirls to approach? She hates them
    and I'd recount the origin of her hatred, if she'd let me.
Daughter of Cadmus, one of your handmaidens often used
    to submit to your husband's embraces.
Shameless Athamas loved her on the sly. From her he found out   555
    that you had given his farmers toasted seed corn.
Of course you denied it, but gossip gave the story credence.
    This is why you hate slaves as a group.
Not to her should a dutiful mother pray for her offspring;
    she's proved too little lucky a mother herself.   560
You'll do better to entrust her with another woman's child;
    she did more good for Bacchus than for her own.

"Where are you rushing?" she asked Rutilius. "On my feast day
    you're going to fall while consul to a Marsian foe."
The outcome agreed with her words, and the Tolenus river   565
    ran crimson with the blood mixed in its waters.
The next year came. On that very same day Didius
    was killed and doubled the power of the foe.

The same dedication day, founder and locale belongs to Fortune,
    but who's that hiding under a pile of togas?   570
It's King Servius, that much is for sure, but the reason he's hiding
    is disputed and keeps my mind uncertain too.
Although the goddess shudders to admit her clandestine affair
    and the shame of bedding down, goddess with mortal
(an overwhelming desire for the king set her on fire   575

and for this man alone Fortune wasn't blind),
at night she used to enter his house by a little window
    which gave the Fenestella Gate its name.
Now from shame she veils her lover's features to hide them,
    and the king's face is covered with a lot of toga.   580
Or is it true instead that after Servius' funeral his people
    were in disarray at their gentle leader's death?
Their grief was boundless and grew at the sight of his statue,
    until they hid him from view by piling on togas.
I have to recount a third explanation at greater length,   585
    but I'll keep my horses reined in tight.
After Servius' daughter had got marriage as her prize for crime,[11]
    she used to goad her husband with words like these:
"What's the good of our fine match, murderers of our respective
    siblings, if the dutiful life is now appealing?   590
They should have lived, my husband and your wife,
    if we weren't going to risk any greater exploit.
My father's life and kingdom I stipulated as my dowry.
    If you're a man, collect the dowry you bargained for.
Crime is the stuff of kings. Kill my father, seize his kingdom,   595
    and stain our hands in your father-in-law's blood."
Fired up like that he sat on the throne he had no claim to.
    In shock the masses rushed to arms.
Murder and mayhem ensued, and weak old age was vanquished.
    Servius' scepter was stolen by his proud son-in-law,[12]   600
and he fell murdered at the foot of the Esquiline near his palace,
    covered with blood on the hard ground.
Intending to enter her father's home, his daughter was riding
    with haughty defiance in a carriage through the street.
When her driver caught sight of the corpse, he halted as his tears   605
    poured out. She rebuked him as follows:
"Go on. Are you waiting for devotion's bitter reward? Drive
    your reluctant wheels, I say, right over his face."
There's definite proof of the deed: the Street of Crime is named
    for her, and that affair bears a permanent stigma.   610
But later she dared set foot in the temple that her father built.
    What I'm going to say is amazing but true.
A statue of Servius sitting on his throne was there.
    They say it covered its eyes with its hands,

and a voice was heard saying, "Hide my face to keep me   615
    from seeing my daughter's unspeakable features."
A robe was supplied to cover him. Fortune forbad its removal
    and spoke like this from her temple:
"The first day that Servius' features are unveiled and exposed
    will be the first day decency is discarded."   620
Ladies, refrain from laying hands on the forbidden robe—
    it's enough to set prayers in solemn motion—
and always keep covered with a Roman robe the head
    of him who was our city's seventh king.
This temple had burned down, but the fire spared the statue;   625
    Vulcan himself brought help to his son.
For Vulcan was Servius' father, his mother, Ocresia,
    an outstandingly beautiful woman from Corniculum.
After Queen Tanaquil had duly performed a ritual with her help,
    she ordered her to pour wine on the decorated hearth.   630
Here in the ashes either there was the shape of a man's nasty thing
    or there seemed to be, but probably there really was.
The slave sat on the hearth as ordered. Conceived by her,
    Servius got the seeds of his family from heaven.
His sire gave a sign when he touched his head with flickering fire   635
    and a point of flame blazed in his hair.

The Empress Livia dedicated a splendid shrine to Concord,
    which she provided her beloved husband.[13]
Listen to this, you ages to come: where Livia's colonnade
    is now, once was covered by a vast house.   640
That single house on the scale of a city took up more room
    than the walls of many a small town.
It was levelled to the ground, not to punish an act of treason,[14]
    but its extravagance seemed a bad influence.
The Emperor put up with tearing down such a hulk of a building   645
    and wrecking such a property bequeathed to him.
That's how the censorship is run, that's how examples are set,
    when the disciplinarian practices what he preaches.

12 June

There's nothing remarkable to say about the following day.

169

13 June

On the Ides a temple was given to Jupiter the Unconquerable.   650
And now I am bidden to tell the story of the lesser Quinquatrus.
    Now, blond Minerva, be with this venture of mine.
"Why do the flutists wander in procession throughout the city?
    What do the masks mean, and the long robes?"
That from me, this from Athena when she put down her spear   655
    (I hope I can report the accomplished goddess' words):
"In the time of your venerable ancestors, flutists had much
    employment and always were held in much esteem.
The flute used to play at temples, it played for shows at the theater,
    the flute used to play at mournful funerals.   660
The work was sweetened by its compensation. But a time ensued
    to suddenly wreck the practice of that welcome craft.
Besides, an aedile[15] had ordered that only ten performers
    were to accompany a funeral procession.
They exchanged the city for exile and withdrew to Tivoli: 665
    nearby Tivoli was once a place of exile.
The hollow flute was missed on the stage, it was missed at the altars,
    no dirge conducted the corpse on its final bed.
At Tivoli, a former slave, worthy of any rank
    you like, had long since been a free man.   670
He was getting a banquet ready at his country place and invited
    that group of musicians. They came to the festive banquet.
It was nighttime and their eyes and wits were swimming from the wine
    when a messenger came with a pre-arranged story,
and spoke like this: 'Why are you waiting to break up the party?   675
    Because, look, the man who freed you is coming.'
At once the guests bestirred legs that were shaky from the liquor.
    They stood up and stumbled on unsteady feet.
But the head of the house said, 'Get out,' and supplied
    the dawdlers a wagon with a broad wicker bed.   680
The late hour, the swaying, and the wine lulled them to sleep,
    and the drunken group thought they'd got back to Tivoli.
They'd already entered the city of Rome by way of the Esquiline.
    In the morning the wagon was in the middle of the Forum.
In order to fool the Senate about their appearance and numbers,   685
    Plautius told them to mask their faces,

and mixed in others, and, so that female flutists could increase
    this company, had them appear in long robes.
The returning exiles could thus be well-protected from censure
    for coming back against his colleague's edict.   690
The scheme won approval, and so on the Ides they can employ this strange
    get-up, and sing ribald lyrics to ancient melodies."
When Minerva finished this lesson, I said, "I still have to learn
    why that day has been called the Quinquatrus."
"In March," she said, "a festival of mine by that name takes place.   695
    This group of flutists is another among my discoveries.
I was the first to make the long flute produce sounds
    by drilling holes at intervals in boxwood.
I liked the sound. When my face was reflected in clear water
    I saw my girlish cheeks puffed out.   700
'Too high a price for art; so long, flute of mine,' I said;
    the turf on the bank caught what I'd discarded.
A satyr was perplexed when first he found it and didn't know its function,
    but he noticed it produced sound when he blew it.
But soon by fingering he let out air or held it in,   705
    and already he bragged of his skill to the nymphs.
He even challenged Apollo. When Apollo won, he was strung up
    and his flayed skin fell away from his flesh.
But still, I am the inventor and the founder of this music,
    which is why that art observes my holiday."   710

15 June

The third night will come, on which you'll stand out visible,
    you Hyades from Dodona, on the brow of Europa's Bull.
This is the day on which you'll send the scourings of Vesta
    seaward, Tiber, by your Tuscan waters.

16 June

If one can trust winds at all, sailors, give your canvas to the West Wind.   715
    Tomorrow it will come up favorable on your waters.

17 June

But when the father of Phaethon's sisters has soaked his rays
    in the waves, and peaceful stars ring the twin poles,

Orion will raise his mighty arms from the ground.
On the following night the Dolphin will be visible. 720
As everyone knows, this date once witnessed Volscians and Aequi
routed in the fields of Mount Algidus' territory.
From there Tubertus, famed for his victory over neighbors of Rome,
afterward rode in triumph on snow white horses.

19 June

By now six days and six again are left of the month, 725
if you just add one day to that number.
The sun is leaving the Twins and the sign of the Crab grows red.
Minerva's worship on the Aventine began today.

20 June

Laomedon's daughter-in-law Aurora now rises and banishes
the night, and the damp dew flees the meadows. 730
A temple, they say, was rendered to Summanus, whoever he is,
at the time when Romans had Pyrrhus to fear.[16]
When the Nereids have welcomed this day too in their father's waves,
and the earth is filled with untroubled rest,
the young man blasted by his grandfather Jupiter's weapons rises 735
and reaches out hands that are bound by twin snakes.
Phaedra's love for Hippolytus is famous, famous is Theseus' harm:
that gullible man invoked a curse on his own son.
Punished for respecting his father, the young man was driving to Troezen.
A bull came breasting through the opposing waters. 740
The skittish horses are terrified—it's useless to rein them in—
they drag their master over crags and boulders.
Hippolytus fell from the chariot, but his arms and legs stayed strapped
so he was carried along by his mangled body
and gave up his life, much to Diana's outrage. "No reason 745
for grief," says Apollo's son Aesculapius,
"for I will give this pious young man his life back unscathed,
and the grim Fates will yield to my skill."
At once he brought out from an ivory casket the herbs
which had previously profited the spirit of Glaucus 750
when the seer Polyidus resorted to herbs he'd observed
one snake bring to the aid of another.
Thrice he daubed Hippolytus' chest, thrice spoke words of healing.

He lifted his head from the ground where he'd let it drop.
Diana hid him a long way back in her grove and glade: 755
    at the Lake of Aricia he is called Virbius.
But Pluto and the Fates were aggrieved, they for an interrupted
    life-thread, he for decrease in his realm's authority.
Fearing a precedent, Jupiter aimed his lightning at the one
    who had wielded the power of too much skill.   760
You kept complaining, Apollo. Your son's a god, make up with your father:
    for your sake he did the very thing he forbad.

22 June

No matter your hurry to conquer, Augustus, I would not want you
    to strike camp if the bird report forbids it.
Let Flaminius and the shores of Lake Trasimene be your evidence   765
    that the impartial gods use birds for many a warning.
If you want to know the reckless date of that ancient disaster,[17]
    it's the tenth day from the end of the month.

23 June

The following day is better. Our ally Masinissa defeated Syphax
    and Hannibal's brother fell by his own sword.   770

24 June

Time slips away and we grow old in the course of the noiseless
    years, and the days, unbridled, run away.
How quickly the day for honoring Fors Fortuna has come!
    After seven more days June will be over.
Go on, citizens, joyfully celebrate the goddess of Fortune.   775
    Her temple across the Tiber was a gift from a king.
Hurry on down, some on foot, and some aboard swift skiffs,
    and don't be ashamed to get home drunk from there.
You garlanded boats, bring over parties of young men.
    Drink lots of wine out on the water.   780
The people worship her, since her temple's founder was a man of the people,
    and rose to the throne from a lowly station.
She suits slaves too, since Servius, the son of a slavewoman,
    set up the nearby temple for the changeable goddess.

25–26 June

Look, someone not at all sober coming home from the temple   785
    across the river tosses off this remark to the stars:
"Your belt is hidden now, and tomorrow perhaps it will be.
    But then, Orion, you'll have to let me see it."
If he hadn't been drunk, he would have said that the date
    of the solstice would come the same day.   790

27–28 June

Next morning comes the date when the Lares were given a temple,
    here where accomplished hands lay many a garland.
Jupiter the Stayer has the same foundation date for the temple
    Romulus established facing the Palatine hill.

29 June

As many days of the month remain as the Fates have names,   795
    when a temple was given to Quirinus of the royal robe.

30 June

Tomorrow the Kalends of July will have its birthday.
    Muses, add the last details to my venture.
Tell me, Muses, who assigned your custody to that hero
    whose stepmother unwillingly conceded defeat?   800
Clio answered: "You see the monument of illustrious Phillipus
    from whom virtuous Marcia[18] derives her rank,
Marcia, a name come down from priestly King Ancus.
    Her features are the equal of her noble rank.
Equally her beauty corresponds to her soul; in her   805
    are rank and beauty and character all together.
Don't think it's disgraceful for us to praise beauty;
    we praise goddesses on this point as well.
The Emperor's aunt was once married to Philippus' father.
    What a glorious woman, worthy of this hallowed household!"   810
That's what Clio sang, and her accomplished sisters agreed.
    Hercules approved with a twang of his lyre.

Glossary of Proper Names

Acastus: purified Peleus of involuntary homicide

Acca: foster mother of Romulus and Remus; also called Acca Larentia

Achates: companion of Aeneas

Achilles: Greek hero of the Trojan War; son of Peleus and Thetis

Acis: river in Sicily

Adonis: son of Myrrha by her own father Cinyras; loved by Venus; became a flower

Adrastus: king of Argos, father-in-law of Tydeus, grandfather of Diomedes

Aeacus: grandfather of Achilles

Aegeus: king of Athens, father of Theseus

Aeneas: son of Venus and Anchises; refugee to Italy after Trojan War; Roman national hero

Aeolus: king of the winds

Aequi: ancient mountain people of Italy, conquered by Rome in the 4th century BC

Aequiculi: another name for the Aequi (see above)

Aesculapius: in Greek, Asclepius; son of Apollo and Coronis; as a constellation, called Ophiuchus, the "Serpent Holder" (6.733-62)

Aethra: mother of the Hyades

Africa: for the Romans, this was *North* Africa

"Africanus": *cognomen* of P. Cornelius Scipio the Elder for victory over the Carthaginian Hannibal in 202 BC, and of his adopted son, P. Cornelius Scipio Aemilianus the Younger, for the final conquest of Carthage in 146 BC

Agamemnon: king of Mycenae, leader of Greek expedition against Troy

Agnalia: a supposed earlier variant of the Agonalia (see below), derived from *agnus* ("lamb")

Agonal: related to the Agonalia (see below)

Agonalia: the name (meaning unknown) for festivals in January, March, May, and December, for a different deity on each occasion

Agrigento: modern name for Acragas in Sicily

Agrippa: an Alban king; a descendant of Aeneas' son Julus

Alba: great-grandson of Julus, Aeneas' son

Alba Longa: old town in Latium, birthplace of Romulus and Remus

Albans: inhabitants of Alba Longa (see above)

Albula: earlier name for the Tiber River

Alcmaeon: son of Amphiaraus; murdered his mother Eriphyle for her betrayal of his father, purified of blood-guilt by river Achelous

Alcyone: one of the Pleiades

Alernus: a god, otherwise unknown, with a grove beside the Tiber

Algidus (Mount): Alban hill between towns of Velletri and Tusculum

Almo: river, tributary of the Tiber

Altar of Peace: Altar of Augustan Peace, dedicated in the Campus Martius on 30 January 9 BC in honor of Augustus' safe return from Gaul and Spain in 13 BC

Amalthaea: Cretan Naiad; hid infant Jupiter whom her she-goat nursed

Amenanus: river in Sicily

Ampelos: a boy loved by Bacchus

Amulius: usurped Alban throne from his brother Numitor; uncle of Silvia; ordered Romulus and Remus drowned at birth

Anapus: river in Sicily

Anchises: father of Aeneas

Ancus (King): Ancus Martius, fourth king of Rome

Andromache: wife of the Trojan hero Hector; daughter of Eetion, king of Mysia

Anna: 1. sister of Dido, queen of Carthage
2. old woman of Bovillae (see below)

Anna Perenna: female personification of the year (*annus*) and the continual (*perennis*) succession of years

Antenor: a Trojan; advised surrendering Helen to make peace with the Greeks; after the war, founder of Padua

Antony: Marcus Antonius (83-30 BC); fought on Caesar's side in civil war against Pompey; in aftermath of Caesar's assassination, fought against Octavian at the siege of Modena in April 43, reconciled with him later that year; ultimately fell out with Octavian and was defeated (with Cleopatra) by him at Actium in 31; committed suicide in 30 BC

Aphidna: scene of the fight between the Gemini and Idas and Lynceus

Aphrodite: goddess of love; in Latin, Venus (see below)

Apollo: god associated with prophecy, medicine, music; called Phoebus ("Shining") and identified with the sun; the epithet *Clarius* (1.20) refers to his oracle in the Ionian town of Claros; he is called *Paeon* (4.263), the name of another healing god; as *Smintheus* (6.425), he was worshipped in a temple at Chryse in the Troad as the defender of farmers against mice (*sminthus* was Trojan for "mouse")

Appius: Appius Claudius Caecus ("the Blind"); as censor in 312 BC, built the Appian Road and Aqueduct; in 279/8, persuaded Senate to reject peace treaty with Pyrrhus (see below)

Apulian: from region of Apulia in southern Italy

Aquarius: constellation

Arcadia: region of Greece, central Peloponnese, area south of isthmus of Corinth

Arcadian: from or in Arcadia; a race of people believed to predate the moon and proverbial for their primitive culture (2.289-300)

Arcas: eponymous hero of Arcadia; son of Jupiter and Callisto (see below); he and his mother became constellations (see "Bear Keeper" below)

Archimedes: Sicilian scientist (3rd century BC)

Ardea: town besieged by King Tarquin; the rape of Lucretia (see below) occurred during the siege

Arethusa: nymph of a spring in Sicily

Argei: human effigies, thrown into the Tiber on 14 May (5.621-62)

Argonaut: crewman on the Argo's voyage in search of the Golden Fleece

Argos: important Greek city in the Peloponnese

Ariadne: daughter of Pasiphae and Minos of Crete; gave Theseus the thread which led him out of the Labyrinth; after Theseus abandoned her on the island of Naxos, Dionysus rescued her and later commemorated her with the constellation of the Crown (3.459-516)

Aricia: town in the Alban hills, on a lake of the same name; site of grove sacred to Diana (3.261-72)

Arion: mythical singer and lyre-player; rescued by a dolphin (2.79-118)

Aristaeus: son of Apollo and nymph Cyrene; a beekeeper, he learned a technique for regenerating his lost swarm (1.363-80)

Ascra (Mount): site in Boeotia (see below) of the epiphany of the Muses to the poet Hesiod

Assaracus: a Trojan; "brother" (actually, distant cousin) of Tithonus (see below)

Athamas: husband of Ino, father of Helle and Phrixus

Athena: goddess of wisdom; in Latin, Minerva (see below)

Atlas: Titan who supports the heavens on his shoulders; father of the Hyades and Pleiades

Atreus: father of Agamemnon and Menelaus

Attalus: Attalus I Soter (269–197 BC); king of Pergamum when Cybele (see below) was brought to Rome

Attis: priest of Cybele whose self-castration explains why her priests are eunuchs (4.221-44)

Augustus: 63 BC–AD 14, first Roman Emperor (see Introduction, pp. 17–22 and *passim*)

Aurora: goddess of dawn

Avenger: epithet of Mars (see below)

Aventine: one of the hills of Rome

Aventinus: an Alban king

Azanis: an Arcadian nymph

Bacchus: Greek god of wine, also called Dionysus; son of Zeus and Semele; identified by Romans with Italian god Liber; worshipped at the Liberalia, in March; epithet *Lyaeus* (1.395) means "the loosener" (i.e., "loosener of cares")

Battus: king of Malta (according to Ovid; usually, one of several kings of Cyrene)

Bear Keeper: constellation Ursa Minor, originally Arcas (see above)

Bear(s): the constellations

Bellerophon: Greek hero who rode Pegasus and killed the Chimera

Bellona: a goddess of war

Berecyntian: of Berecyntia, a Phrygian city and mountain; epithet of Cybele

Boeotia: region of Greece NW of Athens; home of the Muses

Bootes: constellation of the "Herdsman"; another name for Bear Keeper (see above)

Bovillae: town about 12 miles south of Rome on the Appian Way

Bowl: part of a constellation, with Raven and Snake (2.243-66)

Briareus: a hundred-armed giant

Brutus: 1. Lucius Junius Brutus; traditional founder of Roman Republic and its first consul in 509 BC
2. Decimus Junius Brutus; consul, 138 BC; earned *cognomen* "Callaicus" (after the Callaici, a people in Spain) for military successes in Spain

Cacus: monster; son of Vulcan; killed by Hercules at the future site of Rome

Cadmus: founder of Greek city of Thebes

Caelian: one of the hills of Rome

Caesar: Gaius Julius Caesar (100–44 BC); became *pontifex maximus* (3.699) in 73 BC; in coalition, so-called First Triumvirate, with Pompey (see below) and Crassus (see below); consul in 59 BC; war with Gauls, 58–49; civil war, including battle of Thapsus (see below) against Pompey, 49–45; his Julian calendar (3.155-67) went into effect in January 45; named dictator for life in 44; assassinated 15 March 44 (3.697-710); adoptive father of Augustus (3.157)

Calabrian: of Calabria, region in SE Italy

Callaican: of the Callaici, a people of NW Spain (modern Galicia)

Calliope: one of the Muses (epic poetry); explains "May" as derived from "Maia" (5.81-106)

Callisto: a nymph; raped by Jupiter; turned into a bear by Juno, became the Bear constellation (2.155-92)

Calpetus: a descendant of Julus, Aeneas' son

Camere: territory near Crathis river (see below)

Camerina: city on S coast of Sicily

Camillus: Marcus Furius Camillus (4th century BC); as dictator, captured Veii ca. 396 BC (see below); saved Rome from Gallic invasion, 387 BC; dedicated temples of Concord in 367 BC (1.641-44) and Juno Moneta in 344 BC (6.183-84)

Capena Gate: gate at Rome on the Appian Way

Capitol: one of the hills of Rome; location of temple of Jupiter Best and Greatest

Capitoline: another name for the Capitol (see above)

Capricorn: constellation

Capta: epithet of Minerva (see below), "the Captive"; so-called because Romans brought her to Rome as a prisoner after capture of Falerii, headquarters of Italian cult of Minerva (3.843-44)

Capys: 1. father of Anchises
2. a descendant of Aeneas' son Julus

Caristia: festival on 22 February, with a meal renewing ties between living kin; after Feralia the preceding day, the last day of Parentalia (see below)

Carmenta: alternate spelling of Carmentis (see below), which I use for the sake of euphony

Carmental Gate: gate at foot of Capitol, near the shrine and altar of Carmentis (see below); in legend the Fabii marched out its right-hand arch to Cremera (see below)

Carmentis: originally, an Italian goddess of women and childbirth; in myth, an Arcadian goddess of prophecy, mother of Evander (see below); epithets "Porrima" (see below) and "Postverta" (see below)

Carna: very old goddess, whom Ovid misidentifies with Cardea, a goddess of hinges

Carseoli: a town of the Aequi, 42 miles E of Rome; became a Latin colony ca. 298 BC

Carthage: city in N Africa; Rome's enemy in the Punic Wars over control of the western Mediterranean

Carthaginian(s): inhabitant(s) of Carthage

Castor: one of the Gemini (see below)

Cattle Market: district of Rome (in Latin, *Forum Boarium*)

Celaenae: town in Phrygia

Celaeno: one of the Pleiades

Celer: assistant of Romulus who killed Remus

Celeus: received Ceres at Eleusis after her wanderings in search of Proserpina

Centaur: Chiron (see below)

Ceres: goddess of grain, called Demeter in Greek; wandered from Sicily to Eleusis in search of her daughter Proserpina, who was abducted by the god of the Underworld (4.417-618)

Changer of Hearts: epithet of Venus (see below)

Chaos: original formless condition of the universe

Charybdis: a monster, whirlpool, in the straits between Italy and Sicily

Chiron: centaur, tutor of Achilles; became a constellation after he was accidentally poisoned by Hercules' arrow (5.379-414)

Chloris: earlier name of goddess Flora

Cinyras: grandfather (and father, by his own daughter Myrrha) of Adonis

Circe: daughter of the Sun, a witch; encountered by Odysseus on his return home; one tradition located her home on the coast of Latium, at the headland of Circeium

Circus Flaminius: racetrack in the Campus Martius built by Flaminius (see below) when he was censor in 220 BC

Circus Maximus: racetrack in the valley between Palatine and Capitoline Hills

Claudia Quinta: granddaughter of Appius Claudius (see above); involved, miraculously, in the final stage of the Great Mother's arrival in Rome (4.305-44)

Clausus: legendary ancestor of the Claudian family

Clio: one of the Muses (history)

Closer: epithet of Janus (see below)

Colchis: country on SE side of Black Sea; Jason's destination in quest for Golden Fleece

Collatia: Sabine town near Rome

Collatinus: husband of Lucretia

Colline Gate: gate at NE end of Quirinal Hill

Concord: goddess Concordia; temple at W end of Forum (1.637-59) vowed in 367 BC by Camillus (see above), restored in 121 BC, rededicated as Concordia Augusta ("Augustan Concord") by Tiberius in AD 10; her worship gained renewed importance in Augustan propaganda

Consus: god of the grain storage bin; one of his festivals was the occasion for the Rape of the Sabine Women

Corinth: city at isthmus connecting Peloponnese and central Greece

Corniculum: town near Collatia (see above); home of Ocresia, mother of Servius Tullius (see below)

Coronis: nymph; mother of Aesculapius

Corybantes: one of two groups who safeguarded the infant Zeus (Jupiter) by making noise to drown out his crying

Cosyra: island near Malta

Covered Way: (*Via Tecta* in Latin); probably a colonnade on the Appian Way, mentioned only here; not identical with Covered Way in Campus Martius

Crab: constellation Cancer

Cranaë: nymph who became goddess Carna (see above); not mentioned elsewhere, perhaps invented by Ovid

Crassus: Marcus Licinius Crassus Dives (ca. 112–53 BC); made his wealth (hence his *cognomen*, "the Wealthy") on the Sullan side in the civil war against Marius; consul in 70 and again in 55 as member of the coalition called the First Triumvirate; after second consulship, took an army to the East, where he was defeated and killed by Parthians at Carrhae (5.583-84)

Crathis: river at toe of Italy

Cremera: little river in Etruria; scene of ambush and massacre of Fabian clan (2.195-242)

Cretan: of Crete

"Creticus": *cognomen* won by Quintus Caecilius Metellus (consul, 69 BC) for conquest of Crete in 69–67 BC

Crocus: boy transformed into saffron flower

Crown (Ariadne's): constellation

Cupid: son of Venus

Cures: Sabine capital

Curetes: one of two groups who safeguarded the infant Zeus (Jupiter) by making noise to drown out his crying

Curius: vowed the Lares Praestites, otherwise unknown; perhaps not the correct reading

Curtius (Lake): once a pond, dry ground in Ovid's time, in the middle of the Forum

Cyane: a spring in Sicily

Cybele: 1. goddess, also known as the Great Mother
2. mountain in Phrygia

Cyclades: islands in S Aegean

Cyclopes: three mythical smiths

Cyllene (Mount): in Arcadia, birthplace of Mercury (Hermes)

Cynosura: name for one of the Bears

Cynurian: of Cynuria, territory disputed between Sparta and Argos (see Book 2, n. 10 on lines 663-66)

Cythera: island associated with Aphrodite (Venus)

Dardanus: son of Jupiter and one of the Pleiades; Trojan ancestor of Aeneas

Daunus: S Italian king; father-in-law of Greek hero Diomedes

Dawn: besides "Aurora" (see above), Ovid calls her "Eos" (Greek equivalent of "dawn," 3.877), "Pallantias" ("daughter of Pallas," 4.373; only Ovid gives that paternity), "Tithonia" ("wife of Tithonus," 4.943), and "Hyperionis" ("daughter of Hyperion," 5.159)

Delphi: location in Greece of the most famous oracle of Apollo

Deucalion: son of Prometheus; he and his wife Pyrrha were sole survivors of flood sent by Zeus to destroy the human race

Diana: goddess of the moon, the hunt, and childbirth; called Artemis in Greek; Ovid also calls her "Cynthia" (e.g., 2.92, goddess of Mt. Cynthius on Delos, her birthplace), "Phoebe" (e.g., 2.163, identifying her with a Titan later identified with the moon goddess), "Dictynna" (6.755, virgin goddess on Crete, identified with Artemis); "Diana of the Crossroads" is Hecate (see below)

Dicte (Mount): mountain on Crete

Didius: Titus Didius (consul, 98 BC); general in Spain, 98–94 BC; fought in Social War in Campania; died in June 89 BC

Dido: queen of Carthage; sister of Anna; fell in love with Aeneas on his way to Italy

Dindyme: volcanic island N of Sicily

Dindymus: mountain in Phrygia, near Pessinus, the sacred city of Cybele

Diomedes: Greek warrior in the Trojan War

Dis: god of the Underwold, also known as Hades (Greek) or Pluto (Roman)

Dodona: city in NW Greece; site of famous oracle of Zeus; home of the Hyades

Dog Star: Sirius

Dolphin: constellation; rescued the singer Arion

Drusus: 1. Nero Claudius Drusus (38–9 BC); son of Livia, younger brother of Tiberius, father of Germanicus
2. Julius Caesar Drusus (13 BC–AD 23); son of Tiberius, designated as his successor in AD 22, adoptive brother of Germanicus

Dryads: tree nymphs

Earth: Roman earth goddess, in Latin *Tellus* (e.g., 1.671) or *Terra* (e.g., 1.673); involved in ritual at *feriae Sementivae* ("Sowing Day") and Fordicidia

Egeria: a spring nymph and wife of King Numa

Electra: one of the Pleiades

Eleusis: town near Athens; location of Eleusinian Mysteries; rites in honor of Demeter (Ceres) and Persephone (Proserpina)

Elicius: epithet of Jupiter (see below)

Epytus: descendant of Aeneas' son Julus

Equirria: festival in honor of Mars

Erato: one of the Muses (erotic poetry); answers Ovid's questions about Cybele (4.195-372)

Ericthonius: son of Dardanus; one of Aeneas' Trojan ancestors

Erycina: epithet of Venus (see below)

Eryx (Mount): mountain in Sicily

Esquiline: one of hills of Rome

Etna (Mount): volcano on Sicily; believed to rest on Typhoeus, a giant

Etruscan: of Etruria, region of Italy N of Latium, W of Appennines

Euboea: island in Aegean off coast of Boeotia (see above)

Euphrates: river, one of boundaries of ancient Mesopotamia

Europa: sister of Cadmus, abducted by Jupiter disguised as a bull

Evander: Arcadian exile; son of Carmentis, settled at site of Rome

Evening (Star): in Latin, *Hesperos*

Fabian: of the family of the Fabii (see below)

Fabians: 1. Fabii (see below)
2. one of two priestly boards of Luperci (see below)

Fabii: Roman family; traced its descent from Hercules (2.238); 306 members died at Cremera (see above 2.195-96); cf. Introduction, p. 5

Falerian: of Falerii

Falerii: Etruscan city, center of Italian cult of Minerva

Faliscans: people of Falerii

Fate(s): three female deities, presiding over human destiny; sometimes (e.g., 3.801) Ovid uses the Latin name *Parcae*

Father of His Country: in Latin, *pater patriae*, title given Augustus in 2 BC

Faunus: rustic god, identified with Pan; his temple on Tiber Island was dedicated 194 BC; the Lupercalia was a festival in his honor

Faustulus: foster father of Romulus and Remus

"Feast of Fools": alternative name for Quirinalia, in honor of Quirinus, Sabine god identified with apotheosized Romulus

Fenestella Gate: location unknown; "fenestella" means "little window"

Fidius: god whose full name is Semo Sancus Dius Fidius; meaning of "Semo Sancus" is unknown, but "Deus Fidius" is the Zeus (Jupiter) of good faith (*fides* in Latin)

Fish: constellation Pisces; rescued Venus and Cupid

Flaminius: Gaius Flaminius (consul in 223 and 217 BC; censor in 220); defeated at Trasimene by Hannibal, 217 BC, after he disregarded augury before the battle (according to sources hostile to his politics)

Flora: goddess of flowers and plants

182

Formiae: city on coast of Latium

Fors Fortuna: Italian goddess identified with Tyche, Greek goddess of luck; dedication day of her two temples across the Tiber, 24 June, was a festival in her honor (6.771-84)

Fortune: goddess of luck; as Firstborn Public Fortune of the Roman People (*Fortuna Publica populi Romani Primigenia*), she had three temples on the Quirinal (4.375; 5.729); as Fortune the Maiden (*Fortuna Virgo*), she had a temple in the Cattle Market (6.569); as Manly Fortune (*Fortuna Virilis*), she was worshipped along with Venus at the Veneralia (4.145). Outside Rome at Praeneste (modern Palestrina), she had a huge temple complex, including an oracle (6.62)

Forum: original religious, commercial, and governmental center of Rome was the Forum Romanum, with later additions by Caesar, Augustus and other emperors

Furies: avenging spirits

Gabii: city in Latium near Rome; fell to treacherous machinations of Sextus Tarquin

Galli: eunuch priests of Cybele

Gallic: of Gaul (modern France)

Gallus: river in Bithynia

Ganymede: Trojan boy, loved by Zeus (Jupiter); became cup-bearer of the gods

Gela: river in S Sicily

Gemini: Castor and Pollux, twin sons of Jupiter and Leda; fought sons of Leucippus (5.699-720); became constellation of Gemini; also called "Dioscuri" ("sons of Zeus"), they had a temple (Temple of Castor) in the Forum

"Germanicus": *cognomen* of elder Drusus (see above), awarded posthumously in AD 9 for his successes as commander in Germany

Germanicus Caesar: (15 BC–AD 19) born Nero Claudius Germanicus, son of the elder Drusus (see above); became Germanicus Julius Caesar upon adoption by Tiberius in AD 4; had military commands in Germany and the East, where he died; the *Fasti* begins with a dedication to him (see Introduction p. 4)

Germany: for Ovid's original readers, the area bounded by the Rhine and the Danube, an area of military campaigns by Tiberius, Drusus, and Germanicus

Geryon: giant in Spain; his cattle were stolen by Hercules

Giants: children of Earth, who attempted assault on heaven

Glaucus: son of Minos; restored to life by the seer Polyidus (see below)

Good Goddess: *Bona Dea*; had a temple on Aventine; worshipped by women only

Good Sense: *Mens Bona*; had a temple on Capitoline, dedicated 215 BC

Graces: in Greek, *Charites*; goddesses personifying charm, grace, and beauty; Roman painting of three nude Graces is copy of famous Hellenistic original

Grape Picker: constellation, once the boy Ampelos, loved by Bacchus (3.403-14)

Great Bear: constellation, originally Callisto (see above)

Great Mother: also known as Cybele; brought from Pessinus in Phrygia to Rome in 204 BC (4.249-348)

Halaesus: either Agamemnon's companion or his bastard son, who fled to Falerii after Agamemnon's murder

Hannibal: Carthaginian general in Second Punic War; his younger brother Hasdrubal died in battle at Metaurus in 207 BC

Harpies: monsters, part bird and part woman

Hebrus (River): large river in Thrace

Hecate: in classical Athens, a goddess of ghosts and magic; became associated with Artemis, and hence with Diana; one manifestation was as a goddess of crossroads, Trivia

Hector: son of King Priam; chief defender of Troy against the Greeks, pre-eminent Trojan warrior

Helen: wife of Menelaus, "cause" of the Trojan War when Priam's son Paris abducted her

Helice: name for one of the Bear constellations

Helicon: mountain in Boeotia; home of the Muses

Helle: daughter of Athamas; as she and brother Phrixus were escaping their stepmother on the back of the ram with the golden fleece, she fell into the sea

Hellespont: modern Dardanelles, strait between Europe and Turkey, where Helle (see above) fell; the name means "sea of Helle"

Helorus: river in SE Sicily

Henna: town in central Sicily where Rape of Proserpina took place

Hercules: the great hero (Heracles in Greek); emblems are club and lion's skin; Chiron was accidentally poisoned by one of his arrows (5.387-414); visited site of Rome during Evander's reign, killed Cacus, and founded an altar (1.543-82); as Hercules Custos (the Guardian), he had a temple near Circus Flaminius (6.209-12); as Hercules Musarum (of the Muses), he had a temple in which there was a statue of the Muses and him playing a lyre (6.797-812)

Hernician: ancient people of Latium near Lanuvium and Alba

Himera: city on N coast of Sicily

Hippocrene: spring in Boeotia on Helicon created by Pegasus' hoof; the name means "horse spring"

Hippolytus: son of Theseus and an Amazon; his preference for Artemis (Diana) over Aphrodite (Venus) ultimately led to his death (6.737-56); called Virbius at grove of Aricia

Homer: Greek epic poet

Honor: an allegorical figure, one of the parents of "Majesty"

Hyacinthus: Spartan boy loved by Apollo and accidentally killed by him

Hyades: constellation, sisters of Hyas

Hyas: son of Atlas, brother of Hyades (5.169-80)

Hydra: many-headed monster killed by Hercules

Hyrieus: "father" of Orion (see below)

Iarbas: a suitor rejected by Dido

Icarian: of Icarus, Athenian who disseminated knowledge of wine

Icarian (Sea): named for Icarus, son of Daedalus, who fell into it while flying on artificial wings made by his father

Icarus: son of Daedalus, architect of the Labyrinth

Ida (Mount): 1. mountain on Crete associated with Jupiter's infancy (4.207; 5.116)
2. mountain near Troy, seat of the Great Mother (4.79, 182)

Idas: brother of Lynceus; killed by Zeus with thunderbolt during fight with the Gemini

Ides: 15th of March, May, July, and October; 13th of other months

Ilia: mother of Romulus and Remus; also called Silvia

Ilium: another name for Troy

Ilus: founder of Troy; great-grandson of Dardanus (see above)

"Imperator": this honorific title for victorious generals was a sort of temporary *cognomen* during the Republican period; around 45 BC Julius Caesar used it as a permanent *cognomen*; Octavian first won the title in 43 BC (4.673-76) at Modena (see below), and around 40 he began to use it as his *praenomen*, calling himself *Imperator Caesar* (see Introduction p. 20)

Inachus: 1. river in Argos
2. father of Io (see below)

Inhibition: *Metus* in Latin; apparently Ovid's own personification

Ino: daughter of Cadmus, second wife of Athamas; persecuted her stepchildren Helle and Phrixus; sister of Semele, she cared for infant Dionysus; when Athamas went mad, she and son Melicertes escaped and she became sea deity Leucothea or Mater Matuta, worshipped at the Matralia (6.475-550)

Io: raped by Jupiter; as a cow, she wandered, harassed by a gadfly

Ionia: W coast of Asia Minor, settled by Greeks

Ionian (Sea): W of Greece

Iphigenia: Agamemnon's daughter, sacrificed by him at the beginning of the Trojan War

Isis: Egyptian goddess, identified with Io

Ismarus: mountain in S Thrace

Ithacan: inhabitant of the island of Ithaca, kingdom of Ulysses

Itys: son of Procne (see below), murdered by her to avenge her husband Tereus' rape of her sister Philomela

Janiculum: one of the hills of Rome

Janus: a god of beginnings; represented with two heads (e.g., 1.65-66)); epithets "Closer" (*Clusius*, 1.130) and "Opener" (*Patulcius*, 1.129); received sacrifice at Agonalia in January (1.317-18); after raping nymph Cranaë, he compensated her with a magic whitethorn branch (6.119-30); assisted Romans during war with Sabines, 1.259-74); the Janus Geminus or Janus Quirinus was a freestanding gate named for the god on N side of Forum (1.257-58), left open in wartime, but closed in peacetime (1.279-82)

Jason: Greek hero who went on quest for Golden Fleece

Jove: archaic English for Jupiter

Juba: king of Numidia, allied with Pompey in civil war out of resentment for Caesar; he escaped after defeat at Thapsus in N Africa by Caesar in April 46 BC and committed suicide

Julia Augusta: name of Livia (see below) after adoption into imperial family in Augustus' will

Julian: of the family of the Iulii, which included Julius Caesar (by birth) and Augustus (by adoption)

Julius Caesar: see "Caesar" above

Julius Proculus: man to whom deified Romulus first appeared

Julus: son of Aeneas, legendary ancestor of the Julian family

Juno: sister and wife of Jupiter; called Hera in Greek; epithets: "Deliverer" (*Sospita*) 2.55, "Bringer to Light" (*Lucina*), e.g., 2.449, a goddess of childbirth, "Warner" (*Moneta*) 6.183; sometimes (e.g., 1.266) Ovid refers to her as *Saturnia*, i.e., "daughter of Saturn" (see below)

Jupiter: chief deity, identified with Greek Zeus; deposed his father Saturn (3.795-808); spent infancy on Cretan Mount Ida (4.203-10); epithets: "Capitoline" (from temple on Capitoline Hill, 6.186), "Thunderer" (*Tonans*, 2.69), "Victorious" (*Victor*, 4.621), "Baker" (*Pistor*, 6.350), "Unconquerable" (*Invictus*, 6.650), "Stayer" (*Stator*, 6.793), by "Jupiter below" (*Jupiter Stygius*), Ovid refers to god of Underworld (5.448)

Justice: goddess who lived on earth in Golden Age; when human race degenerated, she withdrew to heaven, where she is the constellation Virgo

Juturna: 1. a pool in the Forum; also a spring at Lavinium
2. in myth, sister of Turnus

Kalends: first day of the month

Kite Star: an unidentified constellation, perhaps an error or confusion by Ovid

Labyrinth: Minotaur's "cage" on Crete

Ladon: river in Arcadia

Lady of the Hearths: reference to Vesta (see below)

Laenas: Marcus Popillius Laenas (consul, 173 BC); celebrated games for Flora, which were annual thereafter

Laestrygonians: cannibal giants whom Odysseus encountered on his return home; their king Lamas was legendary founder of Formiae (see above)

Lampsacus: Greek city in Hellespont

Lanuvium: town in the Alban Hills; site of famous temple of Juno Sospes

Laomedon: king of Troy; son of Ilus

Lara: nymph, mother of Lares; originally called "Lala"

Larentalia: festival in honor of Acca Larentia

Larentia: also called Acca Larentia; foster mother of Romulus and Remus

Lares: guardian spirits of farmland, of the home, of crossroads, of the Roman state; epithets "Standby" (*Praestites*), 5.129; "Crossroads" (*Compitales*); Augustus associated worship of his "Genius" with the Lares Compitales in the 265 wards of Rome (5.145-46; see Introduction, pp. 21–22)

Latin(s): inhabitant(s) of Latium; their language

Latinus: 1. king of Laurentum; Aeneas' father-in-law
2. grandson of Julus

Latium: region of central Italy, including Rome

Latona: mother of Apollo and Diana; called Leto in Greek

Laurentian(s): an Italian people, living in the area of Latinus' kingdom, Laurentum, a coastal town in Latium

Lausus: Silvia's brother

Lavinia: daughter of King Latinus, wife of Aeneas

Leaping Priests: Salii, priests of Mars

Learchus: son of Ino and Athamas; killed by his crazed father

Lemnos: island especially dear to Vulcan (Hephaestus)

Lemuria: festival for exorcizing family ghosts

Leo: constellation of the Lion

Leontini: city in Sicily

Lerna: home of the Hydra

Lesbian: of the island of Lesbos

Lesbos: island in the Aegean

Leucippus: father of Phoebe and Hilaeira

Leucothea: Ino's name after she became a sea deity; also, Matuta

Liber: Italian god, became identified with Bacchus

Libera: old Roman goddess, originally paired with Liber, later identified with Ariadne

Liberator: one interpretation of the meaning of "Liber"

Liberty: personification of personal liberty

Libra: constellation of the Scales

Libya: for the Romans, N Africa

Libyan: inhabitant of Libya

Lilybaeum: city on westernmost promontory of Sicily

Livia: Livia Drusilla (58 BC–AD 29); wife of Augustus; mother of Tiberius and Drusus by Tiberius Claudius Nero, whom she divorced in 39 BC in order to marry the future emperor

Lotis: nymph, whose attempted rape by Priapus was foiled by Silenus' donkey (1.391-440)

Luceres: one of three tribes established by Romulus

Lucina: goddess of childbirth; epithet of Juno (see above)

Lucretia: wife of Collatinus; monarchy ended at Rome in the aftermath of her rape by Sextus Tarquin (2.685-852)

Lupercal: cave at foot of Palatine Hill where she-wolf supposedly suckled Romulus and Remus

Luperci: priests who performed rites of Lupercalia in honor of Faunus

Lycaeus (Mount): mountain in Arcadia, location of sanctuary of Pan

Lycaon: father of Callisto; grandfather of Arcas

Lycurgus: Thracian king, punished with madness for persecution of Dionysus and his nurses; he killed his wife and children thinking they were vines, and then attacked himself

Lydian: of Lydia, country in W Asia Minor

Lynceus: brother of Idas

Lyre: constellation

Maenalus (Mount): mountain in Arcadia

Maia: one of the Pleiades; mother of Mercury (Hermes)

Maiden Aqueduct: aqueduct built by Agrippa, began operation in June 19 BC, supplied his baths in the Campus Martius, etc.

Majesty: allegorical figure, the daughter of "Honor" and "Respect"

Malta: modern name for Melite

Mamurius: metalworker, who made replicas of the heaven-sent shield for Numa, and whose name appears in the hymn of the Salii (3.379-92)

Manlius: Marcus Manlius Capitolinus, defended Capitol from Gallic sneak attack in 390 BC, executed for treason in 384 BC; his house was razed and became site for temple of Juno Moneta (6.185-90)

Manly Fortune: in Latin, *Fortuna Virilis*

Marcellus: Marcus Claudius Marcellus, captured Syracuse in 212 BC

Marcia: daughter of Lucius Marcius Philippus the younger; cousin of Augustus; wife of Paullus Fabius Maximus, Ovid's patron; see Introduction, p. 4–5

Marmara: modern name for the Propontus, sea in NW Turkey

Mars: god of war, birth contrived by Flora (5.229-60); father of Romulus and Remus (3.9-45); his bird is the woodpecker (3.37); March named in his honor by Romulus (3.71-78); duped by Anna Perenna (3.677-94); as the "Avenger" (*Ultor*), he had temple in Forum of Augustus, for avenging Caesar's assassination and Crassus' defeat at Carrhae (5.545-98); Ovid also calls him "the Marcher" (*Gradivus*, e.g., 2.861), and "the patron of war" (*pater armipotens*, e.g., 2.481)

Mars' Field: in Latin, Campus Martius; flood plain between Pincian, Quirinal, and Capitoline Hills; named for an early altar of Mars there; used for army musters, drills, meetings of Centuriate Assembly

Marsian: one of the Marsi, a central Italian people

Masinissa: king of Numidia; Roman ally in Second Punic War

Matralia: festival in honor of Mother Matuta (see below)

Matuta (Mother): *Mater Matuta*, Latin name for Ino as a sea deity; in Greek, Leucothea

Maximus: Quintus Fabius Maximus Verrucosus Cunctator (consul in 233, 228, 215, 214, 209 BC); won his *cognomen*, "Delayer," originally an insult, for his strategy of refusing to engage with Hannibal during the Second Punic War

Medea: granddaughter of Sun, who fell in love with Jason and used magic to help him get Golden Fleece

Medusa: snake-haired Gorgon; "mother" of Pegasus

Megalensia: festival in honor of Cybele, Great Mother

Megara: city in Sicily, on coast just north of Syracuse

Meleager: Greek hero who led hunt for the boar Diana sent into Calydon when she failed to receive sacrifice; killed his uncles in dispute over spoils; their sister, his mother, retaliated by throwing his talisman, a log, on the fire, thus killing him

Melicertes: son of Ino and Athamas

Memnon: son of Aurora (Dawn)

Mercury: in Greek, Hermes; wears winged sandals (5.100); invented the lyre (5.103-106), 105-106; stole brother Apollo's cattle on the day he was born (5.692); magic wand, "caduceus" (5.447; hence *Caducifer*, "Caduceus-bearer," 4.605); escort of souls to the Underworld (2.609); father of the Lares (2.611-16); "patron" of thieves (5.103); temple between Aventine and Circus, traditionally founded 495 BC, with which was associated a grain market and merchants' guild (cf. 5.669-72)

Merope: one of the Pleiades

Metanira: mother of Triptolemus

Metellus: Lucius Caecilius Metellus, as *pontifex maximus*, rescued Palladium from temple of Vesta during a fire in 241 BC (6.443); another Metellus, perhaps Quintus Caecilius Metellus Numidicus (consul, 109 BC), restored temple of Great Mother after fire in 111 BC (4.438)

Mezentius: Etruscan ally of Turnus against Aeneas

Minerva: in Greek, Athena; goddess of war and crafts (3.5-6); invented flute (6.697-702); daughter of Jupiter alone (5.231-32); wooed by Mars through Anna Perenna (3.677-96); the Palladium, statue of her from heaven, stolen from Troy during Trojan War, kept at Rome in temple of Vesta (6.421-36); festival of Quinquatrus (3.809-34); festival of Lesser Quinquatrus, including procession of flutists (6.651-710); temple of Capta Minerva (3.835-38); in Latin, Ovid also refers to her by two of Athena's epithets, Pallas (e.g., 3.7) and Tritonia (6.655)

Minos: mythical king of Crete; built Labyrinth for Minotaur

Modena: modern name for Mutina, NW of Bologna; for Octavian's defeat of Antony there in April 43 BC, he was acclaimed "Imperator" for the first time (4.627-28, 673-76)

Moneta: epithet of Juno (see above)

Moon: temple of Luna on Aventine, reportedly founded by Servius Tullius

Moor: one of the Mauri, people of N Africa

Moorish: loosely, Carthaginian

Morning Star: Lucifer, any bright planet seen in the east at dawn

Muse(s): daughters of Zeus and Memory; patrons of arts, inspire poets (e.g., 4.83); haunted Mount Helicon; associated with Apollo; identified with Latin *Camenae* (e.g., 3.275)

Mute Goddess: *dea Muta*, another name for *Tacita*, "the Silent One" (see below)

Mycenae: city in S Greece, capital of Agamemnon's kingdom

Mylae: town on N coast of Sicily

Mysia: country in NW Asia Minor

Naiad: nymph of a river or spring

Narcissus: boy who pined away with love for his own reflection in a pool; became the narcissus flower

Nasica: Publius Cornelius Scipio Nasica; appointed by Senate to receive Cybele when she arrived in Rome

❧ GLOSSARY ❧

Nemesis: personification of divine retribution

Neptune: god of the sea; in Greek, Poseidon

Nereid(s): sea nymph(s)

Nestor: king of Pylos; wise counsellor of Agamemnon at Troy

New Street: actually a very old street, running from Porta Mugonia at NE corner of Palatine to Velabrum and Porta Romana

Night: personification; not a Roman goddess; little is known of the Greek goddess

Nomentum: town about 14 miles NE of Rome

Nonacrine: of Nonacris, mountain in Arcadia

Nones: 7th of March, May, July and October; 5th of other months

North Wind: Boreas

Northwest Wind: Argestes

Numa: second king of Rome; episode with Faunus, Jupiter Elicius, and the shields (3.259-392); episode of incubation and the *forda* (4.641-72)

Numantia: town in Spain, sacked 133 BC

"Numanticus": *cognomen* of Publius Cornelius Scipio Aemilianus for his sack of Numantia (see above)

Numicius: small river in Latium, where Aeneas was supposedly buried

Numidia: country (Roman province) in N Africa, W and S of Carthage

Numidians: inhabitants of Numidia

"Numidicus": *cognomen* of Quintus Caecilius Metellus (consul, 109 BC) for successes over King Jugurtha of Numidia, 109–107 BC

Numitor: king of Alba Longa; grandfather of Romulus and Remus

Nymphs: female nature spirits

Nysa: legendary mountain in India, birthplace of Bacchus

Ocean: a primeval deity, offspring of Sky and Earth

Ocresia: mother of King Servius

Olenian: epithet of Amalthaea's goat

Olenus: one of several places; the most famous, in Achaea, had shrine of Aesculapius with frequent fertility miracles

Olympus: mountain in NE Greece (3.442); abode of the gods (5.27); the sky (3.415; 5.169)

Omphale: queen of Lydia, to whom Hercules was once enslaved; pursued unsuccessfully by Faunus (2.303-58)

Opener: epithet of Janus (see above)

Orion: constellation; on his conception, see 5.493-536, on his astrification, 5.537-44

Ortygia: island at entrance of harbor of Syracuse

Ossa: mountain in Thessaly; in assault on heaven, Giants piled Ossa on Olympus and Pelion (see below) on top of them (1.307-308; 3.439-42)

Oven Festival: the *Fornacalia*

Ovid: Publius Ovidius Naso (43 BC–AD 17); see Introduction, pp. 1–3 and *passim*

Pachynos: SE promontory of Sicily

Padua: modern name for Patavium, city in NE Italy

Paelignian: Ovid's "race" and home region in central Italy

Palaemon: Greek name of Melicertes as a sea deity; in Latin, Portunus

Palatine: one of the hills of Rome

Pales: rustic divinity, honored at Parilia (see below)

Palestrina: modern name for Praeneste, city in Latium ca. 20 miles SE of Rome, with famous oracular shrine of Fortune

Palladium: wooden image of Pallas Athena; stolen from Trojans during Trojan War; stored at Rome in temple of Vesta

Pallas: 1. Evander's son, whose death at Turnus' hand was avenged by Aeneas
2. epithet of Athena (Minerva)

Pan: Arcadian god, half-goat; identified with Roman Faunus

Pangaeum (Mount): mountain in Macedon

Panope: a Nereid

Pantagias: small river in E Sicily, flows past Leontini

Parentalia: festival honoring the dead

Parilia: festival of Pales, 21 April (4.721-806)

Paris: son of King Priam of Troy; judged beauty contest between Athena, Hera, and Aphrodite; abducted Helen

Parrhasian: of Parrhasia, region of Arcadia

Parthian(s): inhabitants of Parthia, country in W Asia S of Caspian Sea; captured Roman standards from Crassus at battle of Carrhae

Patroclus: closest companion of Achilles

Peace: cult of Peace was new creation of Augustan period; see "Altar of Peace" above

Pegasus: winged horse

Peleus: father of Achilles

Pelion: mountain in Thessaly; see "Ossa" above

Peloponnese: part of Greece south of Isthmus of Corinth

Pelorus: promontory forming NE corner of Sicily

Pentheus: son of Agave; cousin of Bacchus, who tried to stamp out his worship at Thebes; driven mad by the god, Agave and her sisters killed and dismembered Pentheus, believing he was a young lion

Perenna: see "Anna Perenna"

Pergamum: ancient Greek kingdom on coast of Asia Minor; bequeathed to Rome by its last king in 133 BC, main part of it was organized as province of "Asia" in 129 BC

Persephone: daughter of Demeter (Ceres); in Latin, Proserpina

Perseus: hero who beheaded Medusa

Persians: inhabitants of Persia

Phaedra: sister of Ariadne; wife of Theseus; stepmother of Hippolytus, with whom she fell in love at Aphrodite's instigation

Phaethon: son of the Sun (Helios/Phoebus), who borrowed his father's chariot and crashed, causing widespread destruction on earth

Philippi: town in E Macedonia where Octavian and Antony defeated Brutus and Cassius in 42 BC

Philippus: 1. Lucius Marcius Philippus the younger (suffect, i.e., honorary, consul, 38 BC); husband of the younger Atia (sister of his father's second wife); father of Marcia
2. Lucius Marcius Philippus the elder (consul, 56 BC); father of the above; second husband of Augustus' mother, the elder Atia

Philyra: mother of the centaur Chiron

Phineus: Thracian king, blinded by the gods and harassed by Harpies (see above); rescued by Argonauts, whom he then advised on their route to Golden Fleece

Phoebe: daughter of Leucippus, sister of Hilaeira

Phoenician: from or of Phoenicia, ancient Mediterranean kingdom in Syria, Lebanon, and Israel; Ovid actually uses the adjectives "Tyrian" (e.g., 1.489) and "Sidonian" (e.g., 3.108), derived from the cities of Tyre and Sidon

Pholoe (Mount): mountain in NW Arcadia

Phrixus: son of Athamas; escaped stepmother Ino with sister Helle (see above) on the back of the ram with the Golden Fleece

Phrygia: country in central and western Asia Minor

Phrygian: of Phrygia

Picus: a rustic Italian deity, involved with Faunus in episode of Numa and Jupiter Elicius (3.285-328)

Piraeus: harbor of Athens

Pisces: constellation of the Fish; rescued Venus and Cupid (2.459-72)

Plautius: Gaius Plautius; censor, 312 BC; involved in fluteplayers' "strike" of 311 BC

Pleiades: constellation of the Seven Sisters, daughters of Atlas; on why only six of the seven usually appear, 4.169-78

Pleione: mother of the Pleiades

Pluto: god of the Underworld; in Greek, Hades

Pollux: one of the Gemini (see above)

Polyhymnia: one of the Muses (mime); derives "May" from "Majesty" (5.9-52)

Polyidus: a seer who restored Glaucus (see above) to life with an herb he saw one snake use to resurrect another

Pompey the Great: Gnaeus Pompeius Magnus (106–48 BC); general and politician, called "the Great" after 81 BC; member of First Triumvirate with Caesar and Crassus; actions as sole consul of 52 BC led to civil war with Caesar; defeated at Pharsalus (48 BC), escaped to Egypt and was murdered

"Porrima": epithet of Carmentis (see above) as goddess of childbirth; Ovid explains her as Carmentis' "sister" or "fellow refugee"

Portunus: Latin name for Melicertes as a sea deity; in Greek, Palaemon

Postumius: Lucius Postumius Albinus (consul, 173 BC); celebrated games for Flora which were annual thereafter

Postumus: Silvius Postumus, son of Julus

"Postverta": epithet of Carmentis (see above) as goddess of childbirth; Ovid explains her as Carmentis' "sister" or "fellow refugee"

Priam: king of Troy

Priapus: ithyphallic god, whose statues were used in gardens as scarecrows (1.391); attempted rape of Lotis (1.391-440) and of Vesta (6.319-46); donkey sacrifice at Lampsacus (1.439-40; 6.345-46)

Proca: an Alban king; attacked by screech-owl as a baby and rescued by Cranaë (6.143-68)

Procne: mother of Itys (see above)

Proserpina: Ceres' daughter; abducted by god of Underworld; in Greek, Persephone

Proteus: shape-changing prophetic sea god

Public Fortune: see "Fortune" above

Publician: 1. of the family Publicius (see below)

             2. road up Aventine

Publicius: family name of two plebeian aediles, Lucius and Manlius Publicius Malleolus, who built the Publician road with fines from violators of Licinian law (5.283-94)

Pygmalion: brother of Dido and Anna

Pygmy: member of race of dwarves in Ethiopia, supposedly always at war with the cranes

Pyrrhus: king of Epirus (319–272 BC); offered Rome honorable peace terms after defeating them in battle in 280 BC, but Appius Claudius persuaded the Senate not to accept

Pythagoras: Greek philosopher; emigrated from Samos to Croton in S Italy ca. 531 BC

Quinquatrus: festivals of Minerva, in March and June

Quintilians: one of two priestly boards of Luperci

Quintilis: earlier name for month of July

Quirinal: one of the hills of Rome

Quirinus: name of the deified Romulus, originally perhaps a Sabine war-god

Quirites: name for Romans in civilian, peacetime capacity

Ram: constellation Aries

Ramneses: one of three "tribes" established by Romulus

Raven: part of constellation of Raven, Snake, and Bowl (2.243-66)

Remulus: grandson of Tiberinus, an Alban king

Remuria: original name of Lemuria

Remus: twin brother of Romulus; killed by Celer during construction of walls of Rome (4.807-56; 5.451-80)

Respect: *Reverentia*, here Ovid's allegorical invention, "mother" of "Majesty"

Rhea: goddess, wife of Saturn (in Greek, Cronos); mother of the Olympian gods, Jupiter, *et al.*

Rhodope: mountain in W Thrace

Rhoeteum: promontory in the Troad on the Hellespont

Romulan: of Romulus (see below)

Romulus: founder of Rome; twin brother of Remus; son of Mars and Silvia

Ruminal: a fig tree in the Lupercal (see above), where the she-wolf suckled Romulus and Remus

Rust: *Robigo*, the spirit of a kind of plant fungus

Rutilius: Publius Rutilius Lupus; consul, 90 BC; fell at the Tolenus River during the Social War, fighting against the Marsian Vettius Scato

Rutulians: ancient people of Latium, with capital at Ardea; in legend, the people of Turnus

Sabine(s): ancient people to NE of Rome, who fought with the Romans (1.259-76; 3.201-28), then merged with them (6.93-96); rape of the Sabine Women (alluded to 3.195-98)

Sacred Mount: 3 miles NNE of Rome; site of the first Plebeian Secession

Sagaritis: nymph with whom Attis was unfaithful to Cybele

Samos: Greek island off coast of Asia Minor, near Ephesus; site of important cult of Hera

Sancus: see "Fidius" above

Sapaeans: tribe in interior of Thrace

Sardinia: large island in Mediterranean, W of Italy

Saturn: in Greek, Cronos; father of the Olympian gods, Jupiter (Zeus) *et al.*; deposed and banished (to Italy, hence the "Saturnian land," e.g., 5.625) by Jupiter (3.796); attempt to evade oracle about being overthrown by his son (4.197-200) foiled by Rhea (4.201-206); emblem was the sickle (5.627)

Saturnian: of Saturn

Satyr: lesser deity, half-god, associated with Bacchus

Scorpio(n): constellation

Scylla: dog-like female sea-monster at Straits of Messina

Scythian: of Scythia, region in SE Europe and Asia, N and E of Black and Caspian Seas

Seasons: divinities who guard heaven's gates (1.125); associated with flowers and spring (5.217)

Security: in Latin *Salus*; one of three deities (including Concord and Peace) to which Augustus set up altars and statues in 10 BC from free-will offerings of Senate and people

Semele: daughter of Cadmus; mother of Dionysus (Bacchus), incinerated in the act of conception

Semo: see "Fidius" above

Senate: deliberative body at Rome, whose members were ex-magistrates

Servius (King): Servius Tullius, seventh king of Rome; founded temples of Mater Matuta (6.479-80) and Fortune (6.569)

Shame: in Latin, *Pudor*; personification

She-Goat's Marsh: traditional scene of Romulus' apotheosis

Sibyl: oracle of Apollo at Cumae, supposed author of Sibylline Books (see below); in myth she was granted long life without accompanying long youth, and grew increasingly aged and decrepit

Sibylline Books: collection of oracles consulted by Romans in times of crisis

Sigean: of Sigeum, town and promontory in the Troad

Silent One: in Latin, *Tacita*; object of magic ritual on the Feralia, which along with her name suggests her identity as an underworld goddess; Ovid connects her with *dea Muta*, or Lala/Lara, mother of the Lares

Silenus: oldest satyr, companion of Bacchus; his donkey foils Priapus' attempted rapes of Lotis and Vesta

Silvia: mother of Romulus and Remus; also called Ilia

Silvius: Silvius Postumus; son of Julus and king of Alba

Sirius: the Dog Star

Sisyphus: married to Merope, one of the Pleiades; in one version, the adulterous father of Odysseus; in the Underworld he was condemned to push a stone uphill for eternity

Sleep: personification

Snake: part of constellation of Raven, Snake and Bowl

Solimus: companion of Aeneas, eponymous founder of Sulmore (see below); perhaps invented by Ovid

South Wind: in Latin, *Auster*

Sowing Day: in Latin, *Feriae Sementivae*; moveable agricultural festival, with sacrifices to Ceres and Tellus (Earth)

Spain: Iberian peninsula, organized into a Roman province 197 BC

Sparta: ancient Greek city in the Peloponnese

Spartan: of Sparta

Sterope: one of the Pleiades

Stimula: ancient Roman goddess with a grove near the Tiber near the Aventine; scene of Bacchic orgies, hence confused or connected with Semele (see above)

Stormy Weather: in Latin, *Tempestas*; Lucius Cornelius Scipio (consul, 259 BC) dedicated a temple to Tempests (*Tempestates*) in gratitude for escape from a storm off Corsica

Stygian: of the Styx

Stymphalus (Lake): lake in N Arcadia

Styx: river in the Underworld, by which the gods swear oaths

Sulla: Lucius Cornelius Sulla (138-78 BC); consul, 88 BC; defeated Mithridates in the East (87-84), reorganized the Roman constitution as a special dictator (81-79); as dictator, took credit for restoration or dedication of the temple of Hercules the Guardian (6.209-12)

Sulmo: Ovid's birthplace, 90 miles NW of Rome

Summanus: god connected with Jupiter by the ancient Romans; received a temple on 30 June (see 6.731-32, n. 16)

Sun: in Greek, Helios, in Latin, Sol; Ovid calls him *Sol* (4.581); *Phoebus,* identifying him with Apollo (1.651), refers to his "sister" Diana (3.109-11); *Hyperion,* a Titan, the father of Helios (1.385); *Titan* (1.617); and *Cynthius,* also identifying him with Apollo (3.345)

Sunion: promontory at S tip of Attica

Symaethus: biggest river in Sicily, flowing S from Catana

Syphax: king of a Numidian tribe, captured by Masinissa (see above) in 203 BC during the Second Punic War; sent to Rome where he died two years later

Syracuse: chief city in ancient Sicily

Syria: roughly, the area between Asia Minor and Egypt, usually including Phoenicia and Palestine; the name of various geopolitical entities in antiquity, including the Roman province organized by Pompey in 64–63 BC

Syrtes: two sandy flats on N African coast between Carthage and Cyrene, a proverbial hazard to navigation

Tanaquil (Queen): wife of king Tarquin

Tantalus: grandfather of Atreus and Thyestes; their dispute over the throne of Mycenae led Atreus to serve Thyestes a banquet of his own children

Taormina: city in Sicily whose ancient name was Tauromenum or Taurominium

Tarpeia: daughter of Roman commander of the Capitol; she betrayed it to a Sabine force

Tarquin: Sextus Tarquin, son of Tarquin the Proud; his rape of Lucretia brought Roman monarchy to an end (2.685-852)

Tarquin (the Proud): the last king of Rome

Tartarus: the Underworld

Tatius: Titus Tatius, Sabine king; led war against Romans, then merged with Romulus' people

Taurus: constellation of the Bull; story of its origin, 5.603-20

Taygete: one of the Pleiades

Telegonus: son of Ulysses (in Greek, Odysseus); legendary founder of Tusculum (see below)

Tenedos: island in the Aegean off the coast of the Troad

Tereus: husband of Procne (see above)

Terminus: god of the boundary; honored at festival of the Terminalia (2.639-84)

Tethys: a Titan; wife of Oceanus, mother of Pleione

Thalia: one of the Muses (comedy)

Thapsus: 1. site in N Africa of battle in 46 BC during civil war between Pompey and Caesar, at which Caesar defeated Juba (see above) and Lucius Scipio
2. city on Sicily between Megara and Syracuse

Theban: of Thebes

Thebes: chief city of Boeotia; the "goddess from Thebes" (6.476) is Mater Matuta, originally Ino (see above)

Themis: primeval goddess, daughter of Earth and Sky

Theseus: hero who killed the Minotaur; abandoned Ariadne (see above) on Naxos; father of Hippolytus

Thessaly: area of N Greece proverbial for witches and magic

Thracian(s): of Thrace, the ancient region in E Balkan peninsula

Thunderer: in Latin, *Tonans*; Jupiter Tonans had a temple on the Capitoline hill, dedicated by Augustus on 1 September 22 BC in thanks for a close escape from lightning in Spain

Tiber: river running through Rome

Tiber Island: island in the Tiber at Rome; location of temples of Aesculapius and Jupiter (1.291-94) and of Faunus (2.194)

Tiberinus (King): Alban king; descendant of Julus; drowned in the Tiber

Tiberius: Tiberius Julius Caesar Augustus (42 BC–AD 37); adopted by Augustus in AD 4; second Roman Emperor (AD 14–37); see Introduction, *passim*

Tiber's Courtyard: in Latin, *Tiberina Atria*; a bend in the river near Ostia (ancient port of Rome); the reason for the name and its exact location are unknown

Tiryns: town in NW Peloponnese; legendary home of Hercules

Titaness: female Titan

Titans: children of Earth and Sky

Tithonus: mortal husband of the Dawn, granted immortality without eternal youth

Titienses: one of Romulus' three "tribes"

Tivoli: town 18 miles ENE of Rome (ancient name, Tibur)

Tmolus: mountain in Lydia

Tolenus: river near Carseoli, scene of the defeat and death of Rutilius (see above)

"Torquatus": *cognomen* of Titus Manlius, who stripped the torque (necklace) from the Gaul he killed in single combat in 361 BC

Trasimene (Lake): scene in Etruria of the massacre of the army of Flaminius (see above) by Hannibal during Second Punic War

Tricrene: mountain in Arcadia

Trinacris: an old name for Sicily

Triptolemus: son of Celeus (see above); bringer of agriculture to mankind (4.559-60)

Troezen: town across Saronic gulf from Athens; Theseus' birthplace and scene of Hippolytus' death

Trojan: of Troy

Tros: eponymous founder of Troy, ancestor of Aeneas

Troy: city in NW Asia Minor, scene of legendary ten-year siege by Greek army

Trumpet Purification: in Latin, *Tubilustrium*; festival for Mars, in March (3.849-50) and May (5.725-26)

Tubertus: Aulus Postumius Tubertus; celebrated a triumph for victory of the Aequi and Volsci at Mount Algidus in 431 BC

Turnus: Aeneas' Italian rival for Lavinia

Tuscan: Etruscan

Tusculum: town in Latium

Twins: constellation Gemini (see above)

Tychius: leatherworker who made Ajax' shield; later regarded as the inventor of shoemaking

Typhoeus: a monster buried under Etna, often confused with the Giants (see above)

Typhon: another name for Typhoeus (see above), who pursued the gods to Egypt

Tyre: ancient Phoenician seaport

Tyrrhenian: Etruscan

Ulysses: Latin name for Greek hero Odysseus

Underworld: realm of the dead

Urania: one of the Muses (astronomy); derives "May" from "majority" (*maiores,* literally, "the elders"), 5.55-78

Urion: original name of Orion

Vacuna: old Sabine goddess

Veii: Etruscan city captured by Camillus (see above) in 396 BC

Vejovis: a god whose temple "between two groves" (3.429-48) on the Capitoline was dedicated in 192 BC

Velabrum: valley between the Palatine and Capitoline; on the route from Capitol of the procession preceding games in Circus Maximus; before drainage by Cloaca Maxima ("Great Sewer"), it was a swampy area

Venus: goddess of love and sex; in Greek, Aphrodite; story of her birth in the sea, 4.93; affair with Mars (Ares), 3.611; her plant is myrtle, 4.15; fight with Diomedes during the Trojan War, 4.119-20; judgment of Paris, 4.121-22; her husband was Vulcan (Hephaestus), 4.153; April is her month, 4.13-14; epithets are *Erycina* (from Mount Eryx on Sicily), 4.865, *Cytherea* (from island of Cythera), 4.673, *Verticordia* ("Changer of Hearts"), 4.160

Vertumnus: Etruscan god

Vesta: goddess of the hearth, perhaps originally as a deity of individual domestic hearth, then as the deity of the king's hearth on behalf of the whole people; new fire lit in her temple in Rome on New Year's Day, 3.143-44; associated with festival of Parilia, 4.732; her "priest" is the *pontifex maximus,* 5.573; festival of Vestalia on 9 June, 6.249-460; conflagration in her temple, 6.437; Augustus became *pontifex maximus* on 6 March 12 BC, and on 28 April he dedicated a shrine to her in his home on the Palatine, 4.949-54

Vestal: virgin priestess of Vesta who tended the sacred flame, etc.

Victories: winged acroterial figures on the Temple of Mars Ultor

Vinalia: wine festival

Virbius: name of Hippolytus at Aricia

Volscians: people of central Italy who fought a series of wars with Rome in the fifth to fourth centuries BC

Vulcan: god of metalworking and the forge; in Greek, Hephaestus

Wars: personification

West Wind: Zepyhr; brother of Boreas, the North Wind; raped, then married, Flora

Zancle: older name for Messene (modern Messana or Messina), city near NE end of Sicily

Notes

INTRODUCTION

1. On the topic of patronage, see Gordon Williams, "Phases of Political Patronage of Literature in Rome," in *Literary and Artistic Patronage in Ancient Rome,* ed. Barbara K. Gold (Austin: University of Texas Press, 1982), pp. 3-27; on the Augustan period and the circles of Maecenas and Messalla, see pp. 13-21.

2. On the authenticity of the letter from Sappho, see Howard Jacobson, *Ovid's Heroides* (Princeton: Princeton University Press, 1974), pp. 277-78 and n. 2. On the pairs of letters, see John Barsby, *Ovid* (Oxford: Clarendon, 1978), p. 13 and p. 18 nn. 2-3.

3. For a succinct and fairly recent discussion of these "charges" and Ovid's self-defense in his elegies from exile, see Sir Ronald Syme, *History in Ovid* (Oxford: Clarendon, 1978), pp. 215-29, in a chapter ironically titled "The Error of Caesar Augustus."

4. John F. Miller, *Ovid's Elegiac Festivals* (Frankfurt am Main: Peter Lang, 1991), pp. 16-21 and the appendix, pp. 143-44.

5. Franz Bömer, ed., *P. Ovidius Naso: Die Fasten* (Heidelberg: Carl Winter, 1958), II (Kommentar), p. 96, commenting on line 2.195. Hereafter cited as "Bömer II."

6. In this paragraph and the following one, I am indebted to Ludwig Braun, "Kompositionskunst in Ovids 'Fasti,'" *Aufstieg und Niedergang der Römischen Welt* II.31.4 (Berlin: Walter de Gruyter, 1981), pp. 2344-83, and Elaine Fantham, "Ovid, Germanicus, and the Composition of the *Fasti,*" *Papers of the Liverpool Latin Seminar* 5 (1985): 243-81, esp. 258-59.

7. Tamas Gesztelyi, "Ianus bei Ovid: Bemerkungen zur Komposition der Fasti," *Acta Classica Universitatis Scientiarum Debreceniensis* 16 (1980): 53-59, discusses the chronological organization of the Janus episode and points out that this is the same principle Ovid used to organize all the material in the *Metamorphoses*. R. J. Littlewood, "Ovid's Lupercalia (*Fasti* 2.267-452): A Study in the Artistry of the *Fasti,*" *Latomus* 34 (1975): 1068, points out that the explanations for the nudity of the Luperci are in chronological order.

8. John F. Miller, "Ritual Directions in Ovid's *Fasti:* Dramatic Hymns and Didactic Poetry," *Classical Journal* 75 (1979-80): 204-14, discusses Ovid's ritual directions for "Sowing Day" and Veneralia.

9. Richard Heinze, *Ovids elegische Erzählung* (Leipzig: B. G. Teubner, 1919). Stephen Hinds, *The Metamorphosis of Persephone: Ovid and the Self-Conscious Muse* (Cambridge: Cambridge University Press, 1987).

10. R. J. Littlewood, "Ovid and the Ides of March (*Fasti* 3.523-710): A Further Study in the Artistry of the Fasti," *Studies in Latin Literature and Roman History* II, ed. Carl Deroux (Brussels: Latomus, 1980), pp. 305-14, treats the episode of Anna as a sequel to the *Aeneid.*

11. The translation is by P. A. Brunt and J. M. Moore, *Res Gestae Divi Augusti: The Achievements of the Divine Augustus* (Oxford: Oxford University Press, 1967).

12. My discussion of Roman religion is indebted to R. M. Ogilvie, *The Romans and Their Gods in the Age of Augustus* (New York: W. W. Norton, 1969), and H. J. Rose, *Ancient Roman Religion* (London: Cheltenham Press, 1949).

13. Consult the glossary under the name of the deity (e.g., Venus) for the cult-titles used in the *Fasti*.

14. F. E. Adcock, *Roman Political Ideas and Practice* (Ann Arbor: University of Michigan, 1959), p. 16.

15. My discussion of the Roman calendar is indebted to H. H. Scullard, *Festivals and Ceremonies of the Roman Republic* (Ithaca: Cornell University Press, 1981), pp. 41-48. Part II of this book goes through the festivals month by month; I can recommend Scullard's treatment of January through June (pp. 51-158) as a useful accompaniment to reading the *Fasti*.

16. Edmund Buchner, "Horologium Augusti: Neue Ausgrabungen im Rom," *Gymnasium* 90 (1983): 494-508.

17. Agnes Kirsopp Michels, *The Calendar of the Roman Republic* (Princeton: Princeton University Press, 1967), pp. 19-22.

18. "Über den astronomischen Theil der Fasti des Ovid," *Abhandlungen der königlichen Akademie der Wissenschaften* (Berlin 1825), pp. 137-69.

19. *Ovid's Poetry of Exile* (Baltimore: Johns Hopkins University Press, 1990).

20. On this theory of language in antiquity, see Frederick Ahl, *Metaformations: Soundplay and Wordplay in Ovid and Other Classical Poets* (Ithaca: Cornell University Press, 1985), pp. 9, 22-25 and *passim* for etymological wordplay, mostly in Ovid's *Metamorphoses*.

21. E. H. Alton, D. E. W. Wormell, and E. Courtney, eds., *P. Ovidi Nasonis Fastorum Libri Sex* (Leipzig: B. G. Teubner, 1988). I deviate from the Teubner in five places: at 2.533-34, I read *placate* and *ferte* for *placare* and *ferre*; at 3.200, I read *canes* for *canet*; at 3.576, I read *petenda* for *paranda*; at 3.716, I read *partus* for *parvus*; and at 6.433, I read *genus* for *gener*.

22. Franz Bömer, ed. and trans., *P. Ovidius Naso: Di Fasten* (Heidelberg: Carl Winter, 1957), vol. I; the commentary is vol. II (see above, n. 5). Sir James George Frazer, ed. and trans., *Publii Ovidii Nasonis Fastorum Libri Sex: The Fasti of Ovid* (London: Macmillan, 1929), 5 vols.; hereafter cited as "Frazer I," "Frazer II," etc.

BOOK 1

1. Line 127. "Janus the Doorman": I have supplied "the Doorman" to clarify the etymological connection between "Janus" and the words *ianua* ("door") and *ianitor* ("doorman"). Ovid resumes the etymological wordplay explicitly in line 135 ff. below.

2. Lines 215-16. "On a binge . . . / . . . 'one more for the road.'" I have replaced Ovid's simile of patients suffering from dropsy with the more accessible one of alcoholics. A literal version of this couplet is: "That's the way it is with those whose bellies have swollen with accumulated fluid, the more water they drink, the more they thirst."

3. Line 238. "the lately evicted god": In translating *latente deo,* I have taken liberties to preserve the etymology of "Latium." Literally, the phrase means "from the god in hiding."

4. Line 319. "The origin of the name": Lines 319-32 is the first of many passages of etymological speculation in the *Fasti*. I have taken some liberties in order to preserve the etymology. The first derivation (322) relates Agonalia to the verb *ago*; literally it means, "he always asks whether he should do (*agatne*) [it] and doesn't do (*agit*) [it] unless he's been ordered." The second derivation (323-34) involves the same verb; literally the couplet means, "Because the cattle do not come unless they are driven (*agantur*), some believe the Agonal day gets its name from driving (*actu*)." The fourth explanation (328-29) implies the Greek verb *agōniaō* "to fear" (Bömer II, 39, on line 327); I have followed Frazer in making

this explicit by rendering *metu* (328; literally, "anxiety") as "agony." The fifth derivation (329-30) is also implicitly from the Greek word *agon*; to convey this, I have rendered Ovid's phrase *de ludis* (330; literally, "from games") as "antagonistic contests."

5. Line 336. "'hostage'. . . hosts": I have taken liberties to preserve the derivation of *hostia* ("sacrificial victim") from *hostibus* ("enemies").

6. Lines 453-54. This couplet alludes to a legendary occasion when the honking of geese on the Capitoline Hill alerted the Roman defenders to a sneak attack by Gauls.

7. Line 467. "you whose name derives from the charms of song": The etymological connection is between "Carmenta" and *carmen,* the Latin word for "song," which is also the word for a magical incantation and an oracular prediction. In line 474 below, the word I have translated as "predictions" is *carmina.*

8. Lines 529-31. "The time will come . . . a ward of Augustus": These lines refer to Augustus' role as *pontifex maximus.* My phrase "a ward of Augustus" preserves the technical legal connotations of the phrase *patriae tutela* (531; literally, "guardianship of the fatherland"). The verb in line 529 which I have translated "will be your guardian" is *tuebitur* (literally, "he will safeguard") and is cognate with the noun *tutela.*

9. Lines 591-606: The "family portraits" (591) are the wax funeral masks (Ovid's Latin word here is simply *ceras,* "waxes") displayed in the entrance of homes of the nobility. The word I have translated as "title" (592) is more literally "name," and refers to the *cognomen,* the third part of the typical three-part Roman name, e.g., Publius Ovidius Naso. Originally these were personal nicknames, given for some physical feature ("Naso" means "nose") or accomplishment. Many of the Roman *cognomina* were awarded in honor of military victories, and it is these which Ovid lists in the lines that follow. Because these were the *cognomina* of famous individuals and families, Ovid does not have to mention them explicitly, as I have done, but only alludes to them by reference to the achievement. My addition of the *cognomina* has lengthened some lines, so I have cut a bit: Ovid alludes in lines 593-94 not only to "Africanus" and "Creticus," but also to "Isauricus," in 595-96 not only to "Numidicus" and "Numanticus," but also to "Messala," and in 601-02 to both "Torquatus" and "Corvus" (whose name derives from a raven, *corvus* in Latin, that landed on his helmet). In line 597, the "Drusus, called 'Germanicus'" is the father of the Germanicus to whom Ovid rededicated the *Fasti* when he revised Book 1. For details on the *cognomina* which Ovid cites in this passage, and the individuals who earned them, see the "Glossary" and the notes in Frazer IV, pp. 224-28, and Bömer II, 67-68.

10. Lines 635-36. This couplet preserves the etymological connections with the names *Porrima* and *Postverta.* A literal translation is: "The one is thought to have predicted what was ahead (*porro*), the other, what was going to come afterwards (*postmodo*)." Actually, these are epithets of Carmenta as a goddess of childbirth. The Roman scholar Varro gives these as *Prorsa* ("Forward"), derived from the normal, headfirst delivery, and *Postverta* ("Backward"), from feet-first delivery (Frazer II, 178-79).

11. Line 638. "Moneta's temple": This is the temple of Juno Moneta on the Capitoline Hill. Because the Roman mint was located near this temple, *moneta* came to be the word for "mint" as well as well as for the "money" coined there; this is the derivation of the English words as well. The ancients themselves interpreted the cult-title "Moneta" as "the Warner," deriving it from the verb *moneo,* "to warn"; supposedly the voice of Juno was once heard in this temple "warning" the people to offer a sacrifice in expiation after an earthquake (Cicero, *de Divinatione* 1.101). Ovid mentions the temple again at 6.183-90.

Beside the staircase leading up to this temple was the temple of Concordia, originally built in 367 BC, then restored in 121 BC, and completely rebuilt by Tiberius (before he became Emperor) with funds from spoils taken in Germany, and dedicated as the temple of Concordia Augusta on 16 January 10 AD. Imperial propaganda such as this temple stressed the harmony between Livia and Augustus, and later between her and Tiberius. Ovid celebrates the harmony between Livia and Augustus in this address to Tiberius in Book 1 on the anniversary of the temple's dedication (638-50) and in another passage addressed to him in Book 6 (637-48), which refers to an otherwise unknown shrine dedicated by Livia to Concordia in or on the Portico dedicated in her honor by Augustus in 7 BC.

BOOK 2

1. Line 23. "the honor guard" here renders *lictor*. Ordinarily that word refers to attendants of Roman higher magistrates, but the reference to "lictors" here is unclear and disputed (Bömer II, 81).

2. Line 154. "the Bear Keeper" here renders *Custodem . . . Ursae*. Below in line 190 the same English phrase renders *Arctophylax*, a transliteration of the Greek name for which *Custodem . . . Ursae* is the Latin. This is the constellation which we call Ursa Minor.

3. Lines 241-42. ". . . by your Fabian tactics": This couplet refers to the Quintus Fabius Maximus whose strategy of non-engagement with Hannibal during the Second Punic War led to the Carthaginian defeat and won him the cogonomen *Cunctator* ("the Delayer"). My phrase, "by your Fabian tactics," renders Ovid's gerund *cunctando* (literally, "by delaying"), which alludes to the *cognomen*.

4. Line 375. "He and his Fabians": "Fabians" here and "Quintilians" in line 378 allude to the names of the two boards of the Luperci, the Fabii or Fabiani and Quintilii or Quinctiliales, founded traditionally by Remus and Romulus, respectively (Frazer II, 365 on 2.377).

5. Lines 449-50. "Lucina . . . from the grove / or from . . . the light": The etymological connection, lost in my translation, is between Lucina and *lucus* ("grove") or *lux* ("light").

6. Line 528. "the Oven Festival" in Latin is *Fornacalia*. I owe my rendering of *curio maximus* as "chief warden" to Frazer's "Prime Warden." The Latin for "ward" (529) is *curia*.

7. Lines 533-34. "Appease . . . / and bring": The word *ferte* hints at an etymology of Feralia from the verb *fero* ("to bring"), which becomes explicit at line 569. My translation there preserves the etymology through sound: "They called this day Feralia because they do what's fair" and also preserves the echo of the apostrophe in line 544 to the "fair-minded Latin" (*iuste Latine*). A literal version of "they do what's fair" (*iusta ferunt*) is "they bring what is due."

8. Line 548. "Parentalia": This period for honoring the dead began on 13 February. It ended on Feralia, "the last day," as Ovid says in line 570, "for appeasing the dead."

9. Line 634. "the dancing Lares": The Latin phrase *incinctos . . . Lares* literally means "girded-up Lares." My translation reflects Bömer's comment on this line (II, 128) that the Lares were frequently represented in art as dancers with short belted togas.

10. Lines 663-66. Cynuria, on the border between Argos and Sparta, was a constant source of strife until the Spartans finally won it in the mid-sixth century BC at the legendary battle of Thyrea (see Herodotus 1.82). Each side sent 300 champions to settle the matter. At the end of the day, the survivors were two Argives, who ran to Argos to report their

supposed victory, and one Spartan, named Othryades, who collected spoils, took them to camp, and waited. When the two armies returned to the scene they both claimed victory, the Argives, because more of them had survived, the Spartans, because their man had taken spoils and held his ground. In the battle that ensued, the Spartans finally did win, but Othryades, ashamed to return when all his original company were dead, committed suicide at Thyrea.

11. Lines 667-70. This alludes to the episode, also reported by the historian Livy (1.55.1-4), which took place when Tarquin the Proud was getting ready to build the temple to Jupiter on the Capitoline Hill. He wanted to deconsecrate shrines to other gods that were already on the Capitoline so that the hill would be sacred to Jupiter alone. The auspices permitted deconsecration of all the shrines except that belonging to Terminus.

12. Line 837. "Brutus 'the dolt'": The Roman name "Brutus" means "dolt." Above in line 717 Ovid plays on this in saying, "Brutus had wisely been playing the fool."

BOOK 3

1. Lines 113-14. "They didn't stand by the constellations . . . , / but by their standards": The Latin word for "constellations" (*signa*) is the same as the word for "standards." To convey this wordplay, I have translated *non . . . tenebant* as "they didn't stand by." A literal version is "They didn't grasp (i.e., understand) the constellations . . . , but held onto their standards."

2. Lines 117-18. "troop bundles of hay attached; / . . . troops attached to their unit": The etymological connection here is between *maniplaris . . . miles* (118), a soldier in the unit of the Roman army called a "maniple," and *maniplos* (117), "bundles of hay." A literal version of the couplet is: "A long pole used to carry bundles of hay that had been hung from it; / hence a soldier of the maniple gets his name."

3. Line 120. "decades that were twenty months short": Literally this is "lustra that were ten months short." A Roman *lustrum* was the five-year period between census-taking.

4. Line 163. "three score": Literally this is "six, ten times."

5. Line 177. "Industrious poet of the Latin calendar, learn what you want": Mars echoes Janus' address to Ovid in 1.101-102.

6. Line 202. "war between in-laws": Mention of warring in-laws would suggest Caesar and Pompey to Ovid's original readers; cf. 6.600. Ovid's Latin phrase *socer generque* ("father-in-law and son-in-law") echoes the same phrase, also referring to Caesar and Pompey, at Catullus 29.24. C. J. Fordyce, *Catullus: A Commentary* (Oxford: Clarendon, 1961), p. 164, comments: "The relationship between the rivals clearly was a byword and became a cliché in later literature." As examples, Fordyce cites *Aeneid* 6.830-31 (where *socer* and *gener* refer to the future Caesar and Pompey as Aeneas sees them in the Underworld); Lucan 1.290, 4.802, 10.417; and Martial 9.70.3.

7. Line 246. "the Esquiline Hill": In Latin there is an etymological connection between "Esquiline" and *excubiae* ("watch").

8. Line 340. "a cabbage": In Latin this is an onion (*cepa*), which I have changed because in English we do not refer to a "head" of onion.

9. Lines 663-64. "The common people . . . / seceded": This plebeian "secession," or walk-out, was the first of several (traditions vary between three and five) that occurred during the "Struggle of the Orders," during which the plebeians asserted their rights against the patrician aristocracy. On this first occasion the plebeians withdrew to the Sacred Mount

(three miles away from Rome), or in other versions, to the Aventine Hill in Rome itself, and were induced to return by the creation of plebeian elected officials, the tribunes (see Livy 2.32-33). The last secession in 287 BC resulted in the final concession, that bills passed by the plebeian assembly had the force of law. For a summary of the Struggle, see *Oxford Classical Dictionary*, ed. N. G. L. Hammond and H. H. Scullard, 2d ed. (Oxford: Clarendon, 1970), s.v. "Rome (History)," paragraph 7.

10. Line 771. "the liberal toga": The *toga liberalis* was also known as the *toga virilis* ("toga of manhood," from the age of the wearers) or the *toga pura* ("the pure toga," from its unadorned white color). See lines 777-78 for the etymological connection Ovid makes between the "liberal toga" and Liber.

11. Line 794. "the Kite Star": The only references to this star are here in Ovid and in the Elder Pliny; the constellation has yet to be identified (Bömer II, 198, on line 793, and Frazer III, 141-42, on line 793).

BOOK 4

1. Line 64. "a greater Greece": Because of the Greek settlements in Southern Italy, it was called *Magna Graecia* ("Great Greece").

2. Line 89. "this season of appearance": I have altered the meaning slightly here, to preserve the etymological wordplay with "April." Literally the phrase *ab aperto tempore* means "from the season which has been opened." Likewise, at the beginning of this sentence, "all things appear in spring" (87) renders *ver aperit . . . omnia* (literally, "spring opens all things").

3. Line 145. "Manly Fortune": *Fortuna Virilis* is not the fortune of men but of women in their relationships with men, as line 149 makes somewhat clearer.

4. Line 160. "'Changer of Hearts'": With the phrase *verso corde* ("from her change of heart"), Ovid alludes to Venus' epithet *Verticordia* ("Changer of Hearts").

5. Line 536. "her initiates take food when the stars appear": The *Homeric Hymn to Demeter*, the model for Ovid's "Rape of Proserpina" here, presents the Eleusinian Mysteries, a cult of Demeter at Eleusis near Athens, as an imitation of the sufferings of the goddess in search of her daughter.

6. Lines 623-24. "Liberty . . . began to have a hall of her own": A temple of *Libertas* was consecrated on the Aventine 13 April in the third century BC, perhaps the same as the Temple of Jupiter Libertas built or restored by Augusutus. Ovid erroneously identifies this with the *Atrium Libertatis* ("Hall of Liberty") near the Forum, which was restored by Gaius Asinius Pollio after 39 BC, and which contained the first public library in Rome (Bömer II, 261-62; Frazer III, 313-14).

7. Line 632. "they also think 'birth' is derived": The holiday Fordicidia gets its name from the sacrificial *forda* (translated "brood cow" in lines 630 and 631). That translation, and my rendition of the etymological wordplay in 631-32, preserve the meaning but lose the obvious connection with "Fordicidia." The Latin *ferens, ferendo* and *fetus* are rendered by "that bears," "by bearing," and "'birth.'"

8. Line 640. "on Pales' day" (*luce Palis*) refers to the holiday Parilia on 21 April (see below, lines 721-862).

BOOK 5

1. Line 19. "from the lower class" renders the phrase *de medio plebe* (literally, "from the midst of the plebs"). The plebeians at Rome were distinguished from the aristocratic patricians. Early in the *Metamorphoses* Ovid uses a similar conceit of divine social distinctions analogous to the Roman ones. After referring to the "palaces of the noble gods" (*deorum / atria nobilium*, 1.171-72), he asserts that "the plebeians live elsewhere" (*plebs habitat diversa locis*, 173).

2. Lines 21-22. "offer his arm . . . the very worst seat": The Latin for the first instance of disrespect is *nec latus . . . adiunxit* (literally, "did not join his side"). This alludes to the practice of a younger man walking on the street side, with the older man on the building side (see below, lines 67-68). I have substituted an analogous, but clearer, courtesy. Themis is slighted by being seated *extremo . . . loco* (literally, "in the last place"). This seems to refer to seating arrangements at Roman dinner parties; the *lectus imus* ("lowest couch") was the antithesis of the place of honor.

3. Line 25. "the goddess Majesty": The Latin word *maiestas* literally means the condition of being bigger or grander. The Romans personified the "Majesty" of such entities as the gods, the Republic, the Roman people, and so on, and in time, extended this practice to the Emperor and the imperial family. Since individuals with "majesty" are owed honor and respect, Ovid appropriately makes Honor and Respect the "parents" of his allegorical figure here.

4. Lines 73-74. "age / of majority . . . May": I have translated freely to preserve the etymological wordplay between *maiores* ("elders") and *Maio* ("May"). A literal version of this couplet is: "Hence I am moved to think that the elders assigned their name to May and paid attention to their age."

5. Line 78. "June, named for the juniors" preserves the Latin etymological wordplay between *Iunius* ("June") and *iuvenum* ("young men").

6. Line 129. "the Standby Lares": The epithet *praestites* (singular *praestes*) literally means "guardian" or "protector." I have rendered it as "standby" for the sake of the etymological wordplay in lines 134-36: "they stand by" (*praestant,* 134); "they stand up for us and stand by" (*stant . . . pro nobis et praesunt,* 135); and "stand at the ready" (*sunt praestites,* 136).

7. Lines 203-204. "The North Wind . . . similar prize from Athens": This alludes to the myth of Boreas (the North Wind) and Orithyia, daughter of the Athenian king Erechtheus. Ovid's version appears at *Metamorphoses* 6.682-713.

8. Lines 207-208. "I enjoy . . . constant fodder": These lines, and 273-74 below, are bracketed as spurious by the Teubner editors.

9. Line 281. "whence the financial terms 'stock' and 'holdings'": This free translation preserves the etymological wordplay in a line which literally means "hence a 'wealthy man' (*locuples*) is called, hence 'money' (*pecunia*) itself." The word *locuples* comes from *locus* ("place," i.e., "land") and *pleo* ("to fill," i.e., "full of land"). The word *pecunia* is related to *pecus* ("cattle").

10. Lines 283-89. To pasture livestock on public land, the owners were required to register and pay a tax. Further, the Licinian Law of 367 BC limited the number of animals a single owner could pasture. Apparently fraud became endemic, until two plebeian aediles

(the officials in charge of enforcing the Licinian Law), Publius and Manlius Publicius Malleolus, prosecuted violators in 238 BC (Frazer IV, 24-26).

11. Line 486. "the season of All Souls" renders *ferali tempore* ("the season of the dead") and alludes to the Feralia in February.

12. Line 552. "temple in the Forum of Augustus": Octavian vowed the Temple of Mars the Avenger at the beginning of the campaign to avenge Julius Caesar's assassination (cf. lines 569-77). Construction began in 37 BC, but it was not dedicated until 2 BC. Ovid provides information which supplements that in ancient literary sources (e.g., Suetonius *Life of Augustus*) and from archeological excavations. In the Temple, the Senate deliberated on wars and triumphs; from it, governors with military commands departed for their provinces; to it, as formerly to the Temple of Jupiter Best and Greatest, victorious generals brought the spoils of triumph (Suetonius, *Aug.* 29.2); Ovid alludes to these uses in lines 556-58 and 561-62.

The Temple was flanked by two colonnades with niches for statues of ancient Roman leaders, which Augustus intended as an encouragement to emulation of the standards they had set (Suetonius, *Aug.* 31.5). From Ovid, we learn the arrangement of those statues in two groups, headed by Aeneas and Romulus respectively (lines 563-66); excavations have unearthed some of the statues and accompanying inscriptions. Romulus' "spoils from a general" (line 565, *ducis arma*) are called technically *spolia opima* ("the triumphal spoils"). Romulus was the first Roman general (there were only two others afterward) to kill an enemy general in combat; he dedicated the Temple of Jupiter Feretrius to commemorate this deed (Livy 1.10).

Although the facade does not survive intact, evidence for its appearance is provided by a relief on the Ara Pietatis Augustae ("Altar of Augustan Piety"). This shows winged acroterial figures on the roof (see lines 559-60, where "Victories" is my translation for *invictas . . . deas*, "unconquered goddesses"). Lines 567-68 suggest that there was an inscription, perhaps like the one on the Pantheon, but the Ara Pietatis does not show this.

For a discussion of the Forum of Augustus, including the Temple of Mars, see James C. Anderson, *The Historical Topography of the Imperial Fora* (Brussels: Collection Latomus 182, 1984), pp. 65-100. For an illustration of the Ars Pietatis, see Paul Zanker, trans. Alan Shapiro, *The Power of Images in the Age of Augustus* (Ann Arbor: University of Michigan Press, 1988), p. 105, fig. 86 and p. 196, fig. 150.

13. Line 617. "The Bull entered heaven while Jupiter entered the Phoenician": The zeugma, a figure of speech which plays on two different meanings of the same verb, is a typical feature of Ovidian wit. No zeugma actually occurs in this passage, where I have supplied it to convey the effect of a different play on two occurrences of another verb. In line 609, "The breeze made her robe billow" is my version of *aura sinus implet* (literally, "the breeze fills her bodice"). The verb *implet* also occurs in the Latin of line 617, . . . *te, Sidoni, Iuppiter implet* (literally, "Jupiter fills you, Sidonian woman").

14. Line 622. "from the wooden bridge": This is the Sublician Bridge, the oldest Roman bridge across the Tiber. The next line, "Whoever believes that carcasses were tossed to death at age sixty," alludes to one interpretation of the proverb "sixty-year-olds off the bridge." The couplet 633-34 refers to a less deadly explanation: "Others think the young men pitched the feeble old ones / off the gangways in order to monopolize the voting." These "gangways" led to the voting booths for the Centuriate Assembly. The Latin word for such a "gangway" is *pons*, which is also the word for "bridge," as in line 622.

15. Line 724. "I've explained its origin in another entry": The other entry, which refers to the Dog Star Sirius, is 4.939-41, but that does not really "explain its origin," except to refer to it as "Icarian," no fuller an explanation than referring to it here as "the Erigonian dog" (*canis Erigoneius*, which I have glossed as "Sirius").

16. Lines 727-28. "four letters, the acronym / for a ritual custom or a king's expulsion": The four letters are Q.R.C.F., standing for either *quando rex comitiavit fas* ("when it is right for the king to [do something having to do with the comitium]") or *quando rex comitio fugerit* ("when the king will have fled the comitium"). The "king" is the *rex sacrorum,* but even in antiquity the meaning of *comitiavit* was uncertain (Bömer II, 335 on line 727). Ovid's second interpretation, associating this with the flight of Tarquin, the last king, from Rome (*fuga regis;* for Ovid's narrative of that episode, see 2.685-852) was a common error in antiquity (Frazer IV, 123-24).

BOOK 6

1. Line 13. "professor of ploughing" refers to the Greek poet Hesiod and his didactic *Works and Days.* The Latin phrase *praeceptor arandi* literally means "instructor of ploughing." In his own earlier didactic *Art of Love,* Ovid refers to himself as *praeceptor amoris* ("instructor of love"). Hesiod's encounter with the Muses has special significance for Roman poets because Callimachus alludes to it in the opening of his *Aitia.*

2. Line 40. "the Lady, the Bringer to Light" renders Juno's cult title "Lucina," which the ancients related etymologically to the word for "light" (*lux*). The phrase I have translated as "days light up the months" in line 39 literally means "lights [or, "days"] make a month." In the original text line 39, Ovid stresses the etymological connection by word order: *facient mensem luces, Lucina,* which juxtaposes *luces* ("lights" or "days") and *Lucina.*

3. Line 66. "looking as youthful as she is": With the phrase *in voltu signa vigoris* (literally, "marks of vitality on her face"), Ovid alludes to the name of "Hercules' wife," Hebe in Greek and Iuventus in Latin, both of which mean "youth."

4. Line 96. "'June . . . is named for their union'": Literally, the Latin means "June (*Iunius*) has its name because these (i.e., Romans and Sabines) were joined (*iunctis*)."

5. Line 101. "a cardinal goddess": The Latin phrase *dea cardinis* ("goddess of the hinge") hints at an etymological connection with the name Carna.

6. Line 161. "A heart for a heart, I pray you deliver, a liver for a liver": This captures the rhyming jingle in the Latin, which in turn conveys the jingle of that sort of incantation: *cor pro corde, precor, pro fibris sumite fibras* (literally, "a heart for a heart, I pray, for a liver take a liver").

7. Line 299-300. "The earth is very stable. From being very stable, Vesta gets her name, / as in Greek she's Hestia from her heavy resting": I have rendered line 299 somewhat freely to preserve the etymology. The Latin *stat vi terra sua: vi stando Vesta vocatur* literally means, "The earth stands by its own force; from standing by force, Vesta is named." In line 300, I have been even freer, to make explicit Ovid's allusive etymology for Vesta's Greek "opposite number" Hestia, from the Greek verb *histēmi.* The original of line 300, *causaque par Grai nominis esse potest,* literally means "and there can be a like reason for her Greek name."

8. Line 402. "storm sewer": This ditch (*fossa*) alludes to the Cloaca Maxima, the sewer

dating back to Etruscan occupation of Rome. Originally, the covered sewer was an open storm sewer, part of the drainage project in response to the perennial Roman problem of the flooding Tiber.

9. Line 409. "Yonder god Vertumnus": There was a bronze statue of him in the Velabrum on the Vicus Tuscus ("Tuscan Street"). Ovid does not call "yonder god" (iste . . . deus) by name, but alludes to it in two etymological wordplays, "a name from averting the stream" (ab averso . . . amne), "a name . . . that also fits his versatile shapes" (conveniens diversis . . . figuris). In Propertius 4.2 (where the poet represents the statue as speaking to him), the god himself mentions three possible derivations of his name (verso . . . ab amne, 10; quia vertentis fructum praecepimus anni, "since I got the firstfruits of the turning year," 11; quod formas unus vertebar in omnis, "because, although single, I turn into all forms," 47) and endorses the third. Ovid's phrase ab averso . . . amne obviously echoes Propertius 4.2.10; the idea expressed in the phrase conveniens diversis . . . figuris corresponds to that in another line in the Propertian elegy, when Vertumnus remarks opportuna mea est cunctis natura figuris ("my nature is suitable to all shapes," 21).

10. Lines 503-504. "a grove . . . maybe Stimula's . . .": The goddess Stimula had a grove near the Tiber near the Aventine, which was the scene of Bacchic orgies. Hence, Stimula was connected or confused with Semele, the mother of Bacchus (Frazer IV, 285; Bömer II, 374).

11. Line 587. "marriage as her prize for crime": This is Livy's version of the episode (1.46): King Servius Tullius married his two daughters (both named Tullia, because a Roman woman's name was simply the feminine form of her father's family name) to the two sons of his predecessor Tarquin. The younger Tullia and her brother-in-law Tarquin were the more ambitious of the two, and at her instigation, they murdered their spouses so that they could marry each other.

12. Line 600. "Servius' scepter was stolen by his proud son-in-law" is a freer rendering of sceptra gener socero rapta Superbus habet (literally, "the Proud son-in-law has the scepter stolen from his father-in-law"). The "Proud son-in-law" alludes to the name of Rome's last king, Tarquin the Proud. On rivalrous in-laws, see 3.202 and the note to that line above.

13. Lines 637-38. "Concord, / which she provided her beloved husband": I have endeavored to preserve the ambiguity between "Concord," the deity, and the state of marital "concord." The antecedent of the relative pronoun "which" (quam) is both "shrine" and "Concord."

14. Line 643. "to punish an act of treason": Bömer II, 379, commenting on this line, compares the fate of the house of Manlius Capitolinus (see lines 185-86 above).

15. Line 663. "an aedile": Aediles were officials who regulated such things as markets and traffic, and conducted public shows. The connection of aediles with this story of the flute-players' "strike" seems to be their responsibility for enforcing a prohibition against extravagant funerals in the Twelve Tables, the earliest Roman law code.

There are two ancient versions of the fluteplayers' "strike." Livy (9.30.5-10) dates it to 311 BC and gives as the grievance an edict of 312 BC by the censors Appius Claudius and Gaius Plautius forbidding the players to be feasted in the temple of Jupiter (cf. "his colleague's edict," 6.690). Plutarch (Quaest. Rom. 55) gives the grievance as the elimination of traditional honors (including the restriction to ten flutists permitted in funeral processions; cf. 6.663-64). Scholars have attempted to reconcile this discrepancy in order to explain Ovid's account; one editor speculated that some lines of text have been lost after line 662 (the transition to 663—"Besides"—is rather abrupt). In line 685, the same scholar emended the *Claudius* of some manuscripts to *Plautius*, based on evidence from a coin minted by a later Plautius which suggests that the Plautian family claimed credit for resolving the crisis. See Frazer IV, 308-309 (on line 665) and 310-11 (on line 685) and Bömer II, 381 (on line 663) and 382 (on line 685).

16. Lines 731-32. "A temple . . . to Summanus": Summanus may actually be an Etruscan god associated with the cult of the dead. The Romans connected him with Jupiter etymologically as a god of lightning at night (deriving "Summanus" from *sub mane*, meaning "near dawn"). The temple dedicated on 30 June may be connected to an event in 278 BC, the same year Pyrrhus crossed to Sicily: lightning struck and beheaded a terra-cotta image of Summanus on the temple of Jupiter on the Capitoline (Frazer IV, 317-19; Bömer II, 384-85).

17. Line 767. "that ancient disaster": The Battle at Lake Trasimene in 217 BC was one of the disastrous defeats dealt the Romans in the Second Punic War by Hannibal.

18. Line 802. "virtuous Marcia": On the praise of Marcia in this passage, see Introduction, pp. 4–5.

BETTY ROSE NAGLE, Associate Professor of Classical Studies at Indiana University, is the author of *The Poetics of Exile: Program and Polemic in the Tristia and Epistulae ex Ponto of Ovid*, as well as numerous articles on Roman literature.